Alexis
Florian

JUNIOR GREAT BOOKS

SERIES 9

D0949276

JUNIOR
GREAT BOOKS®

SERIES 9

The Great Books Foundation
A nonprofit educational organization

Junior Great Books® is a registered trademark of the Great Books Foundation.

Shared Inquiry™ is a trademark of the Great Books Foundation.

The contents of this publication include proprietary trademarks

and copyrighted materials and may be used or quoted only with

permission and appropriate credit to the Foundation.

Copyright © 1992 by The Great Books Foundation

Chicago, Illinois

All rights reserved

ISBN 9781-880323-12-0

1 5   1 4   1 3

Printed in the United States of America

Published and distributed by

THE GREAT BOOKS FOUNDATION
A nonprofit educational corporation

35 East Wacker Drive, Suite 400

Chicago, IL 60601

www.greatbooks.org

CONTENTS

PREFACE

SHARED INQUIRY

In Junior Great Books you will explore a number of
outstanding stories. You will do this in a variety of ways:
by taking notes as you read, by looking at important words
and passages, and by sharing your questions and ideas
about each story with your group. In each of these activities,
you and your classmates will be working together with
your teacher or leader, asking and answering questions about
what the story means. You will be sharing what you discover
with your classmates. This way of reading, writing, and
discussion in Junior Great Books is called Shared Inquiry.™

One of the pleasures of Shared Inquiry is that you can
speak without worrying about whether what you say is
"the right answer." Different ideas and points of view can all
lead to a better understanding of the story. When you speak,
the leader may ask you to back up what you have said,
or urge you to develop your idea further. Others in your class
may also respond to what you say. They, too, may be asked
to support their statements or explain them more clearly.
After listening to what others say, you may change your mind
about your answer. Shared Inquiry gives you the chance to
learn both from the author and from one another.

Sometimes you will focus on a small part of the story; at other times you will think about the story as a whole. As you participate in Shared Inquiry, you will develop your own *interpretation* of what you read—you will be working to discover what the author wants to tell you or make you feel through his or her words.

WHAT IS INTERPRETATION?

Good writers do their work with care. There are reasons for everything they put into their stories. They try to include only what has a point and what fits—things needed to make a story clear, to make it interesting, and to keep it moving along. They waste few words. In really good stories, everything fits. Everything has an explanation. The parts are connected and support one another just as the posts and beams in a building do.

The parts of the story, because they are connected, help to explain one another. Authors do not point out exactly how the parts are connected, nor do they say in so many words why everything in a story happens as it does. For one thing, that would make the story dull. For another, they want stories to be convincing—to seem like real life. In real life, few things that happen come complete with explanations. We have to puzzle out the explanations for ourselves.

Stories, too, ask us to work out many explanations for ourselves. And the answers to our questions are in the story, waiting to be found. Every good author puts into a story all that a reader must know to understand what is happening and why. As we figure out for ourselves why the things an author puts in a story are there, we are interpreting what we read.

To interpret a story is to explain its meaning—what happens in it, and why, and what the story is about.

Some stories are simple and easy for us to understand. Others are more perplexing. In this second kind of story the author is trying to share with us ideas and feelings that are not obvious or easy to describe. You can fully understand such stories only if you actively seek their meaning out by asking questions.

ACTIVE READING

You will need to think hard about the stories you read in Junior Great Books—not just about *what* happens but also about *why* it happens the way it does. You will be reading each story at least twice. When you read a story for the first time, your mind is mainly on the action—on what the characters think, do, and say. As you read, the main question you ask is likely to be "What's going to happen next?" When you read a story for the second time, your mind will be free to raise new and different questions about it, and this will lead you to think of new questions to explore with your group. You will almost always notice details that you missed on your first reading, ones that can make you change your mind about why the characters behave as they do or how you feel about them. A second reading gives you the chance to think about the story as a whole without wondering what will happen next.

In Shared Inquiry, you will need to read with a pencil in hand and to make notes as you read. While you are reading, mark the words and passages in the story that strike you as really important, interesting, or surprising. Mark places that make you think of a question. Mark parts that give you ideas about what the story means. Your teacher or leader may also ask you to watch for particular things during your reading and to give them special attention. Your notes will remind you of your thoughts while reading and help you to find evidence to back up what you say.

As you read the stories in Junior Great Books, many questions will probably occur to you. In some cases your first reading of a story will give you the answer to these questions. But often after the first reading you may find that some of your questions haven't been answered. You will need to look actively for the answers when you read the story again. The second reading will help you bring these questions into focus and begin to look for possible answers to them.

Reading actively is reading with a purpose—to answer your questions about the story and to discover new questions. By reading with a purpose you will be able to draw on all parts of the text and think about what it means as a whole.

QUESTIONS OF FACT, INTERPRETATION, AND EVALUATION

There are three kinds of questions that can be asked about a story in Junior Great Books: questions of fact, questions of interpretation, and questions of evaluation. The examples of each given below are from "Miriam," the first story in this book.

Questions of fact ask you to recall particular details or events from a story. Everything the author puts into the story is a fact in that story, even if some of the things couldn't happen in real life. A question of fact has only one correct answer. Knowing and remembering the facts in a story is important. They are the basis for your opinions about the story's meaning. And you will use them to support your opinions.

Many times a leader will ask a factual question in order to get you to back up what you have said with evidence from the story. Suppose someone says, "Mrs. Miller doesn't do much until she meets Miriam." A leader might then ask, *What does Mrs. Miller do?* This question can be answered by pointing to the place in the story that reads "she kept the two rooms immaculate, smoked an occasional cigarette, prepared her own meals, and tended a canary."

Now and then you will be asked a factual question that cannot be answered by looking at any one passage. For example, the question *Is Mrs. Miller confused about her feelings toward Miriam?* can only be answered "Yes." Although the story does not come right out and say so, Mrs. Miller's behavior shows that she is.

Questions of interpretation hold the central place in Junior Great Books. These are the questions that ask you to think carefully about what happens in a story and to consider what the story means. Unlike factual questions, they have more than a single good answer. Any answer that can be supported by factual evidence from the story will be a good one.

Some interpretive questions focus on a single passage or ask about a single event. Take, for example, this one: *Why does Miriam smash the vase containing the paper roses?* One answer is that she is mad at Mrs. Miller for not wanting to kiss her. Another is that she strongly disapproves of Mrs. Miller's "sad" imitation roses. Still another answer is that she is testing Mrs. Miller to see how she will react.

Other, more basic interpretive questions are asked about the meaning of the story as a whole. The answers will often be drawn from several places in the story. Here is one basic interpretive question for "Miriam": *Why does Miriam come into Mrs. Miller's life?* To answer this question, you need to think about the relationship between Miriam and Mrs. Miller throughout the whole story.

Questions of evaluation ask how the story fits with your own experience and, after you have interpreted it, whether or not you agree with what the story is saying. As you read "Miriam," you might wonder *Is it possible to like and dislike a person at the same time?* In answering a question like this, you will be thinking more about yourself and your beliefs than about the story itself. After reading the story, thinking about evaluative questions can be a good way of deciding how you feel about the author's ideas.

Since understanding literature is the main purpose of Junior Great Books, you will spend most of your time considering questions of interpretation. Questions of fact will help you support your opinions about what a story means. Questions of evaluation will help you put yourself in the place of the characters in the story. You will have many chances to answer evaluative questions in your writing after Shared Inquiry discussion.

SHARED INQUIRY DISCUSSION

After you have read a story twice, taken notes, and shared some of your questions with your classmates, you will be ready to participate in Shared Inquiry discussion. Shared Inquiry discussion begins when the discussion leader asks an interpretive question, a question that can have more than one good answer. The leader is not sure which answer is the best, and hopes to discover several good answers during the discussion. Because there can be more than one good answer, it takes many minds to discover and explore those answers fully. By asking questions, the leader seeks to help everyone in the group think for themselves about what the story means.

THE RULES OF SHARED INQUIRY DISCUSSION

1. **Only people who have read the story may take part in Shared Inquiry discussion.** If you have not read the story, you cannot contribute to the discussion because you are unprepared to offer opinions and to support them with evidence from the story.

2. **Discuss only the story that everyone has read.** If you refer to other works of literature or your own personal experiences, the participants who are not familiar with them will not be able to contribute to the discussion. This rule also enables the group to check the validity of what is said by referring to the assigned story.

3. **Do not introduce outside opinions unless you can back them up with evidence of your own.** If you get an idea about the meaning of a story from an outside source—for example, the opinion of someone you know or an insight from another book—you may bring it up in discussion only if you can express it in your own words and support it with evidence from the story.

4. **Leaders may only ask questions; they may not answer them.** If leaders stated their own opinions about the meaning of a story, you might feel less inclined to think for yourself. You might also be less likely to believe that other equally good answers are possible. As a participant you are not limited to offering answers; you may ask questions, too.

In Shared Inquiry discussion you may speak directly to anyone in the group, and not just to the leader. You may ask questions of anyone but the leader, and you will be answering questions that others ask you. Since you are all working together to search for a story's meaning, try to listen carefully when others are speaking. If you don't understand what they are saying, ask them to repeat their comments or explain them more clearly. If you disagree with what they are saying, you can tell them so, always giving your reasons. Sometimes, too, you will be able to support what another member of the group has said by giving a reason no one else has thought of.

By the end of a good discussion everyone in your group will understand the story better than they did before you began to exchange ideas, build on one another's insights, and work out new interpretations. At the close of a discussion, everyone will seldom agree in every detail on what the story means, but that's part of what makes it interesting and worthwhile to discuss the stories in Junior Great Books.

WRITING YOUR OWN
INTERPRETIVE QUESTIONS

The more you participate in Shared Inquiry, the more you will see problems of meaning in the selections you read. Writing interpretive questions is one of the best ways to think on your own about the meaning of a story. Some of your notes may already be in the form of interpretive questions; others can be developed into questions.

The same responses that lead you to make notes on a story can be good sources of interpretive questions. Some of these sources are listed here, together with questions developed for "Miriam."

Look for words or passages that you think are important and that you wonder about. One reader was surprised and puzzled when Mrs. Miller buys flowers, cherries, and almond cakes for Miriam, but then refuses to let her in. She wrote this interpretive question:

Why does Mrs. Miller prepare for Miriam's arrival but then tell her to go away?

Look for parts of the story that you feel strongly about. As you read a story, ask questions about whatever makes you react with strong feelings. Look for places where you agree or disagree with the characters or with the author. One reader thought that Miriam was acting like a brat when she insisted on keeping Mrs. Miller's cameo brooch, a gift from her late husband, and felt that Mrs. Miller should have protested more. This reader wondered:

Why does Mrs. Miller let Miriam take the cameo brooch?

When you are curious about why a character in the story acts the way he or she does, ask a question about that. One reader observed that at some points in the story Mrs. Miller seems attracted to Miriam, but at other times she acts repelled by her. Being curious about why Mrs. Miller has such contradictory feelings, he asked:

> *Why is Mrs. Miller both attracted to and repelled by Miriam?*

Let questions come out of your ideas about the meaning of the story. As you read, keep asking yourself what the author wants you to think about and experience through his or her words. Ask questions about that. One reader noticed several details in "Miriam" that might suggest the young girl does not actually exist: she has the same name as Mrs. Miller, she appears and disappears mysteriously, and she acts as if she knows Mrs. Miller, even though they have never met. This reader asked:

> *Does Miriam exist, or does Mrs. Miller only imagine her?*

Interpretation begins with questions, the questions that come to you as you read. In working out the answers, you will arrive at a clearer idea of how the parts of the story fit together and have a better idea of its meaning.

characters
- physical apperanu + background info
- inner/outter dialonge
- what they do/deeds
- others opinion

conflicts drive the plot forward
$\uparrow$ [mainevent]

inner $\{$ man vs. god ①
man vs. himself ②

man vs. others

outter $\{$ man vs others
man vs. society
man vs. nature

$\}$ 5 conflicts
(driving force)
creative
problems

setting
- time
- season
- place

MIRIAM

Truman Capote

For several years, Mrs. H. T. Miller had lived alone in a pleasant apartment (two rooms with kitchenette) in a remodeled brownstone near the East River. She was a widow: Mr. H. T. Miller had left a reasonable amount of insurance. Her interests were narrow, she had no friends to speak of, and she rarely journeyed farther than the corner grocery. The other people in the house never seemed to notice her: her clothes were matter-of-fact, her hair iron-gray, clipped and casually waved; she did not use cosmetics, her features were plain and inconspicuous, and on her last birthday she was sixty-one. Her activities were seldom spontaneous: she kept the two rooms immaculate, smoked an occasional cigarette, prepared her own meals, and tended a canary.

Then she met Miriam. It was snowing that night. Mrs. Miller had finished drying the supper dishes and was thumbing through an afternoon paper when she saw an advertisement of a picture playing at a neighborhood theater. The title sounded good, so she struggled into her beaver coat, laced her

1

[handwritten left margin: Spontanious going to movie at night in snow scared of dark]

[handwritten: farther than the corner ↓]

galoshes, and left the apartment, leaving one light burning in the foyer: she found nothing more disturbing than a sensation of darkness. *fears. tension. unknown*

[handwritten left margin: blindly ↓]

The snow was fine, falling gently, not yet making an impression on the pavement. The wind from the river cut only at street crossings. Mrs. Miller hurried, her head bowed, oblivious as a mole burrowing a blind path. She stopped at a drugstore and bought a package of peppermints. *not social tho w*

A long line stretched in front of the box office; she took her place at the end. There would be (a tired voice groaned) a short wait for all seats. Mrs. Miller rummaged in her leather handbag till she collected exactly the correct change for admission. The line seemed to be taking its own time and, looking around for some distraction, she suddenly became conscious of a little girl standing under the edge of the marquee.

Her hair was the longest and strangest Mrs. Miller had ever seen: absolutely silver-white, like an albino's. It flowed waist-length in smooth, loose lines. She was thin and fragilely constructed. There was a simple, special elegance in the way she stood with her thumbs in the pockets of a tailored plum-velvet coat.

[handwritten left margin: why? new friend? little girl?! out of character]

Mrs. Miller felt oddly excited and when the little girl glanced toward her, she smiled warmly. The little girl walked over and said, "Would you care to do me a favor?" *simple request*

"I'd be glad to, if I can," said Mrs. Miller.

"Oh, it's quite easy. I merely want you to buy a ticket for me; they won't let me in otherwise. Here, I have the money." And gracefully she handed Mrs. Miller two dimes and a nickel. *40's*

They went over to the theatre together. An usherette direct-ed them to a lounge; in twenty minutes the picture would be over. *Short*

[handwritten: one screen]

seem out of character
excited - breaking law
yemming - concerned

40's

feels concerned, criminal-esque

"I feel just like a genuine criminal," said Mrs. Miller gaily, as she sat down. "I mean that sort of thing's against the law, isn't it? I do hope I haven't done the wrong thing. Your mother knows where you are, dear? I mean she does, doesn't she?"

silence of show?
not peaceful

The little girl said nothing. She unbuttoned her coat and folded it across her lap. Her dress underneath was prim and dark blue. A gold chain dangled about her neck, and her fingers, sensitive and musical-looking, toyed with it. Examining her more attentively, Mrs. Miller decided the truly distinctive feature was not her hair, but her eyes; they were hazel, steady, lacking any childlike quality whatsoever and, because of their size, seemed to consume her small face.

title
hair
w/o
child eyes

a name
drawings

Mrs. Miller offered a peppermint. "What's your name, dear?"

name of story

more out of character

"Miriam," she said, as though, in some curious way, it were information already familiar.

Same name!

"Why, isn't that funny—my name's Miriam, too. And it's not a terribly common name either. Now, don't tell me your last name's Miller!"

interesting, mysterious

"Just Miriam."

already knows this, it's her

"But isn't that funny?"

"Moderately," said Miriam, and rolled the peppermint on her tongue.

Mrs. Miller flushed and shifted uncomfortably. "You have such a large vocabulary for such a little girl."

"Do I?"

"Well, yes," said Mrs. Miller, hastily changing the topic to: "Do you like the movies?"

"I really wouldn't know," said Miriam. "I've never been before."

inexperienced, yet wise girl

Women began filling the lounge; the rumble of the newsreel bombs exploded in the distance. Mrs. Miller rose,

3

tucking her purse under her arm. "I guess I'd better be running now if I want to get a seat," she said. "It was nice to have met you."

Miriam nodded ever so slightly.

It snowed all week. Wheels and footsteps moved soundlessly on the street, as if the business of living continued secretly behind a pale but impenetrable curtain. In the falling quiet there was no sky or earth, only snow lifting in the wind, frosting the window glass, chilling the rooms, deadening and hushing the city. At all hours it was necessary to keep a lamp lighted, and Mrs. Miller lost track of the days: Friday was no different from Saturday, and on Sunday she went to the grocery: closed, of course.

That evening she scrambled eggs and fixed a bowl of tomato soup. Then, after putting on a flannel robe and cold-creaming her face, she propped herself up in bed with a hot water bottle under her feet. She was reading the *Times* when the doorbell rang. At first she thought it must be a mistake and whoever it was would go away. But it rang and rang and settled to a persistent buzz. She looked at the clock: a little after eleven; it did not seem possible, she was always asleep by ten.

Climbing out of bed, she trotted barefoot across the living room. "I'm coming, please be patient." The latch was caught; she turned it this way and that way and the bell never paused an instant. "Stop it," she cried. The bolt gave way and she opened the door an inch. "What in heaven's name?"

"Hello," said Miriam.

"Oh . . . why, hello," said Mrs. Miller, stepping hesitantly into the hall. "You're that little girl."

"I thought you'd never answer, but I kept my finger on the button; I knew you were home. Aren't you glad to see me?"

confused/concerned

Mrs. Miller did not know what to say. Miriam, she saw, wore the same plum-velvet coat and now she had also a beret to match; her white hair was braided in two shining plaits and looped at the ends with enormous white ribbons.

sense of environment

"Since I've waited so long, you could at least let me in," she said.

demanding demanding, pushy, greedy

"It's awfully late . . ."

persistant young lady

Miriam regarded her blankly, "What difference does that make? Let me in. It's cold out here and I have on a silk dress." Then, with a gentle gesture, she urged Mrs. Miller aside and passed into the apartment.

blank like snow

↓ more white

She dropped her coat and beret on a chair. She was indeed wearing a silk dress. White silk. White silk in February. The skirt was beautifully pleated and the sleeves long; it made a faint rustle as she strolled about the room. "I like your place," she said. "I like the rug, blue's my favorite color." She touched a paper rose in a vase on the coffee table. "Imitation," she commented wanly. "How sad. Aren't imitations sad?" She seated herself on the sofa, daintily spreading her skirt.

me shadow

not fake, sad imitation

"What do you want?" asked Mrs. Miller.

demanding

"Sit down," said Miriam. "It makes me nervous to see people stand."

why? concerned...

Mrs. Miller sank to a hassock. "What do you want?" she repeated.

followed command

"You know, I don't think you're glad I came."

For a second time Mrs. Miller was without an answer; her hand motioned vaguely. Miriam giggled and pressed back on a mound of chintz pillows. Mrs. Miller observed that the girl was less pale than she remembered; her cheeks were flushed.

"How did you know where I lived?"

Miriam frowned. "That's no question at all. What's your name? What's mine?"

real question

"But I'm not listed in the phone book."

same person?
alter ego?
– inner child?

5

"Oh, let's talk about something else."

Mrs. Miller said, "Your mother must be insane to let a child like you wander around at all hours of the night—and in such ridiculous clothes. She must be out of her mind."

[handwritten: Judging her mother, good idea? NO.]

Miriam got up and moved to a corner where a covered bird cage hung from a ceiling chain. She peeked beneath the cover. "It's a canary," she said. "Would you mind if I woke him? I'd like to hear him sing." *[handwritten: birds name]*

"Leave Tommy alone," said Mrs. Miller, anxiously. "Don't you dare wake him."

"Certainly," said Miriam. "But I don't see why I can't hear him sing." And then, "Have you anything to eat? I'm starving! Even milk and a jam sandwich would be fine."

[handwritten: Mrs. Miller is concerned + irritated]

"Look," said Mrs. Miller, arising from the hassock, "look—if I make some nice sandwiches will you be a good child and run along home? It's past midnight, I'm sure."

"It's snowing," reproached Miriam. "And cold and dark."

"Well, you shouldn't have come here to begin with," said Mrs. Miller, struggling to control her voice. "I can't help the weather. If you want anything to eat you'll have to promise to leave."

Miriam brushed a braid against her cheek. Her eyes were thoughtful, as if weighing the proposition. She turned toward the bird cage. "Very well," she said, "I promise."

[handwritten: transaction] *[handwritten: possibly]*

How old is she? Ten? Eleven? Mrs. Miller, in the kitchen, unsealed a jar of strawberry preserves and cut four slices of bread. She poured a glass of milk and paused to light a cigarette. *And why has she come?* Her hand shook as she held the match, fascinated, till it burned her finger. The canary was singing; singing as he did in the morning and at no other time. "Miriam," she called, "Miriam, I told you not to disturb Tommy." There was no answer. She called again; all she heard

[handwritten: smokes]

[handwritten: - why is she fascinated at the burning lint?]

6

was the canary. She inhaled the cigarette and discovered she had lighted the cork-tip end and—oh, really, she mustn't lose her temper, *more out of character*

She carried the food in on a tray and set it on the coffee table. She saw first that the bird cage still wore its night cover. And Tommy was singing. It gave her a queer sensation. And no one was in the room. Mrs. Miller went through an alcove leading to her bedroom; at the door she caught her breath.

"What are you doing?" she asked. *where is the girl?*

Miriam glanced up, and in her eyes there was a look that was not ordinary. She was standing by the bureau, a jewel case opened before her. For a minute she studied Mrs. Miller, *stealing?* forcing their eyes to meet, and she smiled. "There's nothing good here," she said. "But I like this," Her hand held a cameo brooch. "It's charming." *demanding, extremly rude* *rude!* *white elobrate mysterious?*

"Suppose—perhaps you'd better put it back," said Mrs. Miller, feeling suddenly the need of some support. She leaned against the door frame; her head was unbearably heavy; a pressure weighted the rhythm of her heartbeat. The light seemed to flutter defectively. "Please, child—a gift from my husband . . ."

"But it's beautiful and I want it," said Miriam. "Give it to me." *persistant, rude, forceful*

As she stood, striving to shape a sentence which would somehow save the brooch, it came to Mrs. Miller there was no one to whom she might turn; she was alone; a fact that had not been among her thoughts for a long time. Its sheer emphasis was stunning. But here in her own room in the hushed snow-city were evidences she could not ignore or, she knew with startling clarity, resist. *realizing she has nobody and is alone* *cant resist force*

did she give her the brooch?

Miriam ate ravenously, and when the sandwiches and milk were gone, her fingers made cobweb movements over the

7

creepy little gin

plate, gathering crumbs. The cameo gleamed on her blouse, the blond profile like a trick reflection of its wearer. "That was very nice," she sighed, "though now an almond cake or a cherry would be ideal. Sweets are lovely, don't you think?"

taking advantage

Mrs. Miller was perched precariously on the hassock, smoking a cigarette. Her hair net had slipped lopsided, and loose strands straggled down her face. Her eyes were stupidly concentrated on nothing and her cheeks were mottled in red patches, as though a fierce slap had left permanent marks.

"Is there a candy—a cake?"

Mrs. Miller tapped ash on the rug. Her head swayed slightly as she tried to focus her eyes. "You promised to leave if I made the sandwiches," she said. *out of it*

"Dear me, did I?"

little girl makes her sick

"It was a promise and I'm tired and I don't feel well at all."

"Mustn't fret," said Miriam. "I'm only teasing."

She picked up her coat, slung it over her arm, and arranged her beret in front of a mirror. Presently she bent close to Mrs. Miller and whispered, "Kiss me good night."

"Please—I'd rather not," said Mrs. Miller.

very inconsiderate

wow, brave girl

Miriam lifted a shoulder, arched an eyebrow. "As you like," she said, and went directly to the coffee table, seized the vase containing the paper roses, carried it to where the hard surface of the floor lay bare, and hurled it downward. Glass sprayed in all directions, and she stamped her foot on the bouquet.

Then slowly she walked to the door, but before closing it she looked back at Mrs. Miller with a slyly innocent curiosity.

goes to bed angry, confused, upset

Mrs. Miller spent the next day in bed, rising once to feed the canary and drink a cup of tea; she took her temperature and had none, yet her dreams were feverishly agitated; their unbalanced mood lingered even as she lay staring wide-eyed at the ceiling. One dream threaded through the others like an

8

dreaming

elusively mysterious theme in a complicated symphony, and the scenes it depicted were sharply outlined, as though sketched by a hand of gifted intensity: a small girl, wearing a bridal gown and a wreath of leaves, led a gray procession *white* down a mountain path, and among them there was unusual silence till a woman at the rear asked, "Where is she taking us?" "No one knows," said an old man marching in front. "But isn't she pretty?" volunteered a third voice. "Isn't she like a frost flower . . . so shining and white?" *like Miriam*

white, cold, shining

Tuesday morning she woke up feeling better; harsh slats of sunlight, slanting through Venetian blinds, shed a disrupting light on her unwholesome fancies. She opened the window to discover a thawed, mild-as-spring day; a sweep of clean new clouds crumpled against a vastly blue, out-of-season sky; and across the low line of rooftops she could see the river and smoke curving from tugboat stacks in a warm wind. A great silver truck plowed the snow-banked street, its machine sound humming on the air. *Where did she get the $?*

After straightening the apartment, she went to the grocer's, cashed a check, and continued to Schrafft's, where she ate breakfast and chatted happily with the waitress. Oh, it was a wonderful day—more like a holiday—and it would be so foolish to go home. *happy, not secluded!*

She boarded a Lexington Avenue bus and rode up to Eighty-sixth Street; it was here that she had decided to do a little shopping. *no need. out of character*

She had no idea what she wanted or needed, but she idled along, intent only upon the passersby, brisk and preoccupied, who gave her a disturbing sense of separateness. *why? her unmodern look?*

It was while waiting at the corner of Third Avenue that she saw the man: an old man, bowlegged and stooped under an armload of bulging packages; he wore a shabby brown coat and a checkered cap. Suddenly she realized they were *→ –in her dream*

9

exchanging a smile: there was nothing friendly about this smile, it was merely two cold flickers of recognition. But she was certain she had never seen him before.

He was standing next to an El pillar, and as she crossed the street he turned and followed. He kept quite close; from the corner of her eye she watched his reflection wavering on the shop windows.

Then in the middle of the block she stopped and faced him. He stopped also and cocked his head, grinning. But what could she say? Do? Here, in broad daylight, on Eighty-sixth Street? It was useless and, despising her own helplessness, she quickened her steps.

Now Second Avenue is a dismal street, made from scraps and ends; part cobblestone, part asphalt, part cement; and its atmosphere of desertion is permanent. Mrs. Miller walked five blocks without meeting anyone, and all the while the steady crunch of his footfalls in the snow stayed near. And when she came to a florist's shop, the sound was still with her. She hurried inside and watched through the glass door as the old man passed; he kept his eyes straight ahead and didn't slow his pace, but he did one strange, telling thing: he tipped his cap.

"Six white ones, did you say?" asked the florist. "Yes," she told him, "white roses." From there she went to a glassware store and selected a vase, presumably a replacement for the one Miriam had broken, though the price was intolerable and the vase itself (she thought) grotesquely vulgar. But a series of unaccountable purchases had begun, as if by prearranged plan: a plan of which she had not the least knowledge or control.

She bought a bag of glazed cherries, and at a place called the Knickerbocker Bakery she paid forty cents for six almond cakes.

10

Within the last hour the weather had turned cold again; like blurred lenses, winter clouds cast a shade over the sun, and the skeleton of an early dusk colored the sky; a damp mist mixed with the wind, and the voices of a few children who romped high on mountains of gutter snow seemed lonely and cheerless. Soon the first flake fell, and when Mrs. Miller reached the brownstone house, snow was falling in a swift screen, and foot tracks vanished as they were printed.

white roses, white hair, white snow

The white roses were arranged decoratively in the vase. The glazed cherries shone on a ceramic plate. The almond cakes, dusted with sugar, awaited a hand. The canary fluttered on its swing and picked at a bar of seed.

At precisely five the doorbell rang. Mrs. Miller knew who it was. The hem of her housecoat trailed as she crossed the floor. "Is that you?" she called. *→ as if "you" isnt anybody...*

"Naturally," said Miriam, the word resounding shrilly from the hall. "Open this door." *RUDE! again...*

"Go away," said Mrs. Miller.

"Please hurry . . . I have a heavy package."

again... "Go away," said Mrs. Miller. She returned to the living room, lighted a cigarette, sat down, and calmly listened to the buzzer; on and on and on. "You might as well leave. I have no intention of letting you in."

Shortly the bell stopped. For possibly ten minutes Mrs. Miller did not move. Then, hearing no sound, she concluded Miriam had gone. She tiptoed to the door and opened it a sliver; Miriam was half-reclining atop a cardboard box with a beautiful French doll cradled in her arms. *Waited over 10min.*

"Really, I thought you were never coming," she said peevishly. "Here, help me get this in, it's awfully heavy."

It was not spell-like compulsion that Mrs. Miller felt, but rather a curious passivity; she brought in the box, Miriam the

11

doll. Miriam curled up on the sofa, not troubling to remove her coat or beret, and watched disinterestedly as Mrs. Miller dropped the box and stood trembling, trying to catch her breath.

"Thank you," she said. In the daylight she looked pinched and drawn, her hair less luminous. The French doll she was loving wore an exquisite powdered wig, and its idiot glass eyes sought solace in Miriam's. "I have a surprise," she continued. "Look into my box."

Kneeling, Mrs. Miller parted the flaps and lifted out another doll; then a blue dress which she recalled as the one Miriam had worn that first night at the theatre; and of the remainder she said, "It's all clothes. Why?"

WHAT?!

"Because I've come to live with you," said Miriam, twisting a cherry stem. "Wasn't it nice of you to buy me the cherries . . . ?"

"But you can't! For God's sake go away—go away and leave me alone!"

". . . and the roses and the almond cakes? How really wonderfully generous. You know, these cherries are delicious. The last place I lived was with an old man; he was terribly poor and we never had good things to eat. But I think I'll be happy here." She paused to snuggle her doll closer. "Now, if you'll just show me where to put my things . . ."

Mrs. Miller's face dissolved into a mask of ugly red lines; she began to cry, and it was an unnatural, tearless sort of weeping, as though, not having wept for a long time, she had forgotten how. Carefully she edged backward till she touched the door.

never showed emotion

She fumbled through the hall and down the stairs to a landing below. She pounded frantically on the door of the first apartment she came to; a short, redheaded man answered and she pushed past him. "Say, what the hell is this?" he said.

"Anything wrong, lover?" asked a young woman who appeared from the kitchen, drying her hands. And it was to her that Mrs. Miller turned.

"Listen," she cried, "I'm ashamed behaving this way but— well, I'm Mrs. H. T. Miller and I live upstairs and . . ." She pressed her hands over her face. "It sounds so absurd . . ."

The woman guided her to a chair, while the man excitedly rattled pocket change. "Yeah?"

"I live upstairs and there's a little girl visiting me, and I suppose that I'm afraid of her. She won't leave and I can't make her and—she's going to do something terrible. She's already stolen my cameo, but she's about to do something worse—something terrible!" *how does she know?*

The man asked, "Is she a relative, huh?"

Mrs. Miller shook her head. "I don't know who she is. Her name's Miriam, but I don't know for certain who she is."

"You gotta calm down, honey," said the woman, stroking Mrs. Miller's arm. "Harry here'll tend to this kid. Go on, lover." And Mrs. Miller said, "The door's open—5A."

After the man left, the woman brought a towel and bathed Mrs. Miller's face. "You're very kind," Mrs. Miller said. "I'm sorry to act like such a fool, only this wicked child . . ."

"Sure honey," consoled the woman. "Now, you better take it easy."

Mrs. Miller rested her head in the crook of her arm; she was quiet enough to be asleep. The woman turned a radio dial; a piano and a husky voice filled the silence and the woman, tapping her foot, kept excellent time. "Maybe we oughta go up too," she said.

"I don't want to see her again. I don't want to be anywhere near her."

"Uh huh, but what you shoulda done, you shoulda called a cop." *focusing on what "shoulda" been done.*

13

Presently they heard the man on the stairs. He strode into the room frowning and scratching the back of his neck. "Nobody there," he said, honestly embarrassed. "She musta beat it."

"Harry, you're a jerk," announced the woman. "We been sitting here the whole time and we woulda seen . . ." She stopped abruptly, for the man's glance was sharp.

"I looked all over," he said, "and there just ain't nobody there. Nobody, understand?"

"Tell me," said Mrs. Miller, rising, "tell me, did you see a large box? Or a doll?"

"No, ma'am, I didn't."

And the woman, as if delivering a verdict, said, "Well, for cryinoutloud . . ."

Miriam fled?

Mrs. Miller entered her apartment softly; she walked to the center of the room and stood quite still. No, in a sense it had not changed: the roses, the cakes, and the cherries were in place. But this was an empty room, emptier than if the furnishings and familiars were not present, lifeless and petrified as a funeral parlor. The sofa loomed before her with a new strangeness: its vacancy had a meaning that would have been less penetrating and terrible had Miriam been curled on it. She gazed fixedly at the space where she remembered setting the box and, for a moment, the hassock spun desperately. And she looked through the window; surely the river was real, surely snow was falling—but then, one could not be certain witness to anything: Miriam, so vividly there—and yet, where was she? Where, where?

compared her home to a funeral parlor

As though moving in a dream, she sank to a chair. The room was losing shape; it was dark and getting darker and there was nothing to be done about it; she could not lift her hand to light a lamp.

became helpless

14

Suddenly, closing her eyes, she felt an upward surge, like a diver emerging from some deeper, greener depth. In times of terror or immense distress, there are moments when the mind waits, as though for a revelation, while a skein of calm is woven over thought; it is like a sleep, or a supernatural trance; and during this lull one is aware of a force of quiet reasoning: well, what if she had never really known a girl named Miriam? that she had been foolishly frightened on the street? In the end, like everything else, it was of no importance. For the only thing she had lost to Miriam was her identity, but now she knew she had found again the person who lived in this room, who cooked her own meals, who owned a canary, who was someone she could trust and believe in: Mrs. H. T. Miller.

Listening in contentment, she became aware of a double sound: a bureau drawer opening and closing; she seemed to hear it long after completion—opening and closing. Then gradually, the harshness of it was replaced by the murmur of a silk dress and this, delicately faint, was moving nearer and swelling in intensity till the walls trembled with the vibration and the room was caving under a wave of whispers. Mrs. Miller stiffened and opened her eyes to a dull, direct stare.

"Hello," said Miriam. What the heck?

dreaming back to Miriam died? flash to
she was little?! when beginning. not
How she became being alone?
alone?

15

ZOO ISLAND

Tomás Rivera

Jose had just turned fifteen when he woke up one day with a great desire of taking a census count, of making a town and making everybody in it do what he said. All this happened because during the night he had dreamed that it was raining and, since they would not be working in the fields the next day, he dreamed about doing various things. But when he awoke, it hadn't rained at all. Anyway, he still had the desire.

The first thing he did when he got up was to count his family and himself—five. "We're five" he thought. Then he went on to the other family that lived with his, his uncle's— "Five more, and that's ten." Next he counted the people living in the chicken coop across the way. "Manuel and his wife and four more—that's six." And, with the ten he already had— "that's sixteen." Then he took into account the coop where Manuel's uncle lived, where there were three families. The first one, Don Jose's family, had seven, so now there were twenty-three. He was about to count the second family, when they told him to get ready to go to the fields.

It was still dark at five-thirty in the morning, and that day they would have to travel some fifty miles to reach the field

16

overgrown with thistle that they had been working on. And as soon as they finished it, they would have to continue searching for more work. It would be way after dark by the time they got back. In the summertime, they could work up to eight o'clock. Then add an hour on the road back, plus the stop at the little store to buy something to eat. . . . "We won't get back to the farm till late," he thought. But now he had something to do during the day while they were pulling up thistle. During the day, he could figure out exactly how many there were on that farm in Iowa.

"Here come those sonsabitches."

"Don't say bad words in front of the kids, Pa. They'll go around saying 'em all the time. That'd really be something, then, wouldn't it?"

"I'll bust them in the mouth if I hear them swearing. But here come those Whities. They don't leave a person in peace, do they? Soon as Sunday comes, and they come riding over to see us, to see how we live. They even stop and try to peek inside our chicken coops. You saw last Sunday how that row of cars passed by here. Them all laughing and laughing, and pointing at us. And you think they care about the dust they raise? Hell no. With their windows closed, why, they go on by just as fine as you please. And here we are, just like a bunch of monkeys in that park in San Antonio—Parkenrich."

"Aw, let 'em be, Pa. They're not doing nothing to us, they're not doing any harm—not even if they was gypsies. Why you get all heated up for?"

"Well, it sets my blood a-boiling, that's all. Why don't they mind their own business? I'm going to tell the owner to put a lock on the gate, so when they come they can't drive inside."

"Aw, let it go, it's nothing to make a fuss over."

"It sure is."

17

"We're almost to the field. Pa, you think we'll find work after we finish here?"

"Sure, son, there's always a lot of work. They don't take us for a bunch of lazy-bones. You saw how the boss's eyes popped out when I started pulling out all that thistle without any gloves on. Huh, they have to use gloves for everything. So, they're bound to recommend us to the other landowners. You'll see how they'll come and ask us if we want another field to work."

"The first thing I'll do is jot down the names on a list. Then, I'll use a page for each family, and that way I won't lose anybody. And for each bachelor, too, I'll use a page for each one, yeah. I'll also write down everybody's age. I wonder how many men and women there are on this farm, anyway? We're forty-nine field hands, counting the eight- and nine-year-olds. Then, there's a bunch of kids, and then there's the two grandmothers that can't work anymore. The best thing to do is to get Jitter and Hank to help me with the counting. They could go to each coop and get the information, then we could gather up all the numbers. Too, it would be a good idea to put a number on each coop. Then, I could paint the number above each door. We could even pick up the mail from the box and distribute it, and that way the folks could even put the number of their coop on the letters they write. Sure, I bet that would make them feel better. Then we could even put up a sign at the farm gate that'll tell the number of people that live here, but . . . what would we call the farm? It doesn't have a name. I gotta think about that."

It rained the next day, and the following day as well. Therefore, Jose had the time and the opportunity to think over his plan. He made his helpers, Jitter and Hank, stick a pencil behind their ear, strap on a wrist watch—which they acquired easily enough—and shine their shoes. They also spent a half day reviewing the questions they would put to each household head and to each bachelor. The folks became aware of what the youngsters were up to and were soon talking about how they were going to be counted.

"These kids are always coming up with something . . . just ideas that pop into their heads or that they learn in school. Now, what for? What're they going to get out of counting us? Why, it's just a game, plain tomfoolery."

"Don't think that, comadre, no, no. These kids nowadays are on the ball, always inquiring about something or other. And you know, I like what they're doing. I like having my name put on a piece of paper, like they say they're gonna do. Tell me, when's anybody ever asked you your name and how many you got in the family and then write it all down on paper. You better believe it! Let them boys be, let 'em be, leastways while the rain keeps us from working."

"Yeah, but, what's it good for? I mean, how come so many questions? And then there's some things a person just doesn't say."

"Well, if you don't want to, don't tell 'em nothin'. But, look, all they want to know is how many of us there are in this grove. But, too, I think they want to feel like we're a whole lot of people. See here, in that little town where we buy our food there're only eighty-three souls, and you know what? They have a church, a dance hall, a filling station, a grocery store, and even a little school. Here, we're more than eighty-three, I'll bet, and we don't have any of that. Why, we only have a water pump and four outhouses, right?"

"Now, you two are going to gather the names and the information. Y'all go together so there won't be any problems. After each coop, you'll bring me the information right back.

Y'all jot it down on a sheet of paper and bring it to me, then I'll make a note of it in this notebook I got here. Let's start out with my family. You, Hank, ask me questions and jot down everything. Then you give me what you wrote down so that I can make a note of it. Do y'all understand what we're going to do? Don't be afraid. Just knock on the door and ask. Don't be afraid."

It took them all afternoon to gather and jot down the details, then they compiled all the figures by the light of an oil lamp. Yes, it turned out that there were more fieldhands on the farm than there were people in the town where they bought their food. Actually, there were eighty-six on the farm, but the boys came up with a figure of eighty-seven because two women were expecting and they counted them for three. They gave the exact number to the rest of the folks, explaining the part about the pregnant women. Everyone was pleased to know that the farm settlement was really a town and bigger than the one where they bought their groceries every Saturday.

The third time the boys went over the figures they realized that they had forgotten to go over to Don Simon's shack. They had simply overlooked it because it was on the other side of the grove. When old Don Simon had gotten upset and fought with Stumpy, he asked the owner to take the tractor and drag his coop to the other side of the grove, where no one would bother him. The owner did this right away. There was something in Don Simon's eyes that made people jump. It wasn't just his gaze but also the fact that he hardly ever spoke. So, when he did talk everybody listened up so as not to lose a single word.

It was already late and the boys decided not to go see him until the next day, but the fact of the matter was they were a little afraid just thinking that they would have to go and ask him something. They remembered the to-do in the field when Don Simon got fed up with Stumpy's needling him and chased Stumpy all over the field with his onion knife. Then Stumpy, even though he was much younger, tripped and fell, tangling himself in the tow-sacks. Right then, Don Simon threw himself on Stumpy, slicing at him with his knife. What saved Stumpy were the tow-sacks. Luckily, Stumpy came out of it with only a slight wound in his leg; nonetheless, it did bleed quite a bit. When the owner was told what had happened, he ran Stumpy off. But Don Simon explained that it wasn't much to make a fuss over, so he let Stumpy stay but the owner did move Don Simon's coop to the other side of the grove, just like Don Simon wanted. So, that's why the boys were a little afraid of him. But, like they told themselves, just not riling him, he was good folk. Stumpy had been riling Don Simon for some time about his wife leaving him for somebody else.

"Excuse us, Don Simon, but we're taking up the farm census, and we'd like to ask you a few questions. You don't have to answer them if you don't want to."

"All right."

"How old are you?"

"Old enough."

"When were you born?"

"When my mother born me."

"Where were you born?"

"In the world."

"Do you have a family?"

"No."

"How come you don't talk much?"

"This is for the census, right?"

"No."

"What for, then? I reckon y'all think you talk a lot. Well, not only y'all but all the folks here. What y'all do most of the time is open your mouth and make noise. Y'all just like to talk to yourselves, that's all. I do the same, but I do it silently, the rest of you do it out loud."

"Well, Don Simon, I believe that's all. Thanks for your cooperation. You know, we're eighty-eight souls here on this farm. We're plenty, right?"

"Well, you know, I kinda like what y'all are doing. By counting yourself, you begin everything. That way you know you're not only here but that you're alive. Y'all know what you oughta call this place?"

"No."

"Zoo Island."

The following Sunday just about all the people on the farm had their picture taken next to the sign the boys had made on Saturday afternoon and which they had put up at the farm gate. It said: *Zoo Island, Pop. 88½*. One of the women had given birth.

And every morning Jose would no sooner get up than he would go see the sign. He was part of that number, he was in Zoo Island, in Iowa, and like Don Simon said, in the world. He didn't know why, but there was a warm feeling that started in his feet and rose through his body until he felt it in his throat and in all his senses. Then this same feeling made him talk, made him open his mouth. At times it even made him shout. The shouting was something the owner never managed to understand. By the time he arrived sleepy-eyed in the morning, the boy would be shouting. Sometimes he thought about asking him why he shouted, but then he'd get busy with other things and forget all about it.

AT THE PITT-RIVERS

Penelope Lively

They've got this museum in Oxford, called the Pitt-Rivers; I spend a lot of time there. It's a weird place, really weird, stuff from all over the world crammed into glass cases like some kind of mad junk shop—native things from New Guinea and Mexico and Sumatra and wherever you like to think of. Spears and stone axes and masks and a thousand different kinds of fishhook. And bead jewellery and peculiar musical instruments. And a great totem from Canada. You can learn a lot there about what people get up to: it makes you think. Mostly it's pretty depressing—umpteen different nasty ways of killing each other.

I didn't start going there to learn anything; just because it was a nice quiet place to mooch around and be on my own, Saturdays, or after school. It got to be a kind of habit. There aren't often people there—the odd art student, a few kids gawping at the shrunken heads, one or two serious-looking blokes wandering around. The porter's usually reading the *Sun* or having a snooze; there's not a lot of custom. The

23

Natural History Museum is a bigger draw; you have to go through that to get into the Pitt-Rivers. You'll always get an audience for a dinosaur and a few nasty-looking jellyfish in formalin. Actually I'm partial to the Natural History Museum myself; that makes you think, too. All those fossils, and then in the end you and me. I had a go at reading *The Origin of Species* last term, not that I got very far. There's a room upstairs in the museum where Darwin's friend—Huxley—had this great argument with that bishop and the rest of them. It says so on the door. I like that, it seems kind of respectful. Putting up a plaque to an argument, instead of just JOE SOAP WAS BORN HERE or whatever. It should be done more often.

It was in the Natural History Museum—underneath the central whale—that I first saw her, and since my mind was on natural selection I thought she wasn't all that good an example of it. I remember thinking that it was funny it doesn't seem to operate with girls, so you got them getting prettier and prettier, because good-looking girls have a better deal than bad-looking ones, you've only got to observe a bit to see that. I always notice girls, to see if they're pretty or not, and she wasn't. She wasn't specially ugly; just very ordinary— you wouldn't look at her twice. She was sitting on a bench, watching the entrance.

All the girls I know—at school or round where I live—are either attractive or they're not. If they're attractive they have lots of blokes after them and if they're not they don't. It's as simple as that. If they're attractive just looking at them makes you think of all sorts of things, imagine what it would be like and so forth, and if they're not then it doesn't really occur to you, except in so far as it occurs to you a good deal of the time, actually. This girl was definitely not attractive. In the first place she was in fact quite old, not far off thirty, I should think, and in the second she hadn't got a nice figure; her legs

were kind of dumpy and she didn't have pretty hair or anything like that. I gave her a look, just automatically, to check,
and then didn't bother with her.

Until I came alongside, where I could see her face clearly,
and then I looked again. And again. She still wasn't pretty, but
she had the most beautiful expression I've ever seen in my life.
She glowed; that's the only way I can put it. She sat there with
her hands in her lap, watching the door, and radiating away
so that in a peculiar fashion it made you feel good just to look
at her, a bit like you were joining in how she felt. Stupid, I
daresay, but that's how it was.

And I thought to myself: oh ho . . . I mean, I've seen films
and I've read books and I know a bit about things.

As a matter of fact I've been in love myself twice. The first
time was with a girl in my class at school and I suppose it was
a bit of a trial run, really, I mean I'm not altogether sure how
much I was feeling it but it seemed quite important when it
was going on. The second time was last year, when I was fifteen. She came to stay with her married sister who lives round
the corner from us and though it's months and months ago
now I still feel quite faint and weak when I go past the house.

Oh ho, I thought. I felt kindly—sort of benign—and a
bit curious to see what the bloke would be like. I thought he
couldn't be much because of her not being pretty. I mean,
in films you can always tell who's going to fall for who
because they'll be the two good-lookers and while I'm not
saying real life's like that there is a way people match each
other, isn't there, you've only got to look round at married
people. Let me hasten to say that I'm not all that good-
looking myself, only about B+. Not too bad, but not all that
marvellous either.

But he didn't show up and I wanted to get on into the Pitt-
Rivers, so I left her there, waiting. What I haven't said is that

one of the things I go to the Pitt-Rivers for is to write poetry. I write quite a lot of poetry. I could do it at home—I often do—and it's not that I'm coy or anything, my parents know about it and they're quite interested, but I just like the idea of having a special place to go to. It's quiet there, and a bit odd like I've said, and nobody takes any notice of me.

Sometimes I feel I'm getting somewhere with this poetry, and other times it looks to me pretty awful. I showed a few poems to our English master and he was very helpful: he said what was good and pointed out where I'd used words badly, or not worked out what I was thinking very well, so that was quite encouraging. He's a nice bloke. I like his lessons. He's very good at explaining poetry. I mean, I think poetry's amazingly difficult: sometimes you read a thing again and again and you just can't see what the hell the person's getting at. He reads all sorts of poetry to us, our English master, and you really get the hang of it after a bit—hard stuff like Hopkins and *The Hound of Heaven,* and Donne. He read us some of those Donne poems about love the other day which are all very explicit and I must say first time round I hadn't quite got the point—"Licence my roving hands . . ." and so forth—but he wasn't embarrassed or anything, our English master, and when you realise that it's not geography he's talking about, the poet, then as a matter of fact I think that poem's lovely. I got a bit fed up with the way some of my mates were sniggering about it, being all-knowing; truth to tell I doubt if they know any more than I do, it's all just show. And that's a beautiful poem: I mean, if anything makes it clear that there's nothing wrong about sex, that poem does, they ought to make it compulsory reading for some people.

Anyway, I went on into the Pitt-Rivers and I was up on the first floor, in a favourite corner of mine among the arrowheads, when I saw her again, and I must say I got quite a

26

shock. Because the man with her was an old bloke: he was older than my father, fiftyish and more, he must have been at least twenty years older than her. So I reckoned I must have made a mistake. Not that at all.

They were talking, though I couldn't hear what they were saying because they were on the far side of the gallery. They stopped in front of a case and I could see their faces quite clearly. They stood there looking at each other, not talking anymore, and I realised I hadn't made a mistake after all. Absolutely not. They didn't touch each other, they just stood and looked; it seemed like ages. I don't imagine they knew I was there.

And that time I was shocked. Really shocked. I don't mind telling you, I thought it was disgusting. He was an ordinary-looking person—he might have been a schoolmaster or something, he wore those kind of clothes, old trousers and sweater, and he had greyish hair, a bit long. And there was she, and as I've said she wasn't pretty, not at all, but she had this marvellous look about her, and she was years and years younger.

It was because of him, I realised, that she had that look.

I didn't like it at all. I got up, from where I was sitting, with quite a clatter to make sure they heard me and I went stumping off out of the museum. I wasn't going to write any more poetry that day, I could see. I went off home and truth to tell I didn't really think much more about them, that man and the girl, mainly because of being rather disgusted, like I said.

A couple of weeks later they were there again. They were on the ground floor, at the back, by the rush matting and ceremonial gear for with-it tribesmen, leaning up against a glass case that they weren't looking into, and talking. At least he was talking, quiet and serious, and she was listening, and nodding from time to time. I was busy with some thinking I wanted to do, and I tried not to take any notice of them;

I mean, they were neither here nor there as far as I was concerned, none of my business, though I still thought it was a bit creepy. I couldn't see *why*, frankly. You fancy people your own age, and that's all there is to it, is what I thought. What I'd always thought.

So I ignored them, except that I couldn't quite. I kept sneaking a look, every now and then, and the more I did the more I felt kind of friendly towards them; I liked them. Which was a bit weird considering they didn't know I even existed—they certainly weren't interested in *me*—so it was a pretty one-sided kind of relationship. I thought he seemed like a nice bloke, whatever you thought about him and her and all that. It was something about the way he smiled, and the way he told her things (not that I ever heard a word they said, I wasn't eavesdropping, not ever, let's be quite clear about that) that made her look interested and say things back and so on. I thought it was obvious they liked talking to each other, quite apart from anything else. I thought that was nice.

I only took out that girl I mentioned—the one who came to stay with her sister—once, and as a matter of fact we couldn't find much to talk about. I was still in love with her—no doubt about that—but it was a bit sticky, I don't mind admitting. In fact I was quite glad when it was time to take her back to her sister's. In many ways the best part was just thinking about her.

Every time I looked at the girl—the Pitt-Rivers one, that is—I found myself imagining what it must be like being able to feel that you've made someone look like that. Radiant, like she was. Which is what that bloke must have been able to feel. I found myself putting myself in his place, as it were, and wondering. I've done a lot of wondering about things like that—everybody does, I suppose—but mostly it's been more kind of basic. Now, I began to think I didn't really know anything. Looking at those two—watching them, if you like—was a bit like seeing something go on behind a thick glass window, so it was half removed from you. You could see but not hear, hear but not touch, or whatever. I could see, but I didn't know.

I suppose you could say I was envious, in a funny kind of way. I don't mean jealous in that I fancied the girl, or anything like that. As I've said already, she wasn't pretty, or even attractive. And I wasn't envious like you might be envious of someone for being happier than you are, because I'm not specially unhappy, as it happens. I think I was envious of them for being what they were—as though one fossil creature might be envious of a more evolved kind of fossil creature, which of course is a stupid idea.

When I was in the Pitt-Rivers again I looked for them, quite deliberately, but they weren't there. I was disappointed, though I pretended to myself it really didn't matter. I wondered about why they went there in the first place; I mean, people have to meet each other somewhere but why *there*? It doesn't exactly spring to mind as a romantic spot. I supposed there were reasons they didn't want to meet somewhere obvious and public: maybe he was married, I thought, or maybe she was, even. I wondered if that was the only place they met, or did they have others. Once walking through the botanical gardens, I found myself looking for them in the big glasshouses there.

I know the inside of the Pitt-Rivers pretty well by now. Considering it's not anthropology or ethnology or whatever I went there for in the first place, it's quite surprising what a lot I could tell you about the things people believe and do. Primitive people, that is—what the Pitt-Rivers calls primitive people. And I think it's all very sad, actually: sad because it's like children, not understanding how things work and getting it all wrong, and carving each other up because of it a lot of the time. It does actually make you feel things get better— wars and bombs and everything notwithstanding. Nobody wants to go on being a child all their lives.

I was thinking about this—looking at a case full of partic- ularly loony stuff to do with witchcraft—when I saw them again. At least I saw her first, standing by the totem with her hands in her coat pockets, and I didn't have to look at the door to know he'd arrived: her face told you that. He came up to her and gave her a kind of hug—arm round her shoulders and then quickly off again—and they wandered away up the stairs, heads together, talking.

I didn't follow them; it had been nice to see them again, and know they were there, and that was it. I was busy on a poem I'd been writing and unpicking and rewriting for some time. It was a poem about an old man sitting on a bench in a park and getting into conversation with a boy—someone around my age—and they swap opinions and observations (it's all dialogue, this poem, like a long conversation) and it's not till the end you realise they're the same person. It sounds either corny, or pretentious, I know; and what I could never decide was whether to have it as though the old man's looking back, or the boy's kind of projecting forward—imagining himself, as it were. So I went on fiddling about with this, and didn't really think much about the man and the girl, until I saw it was latish and there was no one else in the museum except me and some feet on the wooden floor of the gallery overhead, walking round and round, round and round. Two pairs of feet. They'd been doing that for ages, I realised; I'd been hearing them without registering.

I saw them go past—just their heads, above the glass cases—and something wasn't right. They weren't talking. She had her arm through his, and she was looking straight in front of her, and when I saw her face I had a nasty kind of twinge in my stomach. Because she was miserable. Once, she looked at him, and they both managed a bleak sort of smile. And then they walked on, round the gallery again, and next time past they still weren't talking, just holding on to each other like that, like people who're ill, or very old. And then the attendant rang the bell, and I heard them come down the stairs, and they came past me and went out into the Natural History Museum.

I went after them. I saw them stop—under the central whale, just where I first saw her—and then they did say something to each other. I couldn't see her face; she had her back to me. He went off then, on his own, out through the main entrance, quickly, and she sat down on a bench. For a moment or two she just sat staring at that wretched whale, and then she felt in her bag and got out a comb and did her hair, as though that might help. And then she dropped the comb and didn't seem to have noticed, even, because she just sat; she didn't bother to pick it up or anything. I could see her face then, and I hope I don't ever see anyone look so unhappy again. I truly hope that.

I don't know what had happened. I never will. Somehow, I don't think they were ever going to see each other again, but why . . . well, that's their concern, just like the rest of it was, except that in this peculiar way I'd come to feel it was mine too. I didn't think there was anything disgusting about them anymore, or creepy—I hadn't for a long time. I suppose you could say I'd learned something else in the Pitt-Rivers, by accident. I never did go on with that poem. I tore it up, as far as it had got; I wasn't so sure anymore about that conversation, that there could even be one, or not like I'd been imagining, anyway.

NEW AFRICAN

Andrea Lee

On a hot Sunday morning in the summer of 1963, I was sitting restlessly with my mother, my brother Matthew, and my aunts Lily, Emma, and May in a central pew of the New African Baptist Church. It was mid-August, and the hum of the big electric fans at the back of the church was almost enough to muffle my father's voice from the pulpit; behind me I could hear Mrs. Gordon, a stout, feeble old woman who always complained of dizziness, remark sharply to her daughter that at the rate the air-conditioning fund was growing, it might as well be for the next century. Facing the congregation, my father—who was Reverend Phillips to the rest of the world—seemed hot himself; he mopped his brow with a handkerchief and drank several glasses of ice water from the heavy pitcher on the table by the pulpit. I looked at him critically. He's still reading the text, I thought. Then he'll do the sermon, then the baptism, and it will be an hour, maybe two.

I rubbed my chin and then idly began to snap the elastic band that held my red straw hat in place. What I would really like to do, I decided, would be to go home, put on my shorts, and climb up into the tree house I had set up the day before with Matthew. We'd nailed an old bushelbasket up in the branches of the big maple that stretched above the sidewalk in front of the house; it made a sort of crow's nest where you could sit comfortably, except for a few splinters, and read, or peer through the dusty leaves at the cars that passed down the quiet suburban road. There was shade and wind and a feeling of high adventure up in the treetop, where the air seemed to vibrate with the dry rhythms of the cicadas; it was as different as possible from church, where the packed congregation sat in a near-visible miasma of emotion and cologne, and trolleys passing in the city street outside set the stained-glass windows rattling.

I slouched between Mama and Aunt Lily and felt myself going limp with lassitude and boredom, as if the heat had melted my bones; the only thing about me with any character seemed to be my firmly starched eyelet dress. Below the scalloped hem, my legs were skinny and wiry, the legs of a ten-year-old amazon, scarred from violent adventures with bicycles and skates. A fingernail tapped my wrist; it was Aunt Emma, reaching across Aunt Lily to press a piece of butterscotch into my hand. When I slipped the candy into my mouth, it tasted faintly of Arpège; my mother and her three sisters were monumental women, ample of bust and slim of ankle, with a weakness for elegant footwear and French perfume. As they leaned back and forth to exchange discreet tidbits of gossip, they fanned themselves and me with fans from the Byron J. Wiggins Funeral Parlor. The fans, which were fluttering throughout the church, bore a depiction of the Good Shepherd: a hollow-eyed blond Christ holding three fat pink-cheeked children. This Christ resembled the Christ who stood among apostles on the stained-glass windows of the church. Deacon Wiggins, a thoughtful man, had also provided New African with a few dozen fans bearing the picture of a black child praying, but I rarely saw those in use.

There was little that was new or very African about the New African Baptist Church. The original congregation had been formed in 1813 by three young men from Philadelphia's large community of free blacks, and before many generations had passed, it had become spiritual home to a collection of prosperous, conservative, generally light-skinned parishioners. The church was a gray Gothic structure, set on the corner of a run-down street in South Philadelphia a dozen blocks below Rittenhouse Square and a few blocks west of the spare, clannish Italian neighborhoods that produced Frankie Avalon and Frank Rizzo. At the turn of the century, the neighborhood had been a tidy collection of brick houses with scrubbed marble steps—the homes of a group of solid citizens whom Booker T. Washington, in a centennial address to the church, described as "the ablest Negro businessmen of our generation." Here my father had grown up aspiring to preach to the congregation of New African—an ambition encouraged by my grandmother Phillips, a formidable churchwoman. Here, too, my mother and her sisters had walked with linked arms to Sunday services, exchanging affected little catchphrases of French and Latin they had learned at Girls' High.

In the 1950s many of the parishioners, seized by the national urge toward the suburbs, moved to newly integrated towns outside the city, leaving the streets around New African to fill with bottles and papers and loungers. The big church stood suddenly isolated. It had not been abandoned—on Sundays the front steps overflowed with members who had driven in—but there was a tentative feeling in the atmosphere of those Sunday mornings, as if through the muddle of social change, the future of New African had become unclear. Matthew and I, suburban children, felt a mixture of pride and animosity toward the church. On the one hand, it was a marvelous private domain, a richly decorated and infinitely suggestive playground where we were petted by a congregation that adored our father; on the other hand, it seemed a bit like a dreadful old relative in the city, one who forced us into tedious visits and who linked us to a past that came to seem embarrassingly primitive as we grew older.

I slid down in my seat, let my head roll back, and looked up at the blue arches of the church ceiling. Lower than these, in back of the altar, was an enormous gilded cross. Still lower, in a semicircle near the pulpit, sat the choir, flanked by two tall golden files of organ pipes, and below the choir was a somber crescent of dark-suited deacons. In front, at the center of everything, his bald head gleaming under the lights, was Daddy. On summer Sundays he wore white robes, and when he raised his arms, the heavy material fell in curving folds like the ridged petals of an Easter lily. Usually when I came through the crowd to kiss him after the service, his cheek against my lips felt wet and gravelly with sweat and a new growth of beard sprouted since morning. Today, however, was a baptismal Sunday, and I wouldn't have a chance to kiss him until he was freshly shaven and cool from the shower he took after the ceremony. The baptismal pool was in an alcove to the left of the altar; it had mirrored walls and red velvet curtains, and above it, swaying on a string, hung a stuffed white dove.

Daddy paused in the invocation and asked the congregation to pray. The choir began to sing softly:

Blessed assurance,
Jesus is mine!
Oh what a foretaste
Of glory divine!

In the middle of the hymn, I edged my head around my mother's cool, muscular arm (she swam every day of the summer) and peered at Matthew. He was sitting bolt upright holding a hymnal and a pencil, his long legs inside his navy-blue summer suit planted neatly in front of him, his freckled thirteen-year-old face that was so like my father's wearing not the demonic grin it bore when we played alone but a maddeningly composed, attentive expression. "Two hours!" I mouthed at him, and pulled back at a warning pressure from my mother. Then I joined in the singing, feeling disappointed: Matthew had returned me a glance of scorn. Just lately he had started acting very superior and tolerant about tedious Sunday mornings. A month before, he'd been baptized, marching up to the pool in a line of white-robed children as the congregation murmured happily about Reverend Phillips's son. Afterward Mrs. Pinkston, a tiny, yellow-skinned old woman with a blind left eye, had come up to me and given me a painful hug, whispering that she was praying night and day for the pastor's daughter to hear the call as well.

I bit my fingernails whenever I thought about baptism; the subject brought out a deep-rooted balkiness in me. Ever since I could remember, Matthew and I had made a game of dispelling the mysteries of worship with a gleeful secular eye: we knew how the bread and wine were prepared for Communion, and where Daddy bought his robes (Ekhardt Brothers, in North Philadelphia, makers also of robes for choirs, academicians, and judges). Yet there was an unassailable magic about an act as public and dramatic as baptism. I felt toward it the slightly exasperated awe a stagehand might feel on realizing that although he can identify with professional exactitude the minutest components of a show, there is still something indefinable in the power that makes it a cohesive whole. Though I could not have put it into words, I believed that the decision to make a frightening and embarrassing backward plunge into a pool of sanctified water meant that one had received a summons to Christianity as unmistakable as the blare of an automobile horn. I believed this with the same fervor with which, already, I believed in the power of romance, especially in the miraculous efficacy of a lover's first kiss. I had never been kissed by a lover, nor had I heard the call to baptism.

For a Baptist minister and his wife, my father and mother were unusually relaxed about religion; Matthew and I had never been required to read the Bible, and my father's sermons had been criticized by some older church members for omitting the word "sin." Mama and Daddy never tried to push me toward baptism, but a number of other people did. Often on holidays, when I had retreated from the noise of the family dinner table and sat trying to read in my favorite place (the window seat in Matthew's room, with the curtains drawn to form a tent), Aunt Lily would come and find me. Aunt Lily was the youngest of my mother's sisters, a kindergarten teacher with the fatally overdeveloped air of quaintness that is the infallible mark of an old maid. Aunt Lily hoped and hoped again with various suitors, but even I knew she would never find a husband. I respected her because she gave me wonderful books of fairy tales, inscribed in her neat, loopy hand; when she talked about religion, however, she assumed an anxious, flirtatious air that made me cringe. "Well, Miss Sarah, what are you scared of?" she would ask, tugging gently on one of my braids and bringing her plump face so close to mine that I could see her powder, which was, in accordance with the custom of fashionable colored ladies, several shades lighter than her olive skin. "God isn't anyone to be afraid of!" she'd continue as I looked at her with my best deadpan expression. "He's someone nice, just as nice as your daddy"— I had always suspected Aunt Lily of having a crush on my father—"and he loves you, in the same way your daddy does!"

"You would make us all so happy!" I was told at different times by Aunt Lily, Aunt Emma, and Aunt May. The only people who said nothing at all were Mama and Daddy, but I sensed in them a thoughtful, suppressed wistfulness that maddened me.

After the hymn, Daddy read aloud a few verses from the third chapter of Luke, verses I recognized in the almost instinctive way in which I was familiar with all of the well-traveled parts of the Old and New Testaments. "Prepare the way of the Lord, make his paths straight," read my father in a mild voice. "Every valley shall be filled, and every mountain and hill shall be brought low, and the crooked shall be made straight, and the rough paths made smooth, and all flesh shall see the salvation of God."

He had a habit of pausing to fix his gaze on part of the congregation as he read, and that Sunday he seemed to be talking to a small group of strangers who sat in the front row. These visitors were young white men and women, students from Philadelphia colleges, who for the past year had been coming to hear him talk. It was hard to tell them apart: all the men seemed to have beards, and the women wore their hair long and straight. Their informal clothes stood out in that elaborate assembly, and church members whispered angrily that the young women didn't wear hats. I found the students appealing and rather romantic, with their earnest eyes and timid air of being perpetually sorry about something. It was clear that they had good intentions, and I couldn't understand why so many of the adults in the congregation seemed to dislike them so much. After services, they would hover around Daddy. "Never a more beautiful civil rights sermon!" they would say in low, fervent voices. Sometimes they seemed to have tears in their eyes.

I wasn't impressed by their praise of my father; it was only what everyone said. People called him a champion of civil rights; he gave speeches on the radio, and occasionally he appeared on television. (The first time I'd seen him on Channel 5, I'd been gravely disappointed by the way he looked: the bright lights exaggerated the furrows that ran between his nose and mouth, and his narrow eyes gave him a sinister air; he looked like an Oriental villain in a Saturday afternoon thriller.) During the past year he had organized a boycott that integrated the staff of a huge frozen-food plant in Philadelphia, and he'd been away several times to attend marches and meetings in the South. I was privately embarrassed to have a parent who freely admitted going to jail in Alabama, but the students who visited New African seemed to think it almost miraculous. Their conversations with my father were peppered with references to places I had never seen, towns I imagined as being swathed in a mist of darkness visible: Selma, Macon, Birmingham, Biloxi.

Matthew and I had long ago observed that what Daddy generally did in his sermons was to speak very softly and then surprise everyone with a shout. Of course, I knew that there was more to it than that; even in those days I recognized a genius of personality in my father. He loved crowds, handling them with the expert good humor of a man entirely in his element. At church banquets, at the vast annual picnic that was held beside a lake in New Jersey, or at any gathering in the backyards and living rooms of the town where we lived, the sound I heard most often was the booming of my father's voice followed by shouts of laughter from the people around him. He had a passion for oratory; at home, he infuriated Matthew and me by staging absurd debates at the dinner table, verbal melees that he won quite selfishly, with a loud crow of delight at his own virtuosity. "Is a fruit a vegetable?" he would demand. "Is a zipper a machine?" Matthew and I would plead with him to be quiet as we strained to get our own points across, but it was no use. When the last word had resounded and we sat looking at him in irritated silence, he would clear his throat, settle his collar, and resume eating, his face still glowing with an irrepressible glee.

When he preached, he showed the same private delight. A look of rapt pleasure seemed to broaden and brighten the contours of his angular face until it actually appeared to give off light as he spoke. He could preach in two very different ways. One was the delicate, sonorous idiom of formal oratory, with which he must have won the prizes he held from his seminary days. The second was a hectoring, insinuating, incantatory tone, full of the rhythms of the South he had never lived in, linking him to generations of thunderous Baptist preachers. When he used this tone, as he was doing now, affectionate laughter rippled through the pews.

"I know," he said, looking out over the congregation and blinking his eyes rapidly, "that there are certain people in this room—oh, I don't have to name names or point a finger—who have ignored that small true voice, the voice that is the voice of Jesus calling out in the shadowy depths of the soul. And while you all are looking around and wondering just who those 'certain people' are, I want to tell you all a secret: they are you and me, and your brother-in-law, and every man, woman, and child in this room this morning. All of us listen to our bellies when they tell us it is time to eat, we pay attention to our eyes when they grow heavy from wanting sleep, but when it comes to the sacred knowledge our hearts can offer, we are deaf, dumb, blind, and senseless. Throw away that blindness, that deafness, that sulky indifference. When all the world lies to you, Jesus will tell you what is right. Listen to him. Call on him. In these times of confusion, when there are a dozen different ways to turn, and Mama and Papa can't help you, trust Jesus to set you straight. Listen to him. The Son of God has the answers. Call on him. Call on him. Call on him."

The sermon was punctuated with an occasional loud "Amen!" from Miss Middleton, an excitable old lady whose eyes flashed defiantly at the reproving faces of those around her. New African was not the kind of Baptist church where shouting was a normal part of the service; I occasionally heard my father mock the staid congregation by calling it Saint African. Whenever Miss Middleton loosed her tongue (sometimes she went off into fits of rapturous shrieks and had to be helped out of the service by the church nurse), my mother and aunts exchanged grimaces and shrugged, as if confronted by incomprehensibly barbarous behavior.

When Daddy had spoken the final words of the sermon, he drank a glass of water and vanished through a set of red velvet curtains to the right of the altar. At the same time, the choir began to sing what was described in the church bulletin as a "selection." These selections were always arenas for the running dispute between the choirmaster and the choir. Jordan Grimes, the choirmaster, was a Curtis graduate who was partial to Handel, but the choir preferred artistic spirituals performed in the lush, heroic style of Paul Robeson. Grimes had triumphed that Sunday. As the choir gave a spirited but unwilling rendition of Agnus Dei, I watched old Deacon West smile in approval. A Spanish-American War veteran, he

41

admitted to being ninety-four but was said to be older; his round yellowish face, otherwise unwrinkled, bore three deep, deliberate-looking horizontal creases on the brow, like carvings on a scarab. "That old man is as flirtatious as a boy of twenty!" my mother often said, watching his stiff, courtly movements among the ladies of the church. Sometimes he gave me a dry kiss and a piece of peppermint candy after the service; I liked his crackling white collars and smell of bay rum.

The selection ended; Jordan Grimes struck two deep chords on the organ, and the lights in the church went low. A subtle stir ran through the congregation, and I moved closer to my mother. This was the moment that fascinated and disturbed me more than anything else at church: the prelude to the ceremony of baptism. Deacon West rose and drew open the draperies that had been closed around the baptismal pool, and there stood my father in water to his waist. The choir began to sing:

> We're marching to Zion,
> Beautiful, beautiful Zion,
> We're marching upward to Zion,
> The beautiful city of God!

Down the aisle, guided by two church mothers, came a procession of eight children and adolescents. They wore white robes, the girls with white ribbons in their hair, and they all had solemn expressions of terror on their faces. I knew each one of them. There was Billy Price, a big, slow-moving boy of thirteen, the son of Deacon Price. There were the Duckery twins. There was Caroline Piggee, whom I hated because of her long, soft black curls, her dimpled pink face, and her lisp that ravished grownups. There was Georgie Battis and Sue Anne Ivory, and Wendell and Mabel Cullen.

My mother gave me a nudge. "Run up to the side of the pool!" she whispered. It was the custom for unbaptized children to watch the ceremony from the front of the church. They sat on the knees of the deacons and church mothers, and it was not unusual for a child to volunteer then and there for next month's baptism. I made my way quickly down the dark aisle, feeling the carpet slip under the smooth soles of my patent-leather shoes.

When I reached the side of the pool, I sat down in the bony lap of Bessie Gray, an old woman who often took care of Matthew and me when our parents were away; we called her Aunt Bessie. She was a fanatically devout Christian whose strict ideas on child-rearing had evolved over decades of domestic service to a rich white family in Delaware. The link between us, a mixture of hostility and grudging affection, had been forged in hours of pitched battles over bedtimes and proper behavior. Her worshipful respect for my father, whom she called "the Rev," was exceeded only by her pride—the malice-tinged pride of an omniscient family servant—in her "white children," to whom she often unflatteringly compared Matthew and me. It was easy to see why my mother and her circle of fashionable matrons described Bessie Gray as "archaic"—one had only to look at her black straw hat attached with three enormous old-fashioned pins to her knot of frizzy white hair. Her lean, brown-skinned face was dominated by a hawk nose inherited from some Indian ancestor and punctuated by a big black mole; her eyes were small, shrewd, and baleful. She talked in ways that were already passing into history and parody, and she wore a thick orange face powder that smelled like dead leaves.

I leaned against her spare bosom and watched the other children clustered near the pool, their bonnets and hair ribbons and round heads outlined in the dim light. For a minute it was very still. Somewhere in the hot, darkened church a baby gave a fretful murmur; from outside came the sound of cars passing in the street. The candidates for baptism, looking stiff and self-conscious, stood lined up on the short stairway leading to the pool. Sue Anne Ivory fiddled with her sleeve and then put her fingers in her mouth.

Daddy spoke the opening phrases of the ceremony: "In the Baptist Church, we do not baptize infants, but believe that a person must choose salvation for himself."

I didn't listen to the words; what I noticed was the music of the whole—how the big voice darkened and lightened in tone, and how the grand architecture of the Biblical sentences ennobled the voice. The story, of course, was about Jesus and John the Baptist. One phrase struck me newly each time: "This is my beloved son, in whom I am well pleased!" Daddy sang out these words in a clear, triumphant tone, and the choir echoed him. Ever since I could understand it, this phrase had made me feel melancholy; it seemed to expose a hard knot of disobedience that had always lain inside me. When I heard it, I thought enviously of Matthew, for whom life seemed to be a sedate and ordered affair: he, not I, was a child in whom a father could be well pleased.

Daddy beckoned to Billy Price, the first baptismal candidate in line, and Billy, ungainly in his white robe, descended the steps into the pool. In soft, slow voices the choir began to sing:

Wade in the water,
Wade in the water, children,
Wade in the water,
God gonna trouble
The water.

In spite of Jordan Grimes's efforts, the choir swayed like a gospel chorus as it sang this spiritual; the result was to add an eerie jazz beat to the minor chords. The music gave me goose-flesh. Daddy had told me that this was the same song that the slaves had sung long ago in the South, when they gathered to be baptized in rivers and streams. Although I cared little about history, and found it hard to picture the slaves as being any ancestors of mine, I could clearly imagine them coming together beside a broad muddy river that wound away between trees drooping with strange vegetation. They walked silently in lines, their faces very black against their white clothes, leading their children. The whole scene was bathed in the heavy golden light that meant age and solemnity, the same light that seemed to weigh down the Israelites in illustrated volumes of Bible stories, and that shone now from the baptismal pool, giving the ceremony the air of a spectacle staged in a dream.

All attention in the darkened auditorium was now focused on the pool, where between the red curtains my father stood holding Billy Price by the shoulders. Daddy stared into Billy's face, and the boy stared back, his lips set and trembling. "And now, by the power invested in me," said Daddy, "I baptize you in the name of the Father, the Son, and the Holy Ghost." As he pronounced these words, he conveyed a tenderness as efficient and impersonal as a physician's professional manner; beneath it, however, I could see a strong private gladness, the same delight that transformed his face when he preached a sermon. He paused to flick a drop of water off his forehead, and then, with a single smooth, powerful motion of his arms, he laid Billy Price back into the water as if he were putting an infant to bed. I caught my breath as the boy went back-ward. When he came up, sputtering, two church mothers helped him out of the pool and through a doorway into a room where he would be dried and dressed. Daddy shook the water from his hands and gave a slight smile as another child entered the pool.

One by one, the baptismal candidates descended the steps. Sue Anne Ivory began to cry and had to be comforted. Caroline Piggee blushed and looked up at my father with such a coquettish air that I jealously wondered how he could stand it. After a few baptisms my attention wandered, and I began to gnaw the edge of my thumb and to peer at the pale faces of the visiting college students. Then I thought about Matthew, who had punched me in the arm that morning and had shouted, "No punchbacks!" I thought as well about a collection of horse chestnuts I meant to assemble in the fall, and about two books, one whose subject was adults and divorces, and another, by E. Nesbit, that continued the adventures of the Bastable children.

After Wendell Cullen had left the water (glancing uneasily back at the wet robe trailing behind him), Daddy stood alone among the curtains and the mirrors. The moving reflections from the pool made the stuffed dove hanging over him seem to flutter on its string. "Dear Lord," said Daddy, as Jordan Grimes struck a chord, "bless these children who have chosen to be baptized in accordance with your teaching, and who have been reborn to carry out your work. In each of them, surely, you are well pleased." He paused, staring out into the darkened auditorium. "And if there is anyone out there— man, woman, child—who wishes to be baptized next month, let him come forward now." He glanced around eagerly. "Oh, do come forward and give Christ your heart and give me your hand!"

Just then Aunt Bessie gave me a little shake and whispered sharply, "Go on up and accept Jesus!"

I stiffened and dug my bitten fingernails into my palms. The last clash of wills I had had with Aunt Bessie had been when she, crazily set in her old Southern attitudes, had tried to make me wear an enormous straw hat, as her "white children" did, when I played outside in the sun. The old woman had driven me to madness, and I had ended up spanked and sullen, crouching moodily under the dining-room table. But this was different, outrageous, none of her business, I thought. I shook my head violently and she took advantage of the darkness in the church to seize both of my shoulders and jounce me with considerable roughness, whispering, "Now, listen, young lady! Your daddy up there is calling you to Christ. Your big brother has already offered his soul to the Lord. Now Daddy wants his little girl to step forward."

"No, he doesn't." I glanced at the baptismal pool, where my father was clasping the hand of a strange man who had come up to him. I hoped that this would distract Aunt Bessie, but she was tireless.

"Your mama and your aunt Lily and your aunt May all want you to answer the call. You're hurting them when you say no to Jesus."

"No, I'm not!" I spoke out loud and I saw the people nearby turn to look at me. At the sound of my voice, Daddy, who was a few yards away, faltered for a minute in what he was saying and glanced over in my direction.

Aunt Bessie seemed to lose her head. She stood up abruptly, pulling me with her, and, while I was still frozen in a dreadful paralysis, tried to drag me down the aisle toward my father. The two of us began a brief struggle that could not have lasted for more than a few seconds but that seemed an endless mortal conflict—my slippery patent-leather shoes braced against the floor, my straw hat sliding cockeyed and lodging against one ear, my right arm twisting and twisting in the iron circle of the old woman's grip, my nostrils full of the dead-leaf smell of her powder and black skirts. In an instant I had wrenched my arm free and darted up the aisle toward Mama, my aunts, and Matthew. As I slipped past the pews in the darkness, I imagined that I could feel eyes fixed on me and hear whispers. "What'd you do, dummy?" whispered Matthew, tugging on my sash as I reached our pew, but I pushed past him without answering. Although it was hot in the church, my teeth were chattering: it was the first time I had won a battle with a grownup, and the earth seemed to be about to cave in beneath me. I squeezed in between Mama and Aunt Lily just as the lights came back on in the church. In the baptismal pool, Daddy raised his arms for the last time. "The Lord bless you and keep you," came his big voice. "The Lord be gracious unto you, and give you peace."

What was curious was how uncannily subdued my parents were when they heard of my skirmish with Aunt Bessie. Normally they were swift to punish Matthew and me for misbehavior in church and for breaches in politeness toward adults; this episode combined the two, and smacked of sacrilege besides. Yet once I had made an unwilling apology to the old woman (as I kissed her she shot me such a vengeful glare that I realized that forever after it was to be war to the death between the two of us), I was permitted, once we had driven home, to climb up into the green shade of the big maple tree I had dreamed of throughout the service. In those days, more than now, I fell away into a remote dimension whenever I opened a book; that afternoon, as I sat with rings of sunlight and shadow moving over my arms and legs, and winged yellow seeds plopping down on the pages of *The Story of the Treasure Seekers,* I felt a vague uneasiness floating in the back of my mind—a sense of having misplaced something, of being myself misplaced. I was holding myself quite aloof from considering what had happened, as I did with most serious events, but through the adventures of the Bastables I kept remembering the way my father had looked when he'd heard what had happened. He hadn't looked severe or angry, but merely puzzled, and he had regarded me with the same puzzled expression, as if he'd just discovered that I existed and didn't know what to do with me. "What happened, Sairy?" he asked, using an old baby nickname, and I said, "I didn't want to go up there." I hadn't cried at all, and that was another curious thing.

After that Sunday, through some adjustment in the adult spheres beyond my perception, all pressure on me to accept baptism ceased. I turned twelve, fifteen, then eighteen without being baptized, a fact that scandalized some of the congregation; however, my parents, who openly discussed everything else, never said a word to me. The issue, and the episode that had illuminated it, was surrounded by a clear ring of silence that, for our garrulous family, was something close to supernatural. I continued to go to New African—in fact, continued after Matthew, who dropped out abruptly during his freshman year in college; the ambiguousness in my relations with the old church gave me at times an inflated sense of privilege (I saw myself as a romantically isolated religious heroine, a sort of self-made Baptist martyr) and at other times a feeling of loss that I was too proud ever to acknowledge. I never went up to take my father's hand, and he never commented upon that fact to me. It was an odd pact, one that I could never consider in the light of day; I stored it in the subchambers of my heart and mind. It was only much later, after he died, and I left New African forever, that I began to examine the peculiar gift of freedom my father— whose entire soul was in the church, and in his exuberant, bewitching tongue—had granted me through his silence.

SPONONO

Alan Paton

This very day I received a letter from Sponono, full of reproaches. He asks why I have not answered his previous letter. He writes to me, "Are you then like other people, who, when a man has done wrong, treat him badly? I have always looked upon you as trustworthy, but now I am ashamed in front of my friends." He asks, "Why have you turned? You were always a man of your word, but now you are changed." He concludes that this turning of mine is "wonderful."

I feel I must put up some kind of defence against this indictment which questions qualities of my character of whose existence I have been moderately certain. Whether his friends will ever read it, and refrain from harsh judgments on that account, is very improbable. But it will at least give me the opportunity of describing an engaging rascal, who expected my conduct towards him to surpass in superhuman degree his conduct towards me. How did he ever formulate such noble ideals of behaviour? That I do not know, for he certainly did not practise them. Nevertheless he knew of them, and while he considered himself too frail to practise them, he expected me to do so, and never failed to reproach me when I fell short of them. Yet on one occasion he did practise them, under the most unlikely circumstances, with an ease and grace that would have done credit to a saint.

Sponono was a Xhosa boy, about sixteen years old when he first came to the reformatory. My first intimate encounter with him was certainly extraordinary. He had asked to see the Principal, on urgent private business, and accordingly he was brought to me by the Chief Supervisor, Mr. van Dyk.

"Well, Sponono," I said, "I hear you want to see me."

"Yes, *meneer*,"* he said.

"What is your trouble?" I asked.

"I have no trouble," he said. "I have come to see you about the trouble of Johannes Mofoking."

"Are you a friend of his?" I asked.

"I am not a friend of his," he said, "but I have heard about his case, and it is about his case that I wish to speak with you."

By this time Mr. van Dyk was looking somewhat uncomfortable, because it was a rule that any boy wishing to see me must first state his business clearly to the Chief Supervisor, unless he could claim that the matter was confidential and private. But I told Mr. van Dyk to put himself at ease, and I said to Sponono, "What about Johannes Mofoking?"

"We all know," he said, "that Johannes Mofoking ran away from the reformatory, and that when he was captured and sent back here, he was in possession of a gold watch."

"That is so," I said.

---

* **meneer.** Sir (Afrikaans).

"Some of us think," said Sponono, "that you are being too severe. Johannes admitted that he had stolen the watch, and he did not lie about it. This makes us think that he is not a bad fellow, and he himself does not wish to go to prison, but says he is willing to spend some extra time in the reformatory to atone for what he has done."

"That is very good of him," I said.

"Sir," said Mr. van Dyk, "I had no idea . . ."

"Do not trouble yourself," I said. "Sponono, you must know that I cannot conceal the theft of this watch from the police. Furthermore . . ."

"*Meneer,*" he said, "we do not . . ."

"Excuse me, sir," said Mr. van Dyk. "Sponono, you must not interrupt the Principal when he is speaking. It is not proper."

"I ask pardon," said Sponono, humbly. "I did not mean to interrupt the Principal."

"Go on," I said.

"*Meneer,*" said Sponono, "we do not ask you to conceal the theft of the watch from the police."

"That is good of you," I said.

"*Meneer,*" he said, ignoring my own interruption, "we are satisfied that he should go to court. All we ask is that you should ask the court to send him back to the reformatory. Otherwise, he may grow into a bad fellow, and we are sure you do not wish this to happen."

"He is getting old," I said. "He is nearly twenty."

"I admit he is nearly twenty," said Sponono. "But he is not a bad fellow. But if he goes to prison, I fear he will become hard."

"The reformatory is very full," I said. "We have more than six hundred boys now, and the reformatory is built for only four hundred."

"My room is not full," said Sponono. "He can sleep there."

"That is very good of you," I said. It was the third time I had made such a remark, but of the sarcasm he took as little notice as before.

"I thought it would be wrong to send Johannes to prison," he said. "I told a lie to the Chief Supervisor when I said I had private business, because I knew that if I had told him my real business, he would not have allowed me to see you."

"Do you not think it wrong to tell a lie?" I asked.

"Not to save a person," he said.

"Mr. van Dyk," I said, "bring Johannes to me."

Johannes was brought, and I said to him, "Johannes, I understand that you are ready to go to court, and to plead guilty to stealing this watch, but that you wish to be sent back to the reformatory."

"That is true, *meneer.*"

"But," I said, "you are nearly twenty. And if you have not yet learned to stop stealing, what good will it do to teach you all over again?"

"I am learning," he said, "but not yet enough. If I come back here, I shall learn completely. But if I go to prison, I shall learn to steal more than before."

"In that case," I said, "I shall ask the court to send you back here."

"Thank you, *meneer,*" he said.

"Don't thank me," I said. "Thank Sponono. He was the one who spoke for you."

Johannes turned to Sponono. "Thank you," he said.

"Do not thank me," said Sponono. "Thank the Principal. Without him I could have done nothing."

It was about a month later that Sponono asked to see me again.

53

"Is it more private business?" I asked Mr. van Dyk.

Mr. van Dyk smiled at me in a reproachful manner.

"Sponono wishes to work in your garden," he said.

"William is already working in my garden," I said.

"Your garden is not properly cared for," said Sponono. "William is a good fellow, but he does not fully understand the work of a garden."

"What must I say to William?" I asked. "Must I say to him that you do not approve of his work in the garden, and that you have appointed yourself in his place?"

"I do not say that," said Sponono. "Let me work under him until he is discharged. That will be very soon."

"How do you know that?" I asked.

"He told me," he said.

"Did you arrange it between you?" I asked. And when he did not answer I asked again, "Shall I tell William that he does not understand the work of a garden?"

"That would only make trouble," he said. "Let me work under him."

I must report that Sponono did not prove a good subordinate. William would come and complain to me that Sponono would not do what he was told to do. Sponono would come and complain to me that William was inefficient, lazy, and dishonest. I was compelled to divide the garden into two portions, and I must admit that Sponono proved an excellent gardener. But between him and William there was endless friction, until William was discharged and Sponono took command. Then Sponono began to complain about the new assistant, a very meek fellow named George. But things went reasonably smoothly until Christmas Day.

Christmas Day was a big day at the reformatory, with special meals, a sports meeting with prizes, and gifts of sweets for the younger and tobacco for the older boys. I returned home

54

at sunset after a hot and tiring day, looking forward to our own family Christmas and pleasant relaxation. But I had hardly sat down with our guests when the telephone recalled me to the office, where a harassed Mr. van Dyk introduced me to a distraught Mr. Anderson who told me the following disturbing tale.

Mr. Anderson and his wife had packed a picnic basket that morning, and had found a shady spot on the eastern portion of the reformatory farm, where they had enjoyed a good lunch of Christmas fare and some iced beer, after which they had lain down in the grass for a pleasant siesta. But their siesta was to prove anything but pleasant. They had been wakened rudely by a boy in clothes identical with the reformatory uniform, a khaki shirt and khaki shorts. This boy had menaced them with a large stone, and had snatched up Mrs. Anderson's handbag from the grass and made off into the bushes. In the handbag was sixty pounds, in twelve five-pound notes, a whole month's earnings, and the distress of husband and wife was painful to see.

"I know I should have had permission," said Mr. Anderson, "but there was no one to be seen, and it was an ideal spot for a picnic. At least, we thought it was until this terrible thing happened."

"If it was one of our boys, Mr. Anderson," I said, "I hope we shall be able to find him. Most of the boys were at the sports, and we naturally have to know precisely where each one is on such an occasion. Did you find everything correct, Mr. van Dyk?"

"Everything correct, sir. The only boys not at the sports were the domestic servants. I think, sir, you should hear what Mr. Wessels has to report."

He brought in Mr. Wessels, who reported that he had been on farm duty, and that while visiting the top portion of the farm, he had seen Sponono walking through the trees. Knowing that Sponono worked for me, he had contented himself with asking the boy where he was going, and Sponono had replied that I had given him leave to go walking on the farm. We showed Mr. and Mrs. Anderson several of the photographs of the domestic servants, Sponono's amongst them, but they were unable to identify the boy who had menaced them.

"Bring Sponono here, please," I said to Mr. van Dyk. "Mr. and Mrs. Anderson, and Mr. Wessels, I'll ask you to retire to another office."

"This is the stone that the boy carried," said Mr. van Dyk.

"Please leave it on the table," I said.

When Sponono came in, his attention was immediately attracted by the stone, but thereafter he kept his eyes away from it, by an effort of will, I thought.

"Where did you go this afternoon, Sponono?" I asked.

"I went to the sports," he said.

"Were you there all the time?" I asked.

"The Principal knows I don't like sports," he said, "so after a while I went for a walk."

"Where did you walk?"

He closed his eyes for more perfect remembering.

"Down past the stables," he said, "then down to the fields, then back to the pump-house, then back to the house, *meneer.*"

"Did you see anybody?"

"No one, *meneer.*"

Then Mr. Wessels came in, and Sponono looked at him warily.

"Mr. Wessels saw you at the other end of the farm," I said. "He asked you where you were going, did he not?"

"That is true, *meneer.*"

"But you said you saw nobody."

"Not by the stables," he said. "But I did see Mr. Wessels at the top end of the farm."

"Did you see anybody else?" I asked. "Think carefully before you answer."

"Nobody else," he said.

"Why did you tell Mr. Wessels I had given you leave to take a walk?" I asked.

"I did not quite say that," he said. "Probably Mr. Wessels did not hear me clearly, as I do not speak his language very well. I told him I was looking for something for the Principal."

"For what?" I asked sternly.

Against his will his eyes went back to the stone on the table.

"Stones," he said.

"For what?" I asked.

"For your garden, meneer."

"I did not ask you to get stones for the garden," I said.

"I wanted them for a wall," he said. "I was going to speak to you tomorrow."

I pointed to the stone on the table. "Is that one of the stones you found?" I asked.

He did not answer. The questions were coming rapidly, and he was finding it difficult to judge which of the possible answers were the least dangerous. He was breathing heavily, and he found it impossible entirely to conceal his distress.

"Why do you not answer?" I asked.

"You are frightening me, *meneer*," he protested.

"I am only asking you questions," I said.

"I can see you are angry," he said. "Something bad has happened, and somebody wants to blame me for it."

"What has happened?" I asked.

"Something bad." He would say no more. The sweat was pouring off his face.

"Leave us, Mr. Wessels," I said. I sat down at my table, but I did not look at Sponono.

"The boy Johannes was saved from prison because you told me I was doing wrong. Is that not so?"

"Yes, *meneer.*"

"Now it is your turn to be saved from wrong," I said. "You will not lie to me, will you?"

In a low voice he said, "No, *meneer.*"

"You went walking at the top end of the farm?"

"Yes, *meneer.*"

"You were contemplating nothing evil," I said. "You were thinking only of stones for my garden. You did not wish to hurt anybody."

"No, *meneer.*"

"But," I said, "a great temptation was put in your way. And before you could gather your strength, you had done something wrong."

He was silent, and if ever a silence gave consent, it was this one.

"But now," I said, "you repent of what you have done and would like to make amends."

In the low voice he said, "Yes, *meneer.*"

I stood up. "Let us go and get the money," I said. "It will be a great joy to these two people who thought they would have no Christmas at all."

We went out and got into the car, and he led me straight to the money, all sixty pounds of it. The Andersons were overjoyed, and Mr. Anderson insisted on giving me ten pounds, and when I refused he wanted to give it to Mr. Wessels, who naturally refused also. So he put it on my table, and I said I would send it to one of the Christmas funds.

"I feel almost," said Mr. Anderson, so full was he of relief and gratitude, "like giving something to the boy."

"I understand your feelings," I said drily, "but I fear that the consequences of his act must be quite different."

The consequences of Sponono's act were serious; he lost all his free privileges and was sent back to the security building, so that his term at the reformatory virtually began again. His offence was not reported to the police, because all reformatory offences except the gravest fell within my jurisdiction. Nevertheless he tried to get me to alter my decision.

"If I had run away and spent all this money," he said, "you would not have punished me more severely."

When I had admitted this, he said, "What is more, *meneer*, I showed you where the money was hidden."

"I am not a judge," I said. "My job is to teach you better ways, but I have not yet succeeded, therefore I must begin all over again."

He could find no answer to this contention, so he said to me, "I ask only one thing, *meneer*."

"What is that?"

"I ask, *meneer*, that if I behave well, and if I again receive my freedom, I should be allowed to work again in your garden."

"I am willing to agree to that," I said.

"Is that a promise?" he asked.

I could see that Mr. van Dyk was scandalised, but I smiled at him pacifyingly and said to Sponono, "It is a promise."

He turned to Mr. van Dyk and scandalised him further by saying, "I am satisfied."

Two weeks after that, Sponono had a fight with one of his fellows, and received a serious wound over the eye. The doctor told me that the sight of the eye was impaired, and what was more, that when the wound was healed, the eye itself would not look very pretty.

We investigated the case carefully and came to the conclusion that both Sponono and his antagonist, Tembo, were equally blameworthy; but it was difficult to know how to deal with Tembo, for in a fight which had begun as a bout of fisticuffs, he had suddenly whipped off his heavy belt, and struck directly at Sponono's face.

"What have you to say?" I asked Tembo. "This is a grave offence that you have committed."

"I know it is, *meneer*," said Tembo. "That is why I got permission to go to the hospital so that I could ask Sponono's forgiveness."

"Did you forgive him?" I asked Sponono.

Sponono peered at me from under his bandages.

"I forgave him," he said. "He did not mean to hurt my eye. I might have hurt his eye too, if he had not hurt mine first. It was his bad luck, *meneer*."

"You are a generous fellow," I said to Sponono, "and your forgiving spirit is an example to us. However, your forgiveness is between you and him; but between him and me is another matter."

"You should find it easier to forgive him," said Sponono, "for it was my eye that was hurt, not yours."

"You should have been a lawyer," I said.

He smiled at me from beneath the bandages. "*Meneer*, you are playing with me. I am not clever enough to be a lawyer."

"Listen, Sponono," I said, "you may forgive a person, and I may forgive him, but that does not mean that he should not bear the consequences of his act."

His one eye looked at me sceptically, as though I were propounding a doctrine palpably false, but he was too polite to say so.

"Do you think," I asked, "that if a person is forgiven, his offence is wiped out as though it had never been done?"

"Yes," he said.

"Tembo," I said, "you are dismissed with a reprimand. But your belt will be taken away from you, and a softer one will be given to you. If you will take my advice, you will not wear such a belt for the rest of your life, for your temper is hot, and will one day get you into serious trouble."

Tembo said to me humbly, "Thank you, *meneer.*" Mr. van Dyk took him away, and I said to Sponono, "Where did you get this idea of forgiveness?"

"It is the teaching of Jesus," he said. He apparently had no idea of what I might be expected to know or not to know, for he added, "Shall I get a Bible, so that I can read it to you?"

"No, you tell me," I said.

"Jesus said that we must forgive those who offend against us, even unto seventy times seven."

"Are you a Christian?" I asked.

"I am not," he said. "I am not good enough, but I like to obey the commandments."

"Good luck to you," I said. "You may go."

"Couldn't you forgive me now, *meneer,* instead of making me begin again from the beginning?"

"You committed a grave offence," I said, "for which I have forgiven you, but you must still begin again from the beginning."

"Couldn't you forgive this much, *meneer,* that I could go now to work in your garden?"

"No," I said. "Not until you are free."

He surveyed me out of his one eye, his learned superior who knew so little about the true meaning of forgiveness. What he saw was apparently discouraging, for he shrugged his shoulders.

"Why do you do that?" I asked.

"Because I see you are not ready," he said.

I wished that Mr. van Dyk could have been there, for he often thought I was ready to the point of foolishness. But I was denied that pleasure.

Two months later I took the decision to leave the service of the State, and therefore to leave the reformatory. I was obliged to give three months' notice, and I tried to keep the news as secret as possible, but before long it was widely known. One of my first visitors was Sponono. His eye had healed better than expected, and had given him an incredibly knowing look; it remained half-closed, as though he could have seen more of one's weaknesses had he opened it, but as though out of tolerance he would not do so, even though he would continue to give the impression that he knew all.

"I hear you are leaving, *meneer.*"

"That's true, Sponono."

"You promised me," he said, "that when I was free I could work in your garden."

"That's true," I said, "but I did not know I would be leaving."

"Where are you going to?" he asked.

"I am going to Natal," I said.

"I have never been to Natal," he said, "but I am sure I could work very well there."

I was going to say "that is very good of you," when he suddenly changed his tactics and addressed me gravely.

"I did not regard your promise as merely a promise that I could work in your garden," he said. "It was rather a promise that I could be near you, and that was very important to me, because then I knew I would not get into more trouble."

"You did work near me," I said, "and you threatened two innocent people with a stone and stole sixty pounds from them."

He looked at me as though he were pained by the coarseness and directness of my language.

"You said you had forgiven me for that," he said.

"I have forgiven you," I said. "But I thought I should remind you that being near me did not help you on that occasion."

I could see that he thought that the reminder was unethical. But he did not pursue the argument.

"When I am discharged," he said, "I hope I may come to work for you."

"The people in Natal are Zulus," I said, "and you might not be happy amongst them."

"I shall be quite happy," he said with finality. "There are many Zulu boys here, and I have not fought with any of them."

"When you are discharged," I said, "if I am still in Natal, and if I have a garden, you may come to work for me."

Sponono turned to Mr. van Dyk. "I am satisfied," he said.

I glanced at my Chief Supervisor, but he looked quite noncommittal.

So that was how Sponono came to Natal. He had not been there long before he told me that Cele, the gardener, was an idle and worthless fellow, and that Jane Zondi, who looked after our house, was a loose and dishonest woman. These revelations I bore with fortitude, but his next escapade was beyond reason. He had been invited to a party at Jane's sister's home in the hills behind the coast, and dissatisfied with the food, had killed one of the chickens and made himself a feast. He had also drunk freely, and made advances of an ugly and threatening nature to Jane's sister's daughter. The whole countryside was up in arms against the stranger, and Jane's sister went to the police. The police came to see me, saying that it was difficult to obtain evidence in such cases, but that they had no doubt that Sponono had broken several laws; however, if I would send him back to the reformatory, they would take no further steps in the matter. Jane Zondi also came to see me and asked me to build an extra room for Sponono in another part of the garden, while Cele asked me to buy another garden and install Sponono there as sole and all-powerful gardener, so that he could mismanage both the garden and his private affairs without involving others.

"No one seems to want you," I said to Sponono.

"I can see that," he said. "From the time I came, they have all been against me; from the time they knew I came from the reformatory."

"Who told them that?" I asked. "It must have been you yourself."

"Yes, I told them," he said. "I thought it would make them more patient with me."

"The police say you have a choice," I said, "to go to court, or to go back to the reformatory."

"These people hate me," he said. "It is better for me to go back."

So Sponono went back to the reformatory, and so began my long correspondence with him that has lasted now for ten years.

"Your action was very harsh," he wrote. "Others at the party behaved just as I did. You must not think I was the only one who ate the chicken. Jane's sister's son ate just as much as I did, and he was the one who informed against me."

He also complained bitterly against Jane and Cele, and said that they were of the kind that would never forgive any person who had done wrong, but would hound him down until he was destroyed. Furthermore they were Zulus, and hated him because he was a Xhosa. Also Cele was afraid of him, because it was clear that Cele knew nothing about gardening and was afraid of losing his job to a better person.

"But you," he wrote, "you ought to know better. You have worked with thousands of sinners and have gained a good reputation amongst us. Also you are a white man, and have no reason to hate me. Lastly, you are a writer, not a gardener, and you could never lose your job to a person like myself."

When Sponono had served a further year at the reformatory, it was decided to release him, and he asked to be released to me. However, I declined to take him. I wrote to him and told him that Jane Zondi was still with us, and Cele was still in the garden, and neither of them wished to have him.

"They are unforgiving," he wrote, "but that should not be your nature. Do not be influenced by them. Do not be afraid to take me. Why should I make trouble in my own father's house?"

I fear that my nature remained unforgiving. I wrote to him that he had failed me twice and had twice caused trouble in my house. I asked him whether there was not perhaps some fault in his own character.

"I have many faults in my character," he wrote, "but we are speaking of you, not myself. It is true I have failed you twice, but that is a long way from seventy and seven."

"What can I do?" he asked. "At one stroke you have taken away from me my home and my father."

Now it so happened that I had a friend who was growing citrus in the Eastern Province. He was a tolerant fellow of the kind I had once supposed myself to be, and what is more, his employees were all Xhosas. With him I got Sponono a job, which lasted for exactly six weeks, when he was found guilty of stealing a jacket and money from a fellow employee and was sent to the prison at East London for two years.

"A useless fellow," my friend wrote to me. "If you wanted to fire my enthusiasm for rehabilitation, why did you start off with such a quarrelsome scoundrel? He quarrelled with the other workers from the first day he landed here. His worst characteristic was that he was always reminding me of my paternal duties, which he claimed I had inherited from you. I should have thought that after your thirteen years at a reformatory, you would have known a bad egg when you saw one."

"Your friend is a hard man," wrote Sponono to me. "He had all your sternness but none of your good-heartedness. After all, I offended only once against him."

Sponono was allowed to write one letter a month, and I was his correspondent. I sent him simple books to read, and he discovered that the Superintendent of the prison had known me when I was in the State service. "I admire your letters to Sponono," the Superintendent wrote to me, "but I'm afraid your admonitions are wasted. He is a bad-tempered prisoner, and I have had to give him some spells of solitary confinement for fighting. Nevertheless go on with the good work."

"The Superintendent is a hard man," wrote Sponono. "It is not like the reformatory here. There is no forgiveness for small offences."

I do not know how this letter got past the eagle eye of the prison censor; in any event it was the last of its kind. For Sponono was due to be released, and again he asked if he could come back and work for me.

"Jane and Cele are still here," I wrote, "and they will not agree to your returning."

"Who," he wrote and asked me, "is the master in your house?"

It was some years before I heard from him again. This time he was in Tiger Vlei, a prison for seven-year prisoners, who might however receive quite a generous remission for good behaviour. He was allowed to write only at rare intervals, and I replied to him, but I must admit it was with a waning enthusiasm. For one thing the new Government of South Africa had made it almost impossible for Africans from one part of the country to work in another. For another, I felt that my relationship with Sponono had reached its end.

"You take a long time to answer my letters," he wrote. "What is this change in you? There is no change in me."

Nor did it look as though there ever could be. After five years he wrote that he was shortly to be released and wanted to return to me. By that time I had moved to another part of the country. I had engaged in work that took me frequently away from home. I did not think of saddling my wife with the problem of Sponono.

"I cannot have you," I wrote. "I still have Zulus working for me, and you do not like them. I do not think it would be successful."

It was then that he wrote to me that he had always looked upon me as trustworthy, but that now I made him ashamed amongst his friends.

"Why have you turned?" he asked. "You were always a man of your word, but now you have changed."

"You do not say you cannot forgive me," he wrote, "but that is what you mean. But Jesus taught we must forgive unto seventy times seven."

"I do not quarrel anymore," he wrote. "I have had a change of heart. So have you, but yours is in the wrong direction."

Sponono, we have reached, you and I, what is called, in a game not known to you, a stalemate. You move, and I move, but neither of us will ever capture the other. I gave you your chance, and you would not take it, for reasons that are beyond either of us to explain. You gave me my chance, and I would not take it, for reasons that I thought sound and proper.

But I have no doubt that you wish, as I wish, that the game could have ended otherwise.

BOBBY'S ROOM

Douglas Dunn

Henry Pollock was the only child of only children, and
his four grandparents were dead. When he was twelve, in
1954, he and his parents left Glasgow on a motoring holiday.
They stayed in a succession of hotels all over the Borders and
the southwest of Scotland. At one place, they found that the
hotels and guesthouses were full. It was a town Mrs. Pollock
particularly wanted to visit, and all the rooms were booked
up for some local annual event. Mr. Pollock was irate. His
wife chided him for not having telephoned a reservation in
advance, as, she said, she had suggested in the first place.

"We said potluck was part of the charm, did we not?" was
Henry's father's riposte. Bickering in the car park lasted
almost an hour.

Pollock was a tall man, powerful, proud, and successful;
Henry had got used to his obstinate refusals to give in to his
wife's complaints or preferences, to which, in the end, he
always conformed without seeming to surrender. Harsh words
when they fell out were, Henry knew, a prelude to that kind

of morning on which he didn't see them until it was nearly noon. If these were mornings when he went to school, then his mother hurriedly threw his breakfast together and kissed him on the ear before running back upstairs in her kimono.

Even in the small space of the car, they managed to ignore Henry, and he knew better than to say anything. "If you're in such a hurry to find somewhere, then why don't you drive?" his father asked Mrs. Pollock.

"You know I can't. Don't be so stupid."

"Then allow me to be the judge of when we leave and when we don't. I need petrol, in any case."

"You can't possibly need petrol. You filled up this morning in Dumfries."

Eventually they got under way again, and after a few miles Pollock stopped the car outside a substantial stone-built villa, a house much like their own back in Glasgow; a notice board advertised that it offered accommodations.

"What do you think?" he asked.

"I think it's seen better days, that's what I think," said Mrs. Pollock, who was still simmering. Her husband went to see if there were two rooms available, and to investigate what the place was like. "It doesn't even have a drive," she said to Henry. "Where will we put the car?"

"I don't see any cars," Henry said, "so they must have rooms."

"When I want your opinion, I'll ask for it. *Netherbank*," she said, sounding the name of the house as proof of its unsuitability.

Pollock returned a few minutes later. "It's first-rate," he said with genuine enthusiasm, leaning into the car. "The rooms are large and spotlessly clean, very airy and spacious, and no one else is staying there." Breezily, he listed the qualifications Mrs. Pollock always insisted were necessary for a night's comfort. "We can have the sitting room to ourselves, if we want it, and you'll find the bathroom highly acceptable. I think we should take it. Irene, it's run by a lovely old couple. You'll adore them."

Netherbank was run by a Mrs. Bawden. She was over sixty, silver-haired, round, short, respectable, and, as Mrs. Pollock said afterward, very nicely spoken. She took it in her stride when Mrs. Pollock asked if she could have a look at what she was offering for dinner. "Normally, I prefer a proper restaurant. But my husband's very tired after a day's driving."

"Some people ask me for what they call an 'evening meal,' " Mrs. Bawden said, lifting the lid of a saucepan. "I call it dinner. I've always called it dinner, and I won't change now. Round about here, people call lunch dinner. But I call it luncheon, and I call it luncheon at twelve-thirty. And I call tea tea. I don't know where we'll all end up if we begin to call things by the wrong names." Mrs. Pollock couldn't have agreed more.

They stayed for five nights. Henry knew one of the reasons his parents liked the place so much: Mrs. Bawden was very obliging. Before Mrs. Pollock could ask, Mrs. Bawden offered to keep an eye on Henry if they wanted to go off by themselves for a day, or go to dinner in a hotel restaurant about ten miles away which Mrs. Bawden had heard was outstanding for its seafood. "But Mrs. Bawden, you'll do yourself out of business," his mother said.

"No, no, I won't. You're on holiday, and it'll be my pleasure to help you enjoy yourselves." Mrs. Pollock revelled in being the beneficiary of that sort of consideration. Henry's parents had three days on their own without him, and three evenings at the famous restaurant.

Henry wandered round the hills and farms, and walked the two miles to the sea. He read, and he watched Mr. Bawden at

71

work in his garden. The old man was hard of hearing, or said he was, and when Henry tried to talk to him he pointed to an ear, smiled, and went back to his weeding or hoeing.

These were the last days of their holiday. His parents loved it. "I haven't felt so refreshed and well in years!" said Henry's mother as they drove home. "And Mrs. Bawden—what a wonderful woman! Her cooking's pre-war! We were lucky to find it. It's the sort of place you could drive right past without giving it so much as a moment's notice." After that, she and her husband looked at each other in the way that made Henry feel he wasn't there. A little later, Mrs. Pollock started to sing. She coaxed Henry to join in. When he didn't, she turned round and said, "You'll grow up to be miserable. Why won't you sing, like the rest of us?"

Two years later, there was a week in early June when Henry's father was more thoughtful than usual. After dinner he did a lot of meditative gardening. Tired of that, he sat in the lounge with an open book on his lap. Henry's mother brought him tea or coffee, asked him if he wanted something stronger, or something to eat, and in her busy efforts to leave him alone made a nuisance of herself. It was obvious to Henry that his father was making his mind up about something important. From time to time he saw his parents talk quietly and seriously to each other. They cuddled in the kitchen even more often than usual.

"Why don't I phone her? I kept a note of the number, you know," he heard his mother say one evening.

"Do you think she would?" Pollock asked her. "It's not really what she does."

"Almost three months at her usual rates is probably very good business for her, especially if we add something on for her trouble. I imagine she'll be only too pleased."

"It'd be ideal. But what do we do about the weeks of school he'll have to miss?"

"Darling, I've no intention of being left behind. It's an opportunity to travel I won't let pass by, especially since the offer specifically includes me as well. It's not as if you'll have to fork out for my fare and hotel bills. Some of us were prevented from travelling by the war, you know, not to mention marriage and motherhood."

"If this trip's successful, there will have to be others, as a matter of course. It's a big project. It's not one bridge, it's a network. I don't look forward to going away without you, and I want you to come with me. But the best thing might be to start thinking about boarding school."

"Were Henry younger, I'd say no, naturally. But at his age, boarding school is probably a very adventurous proposition. I know it was for Alice Wylie's brother."

Later that evening, Henry heard the telephone being used. He looked down into the hall from the top of the stairs and saw his mother leaning against the opposite wall while his father spoke into the phone. She was smoking, which she did only in company to be polite, or when she was agitated. Then she, too, went over to the phone and began to speak into it. Later, his mother called him to come down to the sitting room.

"Your mother and I have to go to Singapore," his father said. "We'll be gone for most of July and all of August and September. And I'm afraid it just isn't practical to take you with us."

"You remember Mrs. Bawden, and Netherbank?" His wife spoke sooner than Pollock would have liked. "We've arranged for you to stay with her."

"What about school?" Henry's tone of voice was meant to suggest that weeks of missed classes could be disastrous.

73

"Henry, you're the last person I can imagine slipping behind. A few weeks won't be a setback to you."

His mother's way of speaking to him, her confidence in his maturity and academic excellence, made Henry want to fight back. He felt inclined to be stubborn and obstructive. "There isn't a lot to do at Mrs. Bawden's," he said.

"We both think it's ideal."

"We've no choice but to leave you behind," his father said. "We'll be happier, much happier, knowing you're somewhere we can feel easy in our minds about."

Henry looked at his mother, hoping she would understand that he expected her to stay behind with him. She said, "I'll talk to the headmaster on Monday. You can arrange for your teachers to give you a program of study. You can do it on your own—I'm sure you can. And if you think you can't, you're underrating yourself." He knew enough about her to know that if at his age she had been given a "program of study" she'd have collapsed in tears.

Instead of making it difficult for them, he accepted it, and resigned himself. He knew why they had chosen Mrs. Bawden and Netherbank. They had been happy there, and assumed that he had liked it, too. It was a place and a few days in their lives that meant something in their happiness. He wondered why they could continue to be so ignorant of his feelings. Mrs. Bawden was not a complete stranger, but she was the next thing to it—the landlady of a guesthouse, a species his mother usually loathed.

"Don't feel unwanted," his mother said. "It would suit us better, much better, if you could come with us. But it isn't possible, so we have to make the best of it."

When the time came, they drove him to Mrs. Bawden's with suitcases, books, tennis racquet, binoculars, and field guides to the birds and wildflowers of the British Isles. Nature study was his mother's idea. "When I get back, I want to find you thoroughly up to the mark in country life," she said. "It's a wonderful opportunity for you. I've always been opposed to townies." He tried to think of what it was she craved so determinedly that it made a trip to Singapore necessary to her.

She wept as she said goodbye. Henry felt like weeping on his own account.

"I know you won't give Mrs. Bawden any trouble," she said. It was the wrong thing to have said. Obedient to the point of filial perfection, he had never given anyone the least bit of trouble in his life.

"How long does post take from Singapore?" Mrs. Pollock asked her husband.

"Airmail," he said. "Pretty fast."

"Then I'll write at least once a week, and I'll expect you to do the same," she told Henry. With that, she left for the car, dabbing at her eyes with a handkerchief.

"You haven't left me your address in Singapore," Henry said. Pollock had to call for Mrs. Bawden to bring a piece of paper for him to write it down on. He was embarrassed, talking about rush, last-minute details, oversights.

Henry had reckoned on eating alone in the dining room, like any other guest, but he ate with the Bawdens in their kitchen. "No aunts, no uncles," said Mr. Bawden, as the old couple explored Henry's family. "So no cousins, either. No great loss, if you ask me. A big scatter of kin makes you feel guilty at not keeping in touch, which you can't do, you know, unless you're a man of means and leisure."

"I've second cousins," Henry offered.

"I was closer to two of my second cousins than to any of my first," said Mrs. Bawden.

"I've never met them," said Henry.

"Singapore's a long, long journey," she said, pushing a bowl of cauliflower toward him.

"Homegrown," said Mr. Bawden. "We haven't eaten a tinned vegetable in twenty years."

As he lay awake in bed, Henry pondered his affection for his parents, and decided it was becoming as distant and routine as his parents' love of him. They were his parents, therefore he loved them; he was their son, therefore they loved him—it was as mathematical as that. Cooperation between them was beginning to thin out, like the darkness in the triangle of dawn now at the top of the curtains. His mother prodded him to be the scholar of his class at school, and was proud of his examination victories; but she nagged him for being too studious and staying in when he should have been outside, and complained of his lack of interest in sport. They expected him to be perfect, but they neglected him.

He had a different room from the one he had slept in two years before. It was at the front of the house, under the eaves; from its protruding window he could look at a small wedge of sea and the right-hand tip of an island that could be walked to at low tide over the sands. Darkness turned to a transparent gray, and objects in the room slowly became visible. Shelves in an alcove contained dozens of books of a boyish interest— books on ships and the sea, the Empire, foreign countries, warlike history, wildlife, fishing, landmarks in engineering and exploration, most of them heavy and already obsolete. There was a homemade model warship on a chest of drawers. Pictures on the wall did not quite cover the cleaner paint left behind from those that had been taken down. His dressing gown, on the hook behind the door, looked like another person in the room. He imagined that the owner of the books was a long-lost son of the Bawdens, dead, probably, in the war.

76

"Was my room your son's?" he asked Mr. Bawden, who pointed to his ear as Henry began to repeat his question.

"We thought you'd like it better than the rooms we let to the holidaymakers," he said. "Or *she* did. You'll find out," he said, as if excusing himself in advance for any apparent lack of initiative on his part. "Mrs. Bawden is the boss round here. She wears the trousers."

"Where is he?"

"I haven't the foggiest. Somewhere or other." He jabbed his rake on the dusty ground. "It's good soil for carrots. And there's no better earth for potatoes."

"Is he dead?"

"Good God, no. What gave you that idea? All that's wrong with Bobby is that he's a bit wayward when it comes to writing letters. What made you think he was dead?"

Henry was embarrassed, and with no way of explaining himself. Mr. Bawden shrugged and retreated into his deafness and gardening.

Mrs. Bawden was obviously told of Henry's questions in the garden. At dinner she recounted Bobby's travels—his letters from Australia, where he had spent three years, the good job in Hong Kong he'd thrown up on a whim in order to go to Canada. "We're about due a letter from him soon."

"What's that?" her husband asked.

"I said we're about due a letter from Bobby."

"I'll believe it when I see it," said Mr. Bawden.

When Henry offered to do Mrs. Bawden's shopping, it seemed as if she had been expecting him to ask. She gave him a list, and he pedalled the two miles to the nearest shop on a bicycle that had been Bobby's.

A family of five moved in, and stayed for three nights. They were boisterous, but their liveliness appeared toned down out of respect for someone else's house. Mrs. Bawden had that effect on people. Henry kept out of their way. When he came down to say good night, Mr. Bawden, alone in the kitchen with a book, directed him to the guests' sitting room. He found Mrs. Bawden there with the father and mother of the visiting family.

"And this is Bobby in his uniform," she was saying.

"My, he's a fine-looking young man."

"And here's another one, with some friends of his from the same ship."

"I'm off to bed now," Henry told her.

"Good night, Henry."

He was disconcerted by the sight of Mrs. Bawden on the sofa, with a guest on either side of her, showing photographs of her son to people she had never seen before and might never see again. There was an amiable candor in her affectionate disappointment in Bobby, and it jolted Henry, who saw it as a failure of reticence, an openness that compromised her loyalty to her son. Snapshots of her son were being touted to strangers and were symptoms of an unhappiness she was too proud to notice.

"Is it all right if I take a cup of cocoa upstairs with me?" he asked Mr. Bawden.

"Help yourself," said the old man. Henry boiled the kettle and opened the cocoa tin. "What is it, through there?" Mr. Bawden asked. "Snapshots and airmail letters?"

"What?"

"My wife, what's she doing?"

"She's talking to the guests."

"See any photographs?"

"I think she *is* showing them photographs."

The old man went back to his book.

Henry wondered how Mrs. Bawden selected the people who were treated to her photograph albums. Perhaps everyone was, and perhaps his parents, two years before, had been shown the same photographs, with the same pride, and had listened to the same reminiscences. He felt sure that the visiting couple would have asked who Henry was, and been told that his parents had gone to Singapore, that his father was a civil engineer, and that they had stayed at Netherbank and thought it an ideal place to board their son while they were away. "You ought to come home, Bobby," he said to the vanished son. "Not only does your mother miss you, but she talks about you to people she hardly knows. Worse, she's probably talking about me."

There was a visitors' book on the hall table. Besides putting down their names and addresses, guests over the years had written their comments in a column where remarks were invited. "We had a wonderful time." "Smashing food!" "Highly recommended!" "Excellent." Henry leafed back to two years earlier. "First-class!" his mother had written, in her bold, clear, self-assured handwriting. It was characteristic of her. Any time they travelled by train, his mother made it clear that they went first class as a matter of course, and that some people did not—never would, never could.

As soon as the family of five left, Netherbank was full almost every night. His parents had found the house to their taste because they had it to themselves, and they were lucky. People often had to be told that there were no rooms left.

Henry tried to keep away from the guests as much as he could, but it was impossible not to ask Mrs. Bawden each morning if there was anything she wanted him to do. "Maybe you don't think it's man's work," she said, "but I could fair do with someone to strip the beds this morning and bring the linen down here for me to launder." As the days went by he found himself aproned, pulling linen from beds, vacuuming carpets, dusting furniture, cleaning windows and mirrors, polishing the bannister.

"Next time we hear from you," said Mr. Bawden, "you'll be running a hotel. You've taken to it. But don't tell me you like it. Believe me, I know—no one better. She's a hard woman to refuse."

A girl from Lincolnshire, about Henry's age, passed him in the hall and said, "You must be blind. What's that, then, if it isn't carpet fluff? There," and she pointed. Later the same morning, egged on by a friend who was along on holiday with that family, the girl asked him, "Is this your career? Or is it a punishment?"

"Have you been very bad?" the other girl said, giggling.

"Shoo!" Henry waved a duster at them, and they ran away delighted and laughing.

Breakfast was at seven for the Bawdens and Henry, so that they could eat before the rush of holiday families to the dining room. "The Abercrombie children are sleeping three to a bed," said Mrs. Bawden. "I told Mr. Abercrombie it was the best I could do, and he was only too pleased to accept. The English family are just the same. There'll be eighteen for breakfast. I've never been so busy."

"Why folk go on holidays I'll never know," said Mr. Bawden.

"Do you want me to wait on the tables?" Henry offered.

Mr. Bawden gave him an uncertain look, and shook his head in a gesture of subdued bewilderment. "Eighteen," he said. "She could never cook and serve at the same time—not for eighteen."

"You ask them what they'd like," said Mrs. Bawden, patting his hand appreciatively. "We have fruit juice. We have porridge and packet cereals. This morning we have kippers, and we have eggs, bacon, sausages, and those who want a fried breakfast are to be asked if they want black pudding with it. Some don't like it, others love it. I never need to take a note, but it might be for the best if you were to write down the orders, like a proper waiter. Eggs scrambled, fried, boiled, or poached. Tea or coffee, and toast, jam or marmalade. And if someone high and mighty asks you for kedgeree, look daft and pretend you've never even heard of it."

"Should I get changed?"

"Put on my big white apron and you'll look the part well enough. And don't be nervous. We're not the Ritz," she said.

Mr. Bawden slipped out into the garden with his second cup of tea.

Most guests chose to come down at eight-thirty, and within the space of a few minutes the dining room was full. Henry was surprised that they could be so fussy about what to eat.

"Are the sausages fresh?" a man asked.

"I can't see Mrs. Bawden serving you a bad sausage, sir."

"What's a black pudding?"

"Black pudding," Henry said, with a hesitant shrug.

"But what's it made of?"

"Hold on." He asked Mrs. Bawden what black puddings were made of, and Mr. Bawden, rinsing his cup at the sink, raised his eyebrows.

Henry came back from the kitchen. "Blood and lights,"* he said.

"I'll have two lightly poached eggs. No, wait a minute. Did you say there were scrambled eggs? In that case, I'll have scrambled eggs."

The two girls from Lincolnshire giggled as Henry stood in his apron with his pad and pen poised. The mother ordered

---

* **lights.** Lungs.

them to hurry up. The father looked seriously at Henry, as if he thought he had been up to something.

By ten o'clock, Henry and Mrs. Bawden were alone in the kitchen, tired out and hot and sipping tea. "My twenty-of-everything set of breakfast china came in handy," she said. Most of it was stacked beside the sink. "The Lord be thanked, nobody wants lunch. Rooms next, then laundry. I don't know what I'd do without you, Henry. Next year I'll have to get a village girl to come in."

Mr. Bawden appeared with the mail.

"It's another letter from your mother!" Mrs. Bawden said. She gave it to Henry. "Go on, read it."

His mother's cadences were in every line. They had been here, there, and seen that and other things. They had developed a taste for Chinese and Malayan food, although they'd been a bit suspicious at first.

"Is it so private that you can't read it out to me?" Mrs. Bawden asked. Her husband hurried outside with a cup of tea in one hand and his watering can in the other. "Does she say anything about the climate this time?" she said, remembering the first letter. "Have they got over that exhausting journey? I didn't like the sound of the airport at Karachi."

He glanced through the rest of the letter, to make sure his mother hadn't written anything embarrassing, thinking that it was only to be expected that an old woman who showed her snapshots to all and sundry would take it for granted that a letter should be shared. He read out his mother's account of the strange food, the deliciousness of which his parents had come round to accepting, and the sightseeing. "Daddy's had to fly up to Penang for a couple of days, so I've been left on my own. Everyone's extremely kind, and I've been playing a very great deal of bridge but as yet no mahjongg, thank goodness. We've been out for dinner every night since we arrived, and I shall be quite plump when I see you next. We look forward to a quiet evening by ourselves. Our bungalow is bijou but not quite as colonial as I would have liked. I'm not very geographical, as you know, and I wasn't quite sure where Singapore was, but I know now, Henry, and I don't mind telling you that it's *absolutely tropical.* It was so nice of you to press a flower in your letter. It made me feel quite homesick."

"What a nice young man you are for doing a thing like that," said Mrs. Bawden. She patted his hand. "I knew it," she said. "I knew it'd be hot there."

A girl from an Edinburgh family asked Henry if he played tennis. He said he did. She asked if there was a court. He told her where the nearest one was, two miles away in the village.

"I don't have anyone to play with," she said. She didn't sound as if she wanted particularly to play with Henry.

Her mother appeared at the door of the sitting room. "Are you coming with us, or are you staying behind?" The woman's voice stated these options firmly, and Henry recognized the predicaments of both girl and parents.

Mrs. Bawden came to the sitting room door.

"Have you asked him?" the woman said to her daughter.

"It's two miles away," the girl said, meaning that the court was too far to be practical.

"We'll drop you off at the court," said her father from inside, through a rustle of newspaper.

"You haven't had proper company for nearly a month," Mrs. Bawden said to Henry. "Go and play tennis if you want. I can answer the door and do what needs to be done. I can manage well enough without you."

He ran upstairs, changed, got his racquet and a box of tennis balls. When he came down, the family of three was waiting in the hall, and the front door was open. The breeze disturbed the potpourri in the bowl on the hall table.

"I'm told that your father and mother are in Singapore," said the man when they were in the car. "Very interesting," he said. "Very interesting." Henry had the impression he had been vetted and found to be a suitable companion for the girl.

"What's your name?" he asked her as they strolled to the tennis court.

"Louise," she said.

"I know what it's like. At least yours haven't gone to Singapore."

"I wish they would."

"My mother's forgotten something, and it probably hasn't dawned on her yet. I'll be fifteen in a couple of weeks and she won't be here."

"It isn't much of a tennis court," Louise said.

She got bored and sat down, ignoring Henry's tepid but ironic serves as they bounced close beside her. Looking at her, he thought that there might be two major ways in which only children could turn out: they became either super-obliging, obedient models of courtesy and good behavior or, like Louise, rebelliously surly and aggrieved. He never allowed his own grievances to show, and doubted if he ever would.

"When did your father say he'd pick us up?"

"He didn't."

"What do you think of Mrs. Bawden?"

"She certainly doesn't have any secrets."

"And Mr. Bawden?"

"I didn't know there was one. I thought she was a widow."

"No secrets?"

"I feel sorry for Bobby," she said. "I couldn't stand it if my parents talked about me like that."

84

"She misses him," Henry said charitably, although he was interested that Louise disapproved of Mrs. Bawden's lack of reticence as much as he did.

"I think I'd like to travel," Louise said. "My father says that air travel will grow enormously in the next few years. I would like to be an air hostess."

"It's Bobby's room I've got. I think I'd like him. I imagine myself talking to him. I ask him what he'd do in my circumstances."

"And I suppose you get some sort of mysterious answer," she said sarcastically. "Do they have a gramophone in that house? I haven't heard a single decent record since we came away."

"He doesn't say anything," Henry said. "But I see him winking at me. I don't know what it means. Do you ever try to figure out what your dreams mean?"

"Isn't there somewhere we can get lemonade or something?" she said peevishly. "I'm parched."

"We could buy some in the shop," he said, "but there isn't a café."

"What a dump!"

"I don't think you like being in the country."

"I don't like being with my parents. I'd rather be in the city with my friends. At least there's something to do."

"Is your father coming back for us?"

"I doubt it. I think we're expected to walk."

She was unsympathetic and, Henry decided, stupid. She was also unhappy. It was her unhappiness that made her interesting. Her dislikes, her petulant good looks, her tone of voice gave the impression she was festering on the edge of a bitter family insurrection. He wondered what his father had found appealing in his mother. Louise made him think that his mother might have been like her at that age, twenty years before, in the nineteen-thirties. All that would have been different was that other kinds of music, other friends were being missed.

They walked back slowly. When they reached Netherbank, Louise's father's car was parked outside with several others. Her parents were in the garden with the Bawdens. The clear light peculiar to Galloway seeped out of the hills and fields and met a great arc of early-evening light rising from the sea. Louise's parents were holding hands. Henry thought that if his parents had been there, too, he would have experienced a moment in which the significance of how people exist to each other was clear and unmistakable. People who mattered less clouded the issue. He pressed Louise's hand, but she pulled it away.

At midmorning the following day, Louise's father said to Henry, "Do you keep an address book? If you don't, then you should. Everyone ought to. Say goodbye, you two," he said, looking at Louise. Henry felt that Louise had given a glowing report of him to her parents, even though, in his company, she had been standoffish, pert, and sardonic. "You should exchange addresses and keep in touch," her father added. He was strangely open and affable.

Louise produced her address book, and Henry dictated his address to her.

"I think that's very nice," said Mrs. Bawden. "I think it's so nice," she said to Louise's mother, "that young people should exchange addresses and keep in touch."

Mr. Bawden came in by the front door, surprised to find guests still in the house that late in the morning. He could hardly turn round and go out again, and found himself in the company.

"They're exchanging addresses. Isn't that nice, John?" his wife said.

Mr. Bawden smiled at his wife, with whose obsessive and candid garrulity he was very tenderly and very gently browned off.*

"Write letters," she urged Louise. "Write letters and use the phone only when you have to. Letters are *much* nicer. You can keep letters, but you can't keep phone calls. Have you taken a note of Louise's address?" she asked Henry.

"My book's upstairs. I'll take it from the visitors' book."

As Mrs. Bawden went out of the front door with Louise's parents, Henry followed with Louise. "We don't have to write," he said.

"I'm not good at letters. If you write first, you'll have a wait for an answer."

"I don't think I'll ever forget you," he said, "but I don't know if you'd understand why." She looked at him, and laughed quietly, but she was complimented by a surprising remark that sounded serious and mature. Her wave from the departing car was curious and concerned.

Henry waved back, and then went upstairs to strip those beds that needed to be freshly made for the arrival of new guests in the late afternoon and early evening. He suspected that a time would come when his parents would regret the three months in which they had hived him off to the Bawdens. He thought about the crisis that his awakening independence would cause in their lives; still he doubted if when it arrived they would be able to trace it back to his weeks in that safe, homely, and respectable house, or to that quaint old couple who lived in daily expectation of a letter from their son Bobby, in whose room Henry slept.

---

* **browned off.** British slang for "fed up."

87

A BIRD IN THE HOUSE

Margaret Laurence

The parade would be almost over by now, and I had not gone. My mother had said in a resigned voice, "All right, Vanessa, if that's the way you feel," making me suffer twice as many jabs of guilt as I would have done if she had lost her temper. She and Grandmother MacLeod had gone off, my mother pulling the low box sleigh with Roddie all dolled up in his new red snowsuit, just the sort of little kid anyone would want people to see. I sat on the lowest branch of the birch tree in our yard, not minding the snowy wind, even welcoming its punishment. I went over my reasons for not going, trying to believe they were good and sufficient, but in my heart I felt I was betraying my father. This was the first time I had stayed away from the Remembrance Day parade. I wondered if he would notice that I was not there, standing on the sidewalk at the corner of River and Main while the parade passed, and then following to the Courthouse grounds where the service was held.

I could see the whole thing in my mind. It was the same every year. The Manawaka Civic Band always led the way. They had never been able to afford full uniforms, but they had peaked navy blue caps and sky blue chest ribbons. They were joined on Remembrance Day by the Salvation Army band, whose uniforms seemed too ordinary for a parade, for they were the same ones the bandsmen wore every Saturday night when they played "Nearer, my God, to Thee" at the foot of River Street. The two bands never managed to practice quite enough together, so they did not keep in time too well. The Salvation Army band invariably played faster, and afterward my father would say irritably, "They play those marches just like they do hymns, blast them, as though they wouldn't get to heaven if they didn't hustle up." And my mother, who had great respect for the Salvation Army because of the good work they did, would respond chidingly, "Now, now, Ewen—" I vowed I would never say "Now, now" to my husband or children, not that I ever intended having the latter, for I had been put off by my brother, Roderick, who was two years old, with wavy hair, and everyone said what a beautiful child. I was twelve, and no one in his right mind would have said what a beautiful child, for I was big-boned like my Grandfather Connor and had straight lanky black hair like a Blackfoot or Cree.

After the bands would come the veterans. Even thinking of them at this distance, in the white and withdrawn quiet of the birch tree, gave me a sense of painful embarrassment. I might not have minded so much if my father had not been among them. How could he go? How could he not see how they all looked? It must have been a long time since they were soldiers, for they had forgotten how to march in step. They were old—that was the thing. My father was bad enough, being almost forty, but he wasn't a patch on Howard Tully from the drugstore, who was completely gray-haired and also fat, or Stewart MacMurchie, who was bald on the back of his head. They looked to me like impostors, plump or spindly caricatures of past warriors. I almost hated them for walking in that limping column down Main. At the Courthouse, everyone would sing "Lord God of Hosts, be with us yet, lest we forget, lest we forget." Will Masterson would pick up his old army bugle and blow the "Last Post." Then it would be over, and everyone could start gabbling once more and go home.

I jumped down from the birch bough and ran to the house, yelling, making as much noise as I could.

> I'm a poor lonesome cowboy
> An' a long way from home

I stepped inside the front hall and kicked off my snow boots. I slammed the door behind me, making the dark ruby and emerald glass shake in the small leaded panes. I slid purposely on the hall rug, causing it to bunch and crinkle on the slippery polished oak of the floor. I seized the newel-post, round as a head, and spun myself to and fro on the bottom stair.

> I ain't got no father
> To buy the clothes I wear.
> I'm a poor lonesome . . .

At this moment my shoulders were firmly seized and shaken by a pair of hands, white and delicate and old but strong as talons.

"Just what do you think you're doing, young lady?" Grandmother MacLeod inquired, in a voice like frost on a windowpane, infinitely cold and clearly etched.

90

I went limp, and in a moment she took her hands away. If you struggled, she would always hold on longer.

"Gee, I never knew you were home yet."

"I would have thought that on a day like this you might have shown a little respect and consideration," Grandmother MacLeod said, "even if you couldn't make the effort to get cleaned up enough to go to the parade."

I realized with surprise that she imagined this to be my reason for not going. I did not try to correct her impression. My real reason would have been even less acceptable.

"I'm sorry," I said quickly.

In some families, "please" is described as the magic word. In our house, however, it was "sorry."

"This isn't an easy day for any of us," she said.

Then I remembered that her younger son, my Uncle Roderick, had been killed in the Great War. When my father marched, and when the hymn was sung, and when that ʾbearably lonely tune was sounded by the one bugle and everyone forced themselves to keep absolutely still, it would be that boy of whom she was thinking. I felt the enormity of my own offense.

"Grandmother—I'm sorry."

"So you said."

I could not tell her I had not really said it before at all. I went into the den and found my father there. He was sitting in the leather-cushioned armchair beside the fireplace. He was not doing anything, just sitting and smoking. I stood beside him, wanting to touch the light brown hairs on his forearm, but thinking he might laugh at me or pull his arm away if I did.

"I'm sorry," I said, meaning it.

"What for, honey?"

91

"For not going."

"Oh, that. What was the matter?"

I did not want him to know, and yet I had to tell him, make him see.

"They look silly," I blurted. "Marching like that."

For a minute I thought he was going to be angry. It would have been a relief to me if he had been. Instead, he fixed his eyes above the mantelpiece where the sword hung, the handsome and evil-looking crescent in its carved bronze sheath that some ancestor had once brought from the northern frontier of India.

"Is that the way it looks to you?" he said.

I felt in his voice some hurt, something that was my fault. I wanted to make everything all right between us, to convince him that I understood, even if I did not. I prayed that Grandmother MacLeod would stay put in her room, and that my mother would take a long time in the kitchen giving Roddie his lunch. I wanted my father to myself, so I could prove to him that I cared more about him than any of the others did. I wanted to speak in some way that would be more poignant and comprehending than anything of which my mother could possibly be capable. But I did not know how.

"You were right there when Uncle Roderick got killed, weren't you?" I began uncertainly.

"Yes."

"How old was he, Dad?"

"Eighteen," my father said.

Unexpectedly, that day came into intense being for me. He had had to watch his own brother die, not in the antiseptic calm of some hospital, but out in the open, the stretches of mud I had seen in his snapshots. He would not have known what to do. He would just have had to stand there and look at it, whatever that might mean. I looked at my father with a kind of horrified awe, and then I began to cry. I had forgotten about impressing him with my perception. Now I needed him to console me for this unwanted glimpse of the pain he had once known.

"Hey, cut it out, honey," he said, embarrassed. "It was bad, but it wasn't all as bad as that part. There were a few other things."

"Like what?" I said, not believing him.

"Oh, I don't know," he replied evasively. "Most of us were pretty young, you know, I and the boys I joined up with. None of us had ever been away from Manawaka before. Those of us who came back mostly came back here, or else went no further away from town than Winnipeg. So when we were overseas, that was the only time most of us were ever a long way from home."

"Did you want to be?" I asked, shocked.

"Oh, well," my father said uncomfortably. "It was kind of interesting to see a few other places for a change, that's all."

Grandmother MacLeod was standing in the doorway.

"Beth's called you twice for lunch, Ewen. Are you deaf, you and Vanessa?"

"Sorry," my father and I said simultaneously.

Then we went upstairs to wash our hands.

That winter my mother returned to her old job as nurse in my father's medical practice. She was able to do this only because of Noreen.

"Grandmother MacLeod says we're getting a maid," I said to my father, accusingly, one morning. "We're not, are we?"

"Believe you me, on what I'm going to be paying her," my father growled, "she couldn't be called anything as classy as a maid. Hired girl would be more like it."

"Now, now, Ewen," my mother put in, "it's not as if we were cheating her or anything. You know she wants to live in town, and I can certainly see why, stuck out there on the farm, and her father hardly ever letting her come in. What kind of life is that for a girl?"

"I don't like the idea of your going back to work, Beth," my father said. "I know you're fine now, but you're not exactly the robust type."

"You can't afford to hire a nurse any longer. It's all very well to say the Depression won't last forever; probably it won't, but what else can we do for now?"

"I'm damned if I know," my father admitted. "Beth—"

"Yes?"

They both seemed to have forgotten about me. It was at breakfast, which we always ate in the kitchen, and I sat rigidly on my chair, pretending to ignore and thus snub their withdrawal from me. I glared at the window, but it was so thickly plumed and scrolled with frost that I could not see out. I glanced back to my parents. My father had not replied, and my mother was looking at him in that anxious and half-frowning way she had recently developed.

"What is it, Ewen?" Her voice had the same nervous sharpness it bore sometimes when she would say to me, "For mercy's sake, Vanessa, what is it *now*?" as though whatever was the matter, it was bound to be the last straw.

My father spun his sterling silver serviette ring, engraved with his initials, slowly around on the table.

"I never thought things would turn out like this, did you?"

"Please," my mother said in a low, strained voice, "please, Ewen, let's not start all this again. I can't take it."

"All right," my father said. "Only—"

"The MacLeods used to have money, and now they don't," my mother cried. "Well, they're not alone. Do you think all

94

that matters to me, Ewen? What I can't bear is to see you forever reproaching yourself. As if it were your fault."

"I don't think it's the comedown," my father said. "If I were somewhere else, I don't think it would matter to me, either, except where you're concerned. But I suppose you'd work too hard wherever you were—it's bred into you. If you haven't got anything to slave away at, you'll sure as hell invent something."

"What do you think I should do, let the house go to wrack and ruin? That would go over well with your mother, wouldn't it?"

"That's just it," my father said. "It's the damned house all the time. I haven't only taken on my father's house, I've taken on everything that goes with it, apparently. Sometimes I really wonder—"

"Well, it's a good thing I've inherited some practicality even if you haven't," my mother said. "I'll say that for the Connors—they aren't given to brooding, thank the Lord. Do you want your egg poached or scrambled?"

"Scrambled," my father said. "All I hope is that this Noreen doesn't get married straightaway, that's all."

"She won't," my mother said. "Who's she going to meet who could afford to marry?"

"I marvel at you, Beth," my father said. "You look as though a puff of wind would blow you away. But underneath, by God, you're all hardwood."

"Don't talk stupidly," my mother said. "All I hope is that she won't object to taking your mother's breakfast up on a tray."

"That's right," my father said angrily. "Rub it in."

"Oh, Ewen, I'm sorry!" my mother cried, her face suddenly stricken. "I don't know why I say these things. I didn't mean to."

"I know," my father said. "Here, cut it out, honey. Just for God's sake, please don't cry."

"I'm sorry," my mother repeated, blowing her nose.

"We're both sorry," my father said. "Not that that changes anything."

After my father had gone, I got down from my chair and went to my mother.

"I don't want you to go back to the office. I don't want a hired girl here. I'll hate her."

My mother sighed, making me feel that I was placing an intolerable burden on her, and yet making me resent having to feel this weight. She looked tired, as she often did these days. Her tiredness bored me, made me want to attack her for it.

"Catch me getting along with a dumb old hired girl," I threatened.

"Do what you like," my mother said abruptly. "What can I do about it?"

And then, of course, I felt bereft, not knowing which way to turn.

My father need not have worried about Noreen's getting married. She was, as it turned out, interested not in boys but in God. My mother was relieved about the boys but alarmed about God.

"It isn't natural," she said, "for a girl of seventeen. Do you think she's all right mentally, Ewen?"

My parents, along with Grandmother MacLeod, went to the United Church every Sunday, and I was made to go to Sunday school in the church basement, where there were small red chairs which humiliatingly resembled kindergarten furniture, and pictures of Jesus wearing a white sheet and surrounded by a whole lot of well-dressed kids whose mothers obviously had not suffered them to come unto Him until

every face and ear was properly scrubbed. Our religious obser-
vances also included grace at meals, when my father would
mumble, "For what we are about to receive the Lord make us
truly thankful Amen," running the words together as though
they were one long word. My mother approved of these rit-
uals, which seemed decent and moderate to her. Noreen's
religion, however, was a different matter. Noreen belonged to
the Tabernacle of the Risen and Reborn, and she had got up
to testify no less than seven times in the past two years, she
told us. My mother, who could not imagine anyone voluntarily making a public spectacle of himself, was profoundly
shocked by this revelation.

"Don't worry," my father soothed her. "She's all right. She's
just had kind of a dull life, that's all."

My mother shrugged and went on worrying and trying to
help Noreen without hurting her feelings, by tactful remarks
about the advisability of modulating one's voice when singing
hymns and about the fact that there was plenty of hot water
so Noreen really didn't need to hesitate about taking a bath.
She even bought a razor and a packet of blades and whispered
to Noreen that any girl who wore transparent blouses so
much would probably like to shave under her arms. None of
these suggestions had the slightest effect on Noreen. She did
not cease belting out hymns at the top of her voice, she
bathed once a fortnight, and the sorrel-colored hair continued
to bloom like a thicket of Indian paintbrush in her armpits.

Grandmother MacLeod refused to speak to Noreen. This
caused Noreen a certain amount of bewilderment until she
finally hit on an answer.

"Your poor grandma," she said. "She is deaf as a post.
These things are sent to try us here on earth, Vanessa. But if
she makes it into heaven, I'll bet you anything she will hear
clear as a bell."

Noreen and I talked about heaven quite a lot, and also hell. Noreen had an intimate and detailed knowledge of both places. She not only knew what they looked like, she even knew how big they were. Heaven was seventy-seven thousand miles square, and it had four gates, each one made out of a different kind of precious jewel. The Pearl Gate, the Topaz Gate, the Amethyst Gate, the Ruby Gate—Noreen would reel them off, all the gates of heaven. I told Noreen they sounded like poetry, but she was puzzled by my reaction, and said I shouldn't talk that way. If you said poetry, it sounded like it was just made up and not really so, Noreen said.

Hell was larger than heaven, and when I asked why, thinking of it as something of a comedown for God, Noreen said naturally it had to be bigger because there were a darn sight more people there than in heaven. Hell was one hundred and ninety million miles deep and was in perpetual darkness, like a cave or under the sea. Even the flames (this was the awful thing) did not give off any light.

I did not actually believe in Noreen's doctrines, but the images which they conjured up began to inhabit my imagination. Noreen's fund of exotic knowledge was not limited to religion, although in a way it all seemed related. She could do many things which had a spooky tinge to them. Once when she was making a cake, she found we had run out of eggs. She went outside and gathered a bowl of fresh snow and used it instead. The cake rose like a charm, and I stared at Noreen as though she were a sorceress. In fact, I began to think of her as a sorceress, someone not quite of this earth. There was nothing unearthly about her broad shoulders and hips and her forest of dark red hair, but even these features took on a slightly sinister significance to me. I no longer saw her through the eyes or the expressed opinions of my mother and father, as a girl who had quit school at grade eight and whose life on the farm had been endlessly drab. I knew the truth— Noreen's life had not been drab at all, for she dwelt in a world of violent splendors, a world filled with angels whose wings of delicate light bore real feathers, and saints shining like the dawn, and prophets who spoke in the ancient tongues, and the ecstatic souls of the saved, as well as denizens of the lower regions; mean-eyed imps, and crooked cloven-hoofed monsters, and beasts with the bodies of swine and the human heads of murderers, and lovely depraved jezebels torn by dogs through all eternity.

The middle layer of creation, our earth, was equally full of grotesque presences, for Noreen believed strongly in the visitation of ghosts and the communication with spirits. She could prove this with her Ouija board. We would both place our fingers lightly on the indicator, and it would skim across the board and spell out answers to our questions. I did not believe wholeheartedly in the Ouija board either, but I was cautious about the kind of question I asked, in case the answer would turn out unfavorable and I would be unable to forget it.

One day Noreen told me she could also make a table talk. We used the small table in my bedroom, and sure enough, it lifted very slightly under our fingertips and tapped once for *yes,* twice for *no.* Noreen asked if her Aunt Ruthie would get better from the kidney operation, and the table replied *no.* I withdrew my hands.

"I don't want to do it anymore."

"Gee, what's the matter, Vanessa?" Noreen's plain, placid face creased in a frown. "We only just begun."

"I have to do my homework."

My heart lurched as I said this. I was certain Noreen would know I was lying, and that she would know not by any

99

ordinary perception, either. But her attention had been caught by something else, and I was thankful, at least until I saw what it was.

My bedroom window was not opened in the coldest weather. The storm window, which was fitted outside as an extra wall against the winter, had three small circular holes in its frame so that some fresh air could seep into the house. The sparrow must have been floundering in the new snow on the roof, for it had crawled in through one of these holes and was now caught between the two layers of glass. I could not bear the panic of the trapped bird, and before I realized what I was doing, I had thrown open the bedroom window. I was not releasing the sparrow into any better situation, I soon saw, for instead of remaining quiet and allowing us to catch it in order to free it, it began flying blindly around the room, hitting the lampshade, brushing against the walls, its wings seeming to spin faster and faster.

I was petrified. I thought I would pass out if those palpitating wings touched me. There was something in the bird's senseless movements that revolted me. I also thought it was going to damage itself, break one of those thin wing bones, perhaps, and then it would be lying on the floor, dying, like the pimpled and horribly featherless baby birds we saw sometimes on the sidewalks in the spring when they had fallen out of their nests. I was not any longer worried about the sparrow. I wanted only to avoid the sight of it lying broken on the floor. Viciously, I thought that if Noreen said, "God sees the little sparrow fall," I would kick her in the shins. She did not, however, say this.

"A bird in the house means a death in the house," Noreen remarked.

Shaken, I pulled my glance away from the whirling wings and looked at Noreen. "What?"

"That's what I've heard said, anyhow."

The sparrow had exhausted itself. It lay on the floor, spent and trembling. I could not bring myself to touch it. Noreen bent and picked it up. She cradled it with great gentleness between her cupped hands. Then we took it downstairs, and when I had opened the back door, Noreen set the bird free.

"Poor little scrap," she said, and I felt struck to the heart, knowing she had been concerned all along about the sparrow, while I, perfidiously, in the chaos of the moment, had been concerned only about myself.

"Wanna do some with the Ouija board, Vanessa?" Noreen asked.

I shivered a little, perhaps only because of the blast of cold air which had come into the kitchen when the door was opened.

"No thanks, Noreen. Like I said, I got my homework to do. But thanks all the same."

"That's OK," Noreen said in her guileless voice. "Anytime."

But whenever she mentioned the Ouija board or the talking table after that, I always found some excuse not to consult these oracles.

"Do you want to come to church with me this evening, Vanessa?" my father asked.

"How come you're going to the evening service?" I inquired.

"Well, we didn't go this morning. We went snowshoeing instead, remember? I think your grandmother was a little bit put out about it. She went alone this morning. I guess it wouldn't hurt you and me to go now."

We walked through the dark, along the white streets, the snow squeaking dryly under our feet. The streetlights were placed at long intervals along the sidewalks, and around each pole the circle of flimsy light created glistening points of blue and crystal on the crusted snow. I would have liked to take my father's hand, as I used to do, but I was too old for that now. I walked beside him, taking long steps so he would not have to walk more slowly on my account.

The sermon bored me, and I began leafing through the hymnary for entertainment. I must have drowsed, for the next thing I knew, my father was prodding me, and we were on our feet for the closing hymn.

> Near the Cross, near the Cross,
> Be my glory ever,
> Till my ransomed soul shall find
> Rest beyond the river.

I knew the tune well, so I sang loudly for the first verse. But the music to that hymn is somber, and all at once the words themselves seemed too dreadful to be sung. I stopped singing, my throat knotted. I thought I was going to cry, but I did not know why, except that the song recalled to me my Grandmother Connor, who had died the year before. She had been a very religious woman, but not in any sanctimonious way, and we had all loved her, even Grandfather Connor, who did not seem like the sort of person who would love anybody. I wondered why her soul needed to be ransomed. If God did not think she was good enough just as she was, then I did not have much use for His opinion. "Rest beyond the river"—was that what had happened to her? She had believed in heaven, but I did not think that rest beyond the river was quite what she had had in mind. To think of her in Noreen's flashy heaven, though—that was even worse. Someplace where nobody ever got annoyed or had to be smoothed down and placated, someplace where there were never any family scenes—that would have suited my Grandmother Connor. Maybe she wouldn't have minded a certain amount of rest beyond the river at that.

When we had the silent prayer, I looked at my father. He sat with his head bowed and his eyes closed. He was frowning deeply, and I could see the pulse in his temple. I wondered then what he believed. I did not have any real idea what it might be. When he raised his head, he did not look uplifted or anything like that. He merely looked tired. Then Reverend McKee pronounced the benediction, and we could go home.

"What do you think about all that stuff, Dad?" I asked hesitantly, as we walked.

"What stuff, honey?"

"Oh, heaven and hell, and like that."

My father laughed. "Have you been listening to Noreen too much? Well, I don't know. I don't think they're actual places. Maybe they stand for something that happens all the time here, or else doesn't happen. It's kind of hard to explain. I guess I'm not so good at explanations."

Nothing seemed to have been made any clearer to me. I reached out and took his hand, not caring that he might think this a babyish gesture.

"I hate that hymn!"

"Good Lord," my father said in astonishment. "Why, Vanessa?"

But I did not know and so could not tell him.

Many people in Manawaka had flu that winter, so my father and Doctor Cates were kept extremely busy. I had flu myself, and spent a week in bed, vomiting only the first day and after that enjoying poor health, as my mother put it, with Noreen bringing me ginger ale and orange juice, and each evening my father putting a wooden tongue depressor into my mouth and peering down my throat, then smiling and saying he thought I might live after all.

Then my father got sick himself and had to stay home and go to bed. This was such an unusual occurrence that it amused me.

"Doctors shouldn't get sick," I told him.

"You're right," he said. "That was pretty bad management."

"Run along now, dear," my mother said.

That night I woke and heard voices in the upstairs hall. When I went out, I found my mother and Grandmother MacLeod, both in their dressing gowns. With them was Doctor Cates. I did not go immediately to my mother, as I would have done only a year before. I stood in the doorway of my room, squinting against the sudden light.

"Mother, what is it?"

She turned, and momentarily I saw the look on her face before she erased it and put on a contrived calm.

"It's all right," she said. "Doctor Cates has just come to have a look at Daddy. You go on back to sleep."

The wind was high that night, and I lay and listened to it rattling the storm windows and making the dry and winter-stiffened vines of the Virginia creeper scratch like small persistent claws against the red brick. In the morning, my mother told me that my father had developed pneumonia.

Doctor Cates did not think it would be safe to move my father to the hospital. My mother began sleeping in the spare bedroom, and after she had been there for a few nights, I asked if I could sleep in there too. I thought she would be bound to ask me why, and I did not know what I would say, but she only nodded, and in some way her easy agreement upset me.

That night Doctor Cates came again, bringing with him one of the nurses from the hospital. My mother stayed upstairs with them. I sat with Grandmother MacLeod in the living room. That was the last place in the world I wanted to be, but I thought she would be offended if I went off. She sat as straight and rigid as a totem pole and embroidered away at the needlepoint cushion cover she was doing. I perched on the edge of the chesterfield and kept my eyes fixed on *The White Company* by Conan Doyle, and from time to time I turned a page. I had already read it three times, but luckily Grandmother MacLeod did not know that. At nine o'clock she looked at her gold brooch watch, which she always wore pinned to her dress, and told me to go to bed, so I did that.

I wakened in darkness. At first, it seemed to me that I was in my own bed, and everything was as usual, with my parents in their room, and Roddie curled up in the crib in his room, and Grandmother MacLeod sleeping with her mouth open in her enormous spool bed, surrounded by half a dozen framed photos of Uncle Roderick and only one of my father, and Noreen snoring fitfully in the room next to mine, with the dark flames of her hair spreading out across the pillow, and the pink and silver motto cards from the Tabernacle stuck with adhesive tape onto the wall beside her bed: Lean on Him, Emmanuel Is My Refuge, Rock of Ages Cleft for Me.

Then in the total night around me, I heard a sound. It was my mother, and she was crying, not loudly at all but from somewhere very deep inside her. I sat up in bed. Everything seemed to have stopped, not only time but my own heart and blood as well. Then my mother noticed that I was awake.

I did not ask her, and she did not tell me anything. There was no need. She held me in her arms, or I held her, I am not certain which. And after a while the first mourning stopped, too, as everything does sooner or later, for when the limits of endurance have been reached, then people must sleep.

In the days following my father's death, I stayed close beside my mother, and this was only partly for my own consoling.

I also had the feeling that she needed my protection. I did not know from what, or what I could possibly do, but something held me there. Reverend McKee called, and I sat with my grandmother and my mother in the living room. My mother told me I did not need to stay unless I wanted to, but I refused to go. What I thought chiefly was that he would speak of the healing power of prayer and all that, and it would be bound to make my mother cry again. And, in fact, it happened in just that way, but when it actually came, I could not protect her from this assault. I could only sit there and pray my own prayer, which was that he would go away quickly.

My mother tried not to cry unless she was alone or with me. I also tried, but neither of us was entirely successful. Grandmother MacLeod, on the other hand, was never seen crying, not even the day of my father's funeral. But that day, when we had returned to the house and she had taken off her black velvet overshoes and her heavy sealskin coat with its black fur that was the softest thing I had ever touched, she stood in the hallway and for the first time she looked unsteady. When I reached out instinctively toward her, she sighed.

"That's right," she said. "You might just take my arm while I go upstairs, Vanessa."

That was the most my Grandmother MacLeod ever gave in, to anyone's sight. I left her in her bedroom, sitting on the straight chair beside her bed and looking at the picture of my father that had been taken when he graduated from medical college. Maybe she was sorry now that she had only the one photograph of him, but whatever she felt, she did not say.

I went down into the kitchen. I had scarcely spoken to Noreen since my father's death. This had not been done on purpose. I simply had not seen her. I had not really seen any-one except my mother. Looking at Noreen now, I suddenly recalled the sparrow. I felt physically sick, remembering the fearful darting and plunging of those wings, and the fact that it was I who had opened the window and let it in. Then an inexplicable fury took hold of me, some terrifying need to hurt, burn, destroy. Absolutely without warning, either to her or to myself, I hit Noreen as hard as I could. When she swung around, appalled, I hit out at her once more, my arms and legs flailing. Her hands snatched at my wrists, and she held me, but I continued to struggle, fighting blindly, my eyes tightly closed, as though she were a prison all around me and I was battling to get out. Finally, too shocked at myself to go on, I went limp in her grasp, and she let me drop to the floor.

"Vanessa! I never done one single solitary thing to you, and here you go hitting and scratching me like that! What in the world has got into you?"

I began to say I was sorry, which was certainly true, but I did not say it. I could not say anything.

"You're not yourself, what with your dad and everything," she excused me. "I been praying every night that your dad is with God, Vanessa. I know he wasn't actually saved in the regular way, but still and all—"

"Shut up," I said.

Something in my voice made her stop talking. I rose from the floor and stood in the doorway.

"He didn't need to be saved," I went on coldly, distinctly. "And he is not in heaven, because there is no heaven. And it doesn't matter, see? *It doesn't matter!*"

Noreen's face looked peculiarly vulnerable now, her high, wide cheekbones and puzzled childish eyes, and the thick russet tangle of her hair. I had not hurt her much before, when I hit her. But I had hurt her now, hurt her in some inexcusable way. Yet I sensed, too, that already she was gaining some satisfaction out of feeling sorrowful about my disbelief.

I went upstairs to my room. Momentarily I felt a sense of calm, almost of acceptance. *Rest beyond the river.* I knew now what that meant. It meant Nothing. It meant only silence, forever.

Then I lay down on my bed and spent the last of my tears, or what seemed then to be the last. Because, despite what I had said to Noreen, it did matter. It mattered, but there was no help for it.

Everything changed after my father's death. The MacLeod house could not be kept up any longer. My mother sold it to a local merchant who subsequently covered over with yellow stucco the deep red of the brick. Something about the house had always made me uneasy—its tower room, where Grandmother MacLeod's potted plants drooped in a lethargic and lime-green confusion, its long stairways and hidden places, the attic, which I had always imagined to be dwelt in by the spirits of the family dead, the gigantic portrait of the Duke of Wellington that hung at the top of the stairs. It was never an endearing house. And yet when it was no longer ours, and when the Virginia creeper had been torn down and the dark walls turned to a light marigold, I went out of my way to avoid walking past, for it seemed to me that the house had lost the stern dignity that was its very heart.

Noreen went back to the farm. My mother and brother and I moved into Grandfather Connor's house. Grandmother MacLeod went to live with Aunt Morag in Winnipeg. It was harder for her than for anyone else, because so much of her life was bound up with the MacLeod house. She was fond of Aunt Morag, but that hardly counted. Her men were gone, her husband and her sons, and a family whose men are gone is no family at all. The day she left, my mother and I did not know what to say. Grandmother MacLeod looked even smaller than usual in her fur coat and her black velvet toque. She became extremely agitated about trivialities, and fussed about the possibility of the taxi not arriving on time. She had forbidden us to accompany her to the station. About my father, or the house, or anything important, she did not say a word. Then, when the taxi had finally arrived, she turned to my mother.

"Roddie will have Ewen's seal ring, of course, with the MacLeod crest on it," she said. "But there is another seal as well, don't forget, the larger one with the crest and motto. It's meant to be worn on a watch chain. I keep it in my jewel box. It was Roderick's. Roddie's to have that, too, when I die. Don't let Morag talk you out of it."

During World War II, when I was seventeen years old and in love with an airman who did not love me, and desperately anxious to get away from Manawaka and from my grandfather's house, I happened one day to be going through the old mahogany desk that had belonged to my father. It had a number of small drawers inside, and I accidentally pulled one of these all the way out. Behind it there was another drawer, one I had not known about. Curious, I opened it. Inside, there was a letter written on almost transparent paper in a cramped, angular handwriting. It began, *Cher Monsieur Ewen. . . .* That was all I could make out, for the writing was nearly impossible to read and my French was not good. It was dated 1919. With it, there was a picture of a girl, looking absurdly old-fashioned to my eyes, like the faces on long-discarded calendars or chocolate boxes. But beneath the dated quality of the photograph, she seemed neither expensive nor cheap. She looked like what she probably had been—an ordinary, middle-class girl, but in another country. She wore her hair in long ringlets, and her mouth was shaped into a sweetly sad posed smile like Mary Pickford's. That was all. There was nothing else in the drawer.

I looked for a long time at the girl, and hoped she had meant some momentary and unexpected freedom. I remembered what he had said to me after I hadn't gone to the Remembrance Day parade.

"What are you doing, Vanessa?" my mother called from the kitchen.

"Nothing," I replied.

I took the letter and picture outside and burned them. That was all I could do for him. Now that we might have talked together, it was many years too late. Perhaps it would not have been possible anyway.

As I watched the smile of the girl turn into scorched paper, I grieved for my father as though he had just died now.

THE STRANGE CASE OF
DR. JEKYLL AND MR. HYDE

Published:
January 1886

Robert Louis Stevenson
(1850-1894)

science: king
religion: attack

London

CHAPTER 1

important

STORY OF THE DOOR

Mr. Utterson the lawyer was a man of a rugged counte- *(face)* nance that was never lighted by a smile; cold, scanty, and embarrassed in discourse; backward in sentiment; lean, long, dusty, dreary, and yet somehow lovable. *conversation* *feeling* At friendly meetings, and when the wine was to his taste, something eminently human beaconed from his eye; something indeed which never found its way into his talk, but which spoke not only in these silent symbols of the after-dinner face, but more often and loudly in the acts of his life. He was austere with himself; drank gin when he was alone, to mortify a taste for vintages; and though he enjoyed the theatre, had not crossed the doors of one for twenty years. But he had an approved tolerance for others; sometimes wondering, almost with envy, at the high pressure of spirits involved in their misdeeds; and in any extremity inclined to help rather than to reprove. "I incline to

doesn't judge people

Cain's heresy," he used to say quaintly: "I let my brother go to the devil in his own way." In this character, it was frequently his fortune to be the last reputable acquaintance and the last good influence in the lives of downgoing men. And to such as these, so long as they came about his chambers, he never marked a shade of change in his demeanour.

No doubt the feat was easy to Mr. Utterson; for he was undemonstrative at the best, and even his friendship seemed to be founded in a similar catholicity of good-nature. It is the mark of a modest man to accept his friendly circle ready-made from the hands of opportunity; and that was the lawyer's way. His friends were those of his own blood or those whom he had known the longest; his affections, like ivy, were the growth of time, they implied no aptness in the object. Hence, no doubt, the bond that united him to Mr. Richard Enfield, his distant kinsman, the well-known man about town. It was a nut to crack for many, what these two could see in each other, or what subject they could find in common. It was reported by those who encountered them in their Sunday walks, that they said nothing, looked singularly dull, and would hail with obvious relief the appearance of a friend. For all that, the two men put the greatest store by these excursions, counted them the chief jewel of each week, and not only set aside occasions of pleasure, but even resisted the calls of business, that they might enjoy them uninterrupted.

It chanced on one of these rambles that their way led them down a by-street in a busy quarter of London. The street was small and what is called quiet, but it drove a thriving trade on the week-days. The inhabitants were all doing well, it seemed, and all emulously hoping to do better still, and laying out the surplus of their gains in coquetry; so that the shop fronts stood along that thoroughfare with an air of invitation, like rows of smiling saleswomen. Even on Sunday, when it veiled its more florid charms and lay comparatively empty of passage, the street shone out in contrast to its dingy neighbourhood, like a fire in a forest; and with its freshly painted shutters, well-polished brasses, and general cleanliness and gaiety of note, instantly caught and pleased the eye of the passenger.

Two doors from one corner, on the left hand going east, the line was broken by the entry of a court; and just at that point, a certain sinister block of building thrust forward its gable on the street. It was two storeys high; showed no window, nothing but a door on the lower storey and a blind forehead of discoloured wall on the upper; and bore in every feature, the marks of prolonged and sordid negligence. The door, which was equipped with neither bell nor knocker, was blistered and distained. Tramps slouched into the recess and struck matches on the panels; children kept shop upon the steps; the schoolboy had tried his knife on the mouldings; and for close on a generation, no one had appeared to drive away these random visitors or to repair their ravages.

Mr. Enfield and the lawyer were on the other side of the by-street; but when they came abreast of the entry, the former lifted up his cane and pointed.

"Did you ever remark that door?" he asked; and when his companion had replied in the affirmative, "It is connected in my mind," added he, "with a very odd story."

"Indeed?" said Mr. Utterson, with a slight change of voice, "and what was that?"

"Well, it was this way," returned Mr. Enfield: "I was coming home from some place at the end of the world, about three o'clock of a black winter morning, and my way lay through a part of town where there was literally nothing to be seen but lamps. Street after street, and all the folks asleep—street after street, all lighted up as if for a procession and all as empty as a church—till at last I got into that state of mind

when a man listens and listens and begins to long for the sight
of a policeman. All at once, I saw two figures; one a little
man who was stumping along eastward at a good walk, and
the other a girl of maybe eight or ten who was running as
hard as she was able down a cross street. Well, sir, the two ran
into one another naturally enough at the corner; and then
came the horrible part of the thing; for the man trampled
calmly over the child's body and left her screaming on the
ground. It sounds nothing to hear, but it was hellish to see. It
wasn't like a man; it was like some damned juggernaut. I gave
a view halloa, took to my heels, collared my gentleman, and
brought him back to where there was already quite a group
about the screaming child. He was perfectly cool and made
no resistance, but gave me one look, so ugly that it brought
out the sweat on me like running. The people who had
turned out were the girl's own family; and pretty soon, the
doctor, for whom she had been sent, put in his appearance.
Well, the child was not much the worse, more frightened,
according to the Sawbones; and there you might have supposed would be an end to it. But there was one curious
circumstance. I had taken a loathing to my gentleman at first
sight. So had the child's family, which was only natural. But
the doctor's case was what struck me. He was the usual cut
and dry apothecary, of no particular age and colour, with a
strong Edinburgh accent, and about as emotional as a bag-
pipe. Well, sir, he was like the rest of us; every time he looked
at my prisoner, I saw that Sawbones turn sick and white with
the desire to kill him. I knew what was in his mind, just as he
knew what was in mine; and killing being out of the question,
we did the next best. We told the man we could and would
make such a scandal out of this, as should make his name
stink from one end of London to the other. If he had any
friends or any credit, we undertook that he should lose them.

114

evil animal w/ female face   *references to hell*   *well spoken*

And all the time, as we were pitching it in red hot, we were
keeping the women off him as best we could, for they were as
wild as harpies. I never saw a circle of such hateful faces; and
there was the man in the middle, with a kind of black, sneering coolness—frightened too, I could see that—but carrying
it off, sir, really like Satan. 'If you choose to make capital out
of this accident,' said he, 'I am naturally helpless. No gentleman but wishes to avoid a scene,' says he. 'Name your figure.'
Well, we screwed him up to a hundred pounds for the child's
family; he would have clearly liked to stick out; but there was
something about the lot of us that meant mischief, and at last
he struck. The next thing was to get the money; and where do
you think he carried us but to that place with the door?—
whipped out a key, went in, and presently came back with the
matter of ten pounds in gold and a cheque for the balance on
Coutts's, drawn payable to bearer and signed with a name that
I can't mention, though it's one of the points of my story, but
it was a name at least very well known and often printed. The
figure was stiff; but the signature was good for more than
that, if it was only genuine. I took the liberty of pointing out
to my gentleman that the whole business looked apocryphal,
and that a man does not, in real life, walk into a cellar door at
four in the morning and come out of it with another man's
cheque for close upon a hundred pounds. But he was quite
easy and sneering. 'Set your mind at rest,' says he, 'I will stay
with you till the banks open and cash the cheque myself.' So
we all set off, the doctor, and the child's father, and our
friend, and myself, and passed the rest of the night in my
chambers; and next day, when we had breakfasted, went in a
body to the bank. I gave in the cheque myself, and said I had
every reason to believe it was a forgery. Not a bit of it. The
cheque was genuine."

"Tut-tut," said Mr. Utterson.

115

who drew that check?

"I see you feel as I do," said Mr. Enfield. "Yes, it's a bad story. For my man was a fellow that nobody could have to do with, a really damnable man; and the person that drew the cheque is the very pink of the proprieties, celebrated too, and (what makes it worse) one of your fellows who do what they call good. Blackmail, I suppose; an honest man paying through the nose for some of the capers of his youth. Blackmail House is what I call that place with the door, in consequence. Though even that, you know, is far from explaining all," he added, and with the words fell into a vein of musing.

From this he was recalled by Mr. Utterson asking rather suddenly: "And you don't know if the drawer of the cheque lives there?"

"A likely place, isn't it?" returned Mr. Enfield. "But I happen to have noticed his address; he lives in some square or other."

"And you never asked about the—place with the door?" said Mr. Utterson.

"No, sir: I had a delicacy," was the reply. "I feel very strongly about putting questions; it partakes too much of the style of the day of judgment. You start a question, and it's like starting a stone. You sit quietly on the top of a hill; and away the stone goes, starting others; and presently some bland old bird (the last you would have thought of) is knocked on the head in his own back garden and the family have to change their name. No, sir, I make it a rule of mine: the more it looks like Queer Street, the less I ask."

"A very good rule, too," said the lawyer.

"But I have studied the place for myself," continued Mr. Enfield. "It seems scarcely a house. There is no other door, and nobody goes in or out of that one but, once in a great while, the gentleman of my adventure. There are three windows looking on the court on the first floor; none below;

my: not to get into things

the windows are always shut but they're clean. And then there is a chimney which is generally smoking; so somebody must live there. And yet it's not so sure; for the buildings are so packed together about that court, that it's hard to say where one ends and another begins."

The pair walked on again for a while in silence; and then "Enfield," said Mr. Utterson, "that's a good rule of yours."

"Yes, I think it is," returned Enfield.

"But for all that," continued the lawyer, "there's one point I want to ask: I want to ask the name of that man who walked over the child."

"Well," said Mr. Enfield, "I can't see what harm it would do. It was a man of the name of Hyde."

"Hm," said Mr. Utterson. "What sort of a man is he to see?"

a words, alliteration

"He is not easy to describe. There is something wrong with his appearance; something displeasing, something downright detestable. I never saw a man I so disliked, and yet I scarce know why. He must be deformed somewhere; he gives a strong feeling of deformity, although I couldn't specify the point. He's an extraordinary looking man, and yet I really can name nothing out of the way. No, sir; I can make no hand of it; I can't describe him. And it's not want of memory; for I declare I can see him this moment."

why can't he make the connection

Mr. Utterson again walked some way in silence and obviously under a weight of consideration. "You are sure he used a key?" he inquired at last.

"My dear sir . . ." began Enfield, surprised out of himself.

"Yes, I know," said Utterson; "I know it must seem strange. The fact is, if I do not ask you the name of the other party, it is because I know it already. You see, Richard, your tale has gone home. If you have been inexact in any point, you had better correct it."

"I think you might have warned me," returned the other with a touch of sullenness. "But I have been pedantically exact, as you call it. The fellow had a key; and what's more, he has it still. I saw him use it, not a week ago."

Mr. Utterson sighed deeply but said never a word; and the young man presently resumed. "Here is another lesson to say nothing," said he. "I am ashamed of my long tongue. Let us make a bargain never to refer to this again."

"With all my heart," said the lawyer. "I shake hands on that, Richard."

CHAPTER 2

SEARCH FOR MR. HYDE

That evening Mr. Utterson came home to his bachelor house in sombre spirits and sat down to dinner without relish. It was his custom of a Sunday, when this meal was over, to sit close by the fire, a volume of some dry divinity on his reading desk, until the clock of the neighbouring church rang out the hour of twelve, when he would go soberly and gratefully to bed. On this night, however, as soon as the cloth was taken away, he took up a candle and went into his business room. There he opened his safe, took from the most private part of it a document endorsed on the envelope as Dr. Jekyll's Will, and sat down with a clouded brow to study its contents. The will was holograph, for Mr. Utterson, though he took charge of it now that it was made, had refused to lend the least assistance in the making of it; it provided not only that, in case of the decease of Henry Jekyll, M.D., D.C.L., L.L.D., F.R.S., etc., all his possessions were to pass into the hands of his "friend and benefactor Edward Hyde," but that in case of Dr. Jekyll's

118

knowledge >ignorance

"disappearance or unexplained absence for any period exceeding three calendar months," the said Edward Hyde should step into the said Henry Jekyll's shoes without further delay and free from any burthen or obligation, beyond the payment of a few small sums to the members of the doctor's household. This document had long been the lawyer's eye-sore. It offended him both as a lawyer and as a lover of the sane and customary sides of life, to whom the fanciful was the immodest. And hitherto it was his ignorance of Mr. Hyde that had swelled his indignation; now, by a sudden turn, it was his knowledge. It was already bad enough when the name was but a name of which he could learn no more. It was worse when it began to be clothed upon with detestable attributes; and out of the shifting, insubstantial mists that had so long baffled his eye, there leaped up the sudden, definite presentment of a fiend.

bugged him b/c he didn't understand why

"I thought it was madness," he said, as he replaced the obnoxious paper in the safe, "and now I begin to fear it is disgrace." *Why would he associate w/ him?*

With that he blew out his candle, put on a greatcoat, and set forth in the direction of Cavendish Square, that citadel of medicine, where his friend, the great Dr. Lanyon, had his house and received his crowding patients. "If anyone knows, it will be Lanyon," he had thought.

The solemn butler knew and welcomed him; he was subjected to no stage of delay, but ushered direct from the door to the dining room where Dr. Lanyon sat alone over his wine. This was a hearty, healthy, dapper, red-faced gentleman, with a shock of hair prematurely white, and a boisterous and decided manner. At sight of Mr. Utterson, he sprang up from his chair and welcomed him with both hands. The geniality, as was the way of the man, was somewhat theatrical to the eye;

but it reposed on genuine feeling. For these two were old friends, old mates both at school and college, both thorough respecters of themselves and of each other, and, what does not always follow, men who thoroughly enjoyed each other's company.

After a little rambling talk, the lawyer led up to the subject which so disagreeably preoccupied his mind.

"I suppose, Lanyon," said he, "you and I must be the two oldest friends that Henry Jekyll has?"

"I wish the friends were younger," chuckled Dr. Lanyon. "But I suppose we are. And what of that? I see little of him now."

"Indeed?" said Utterson. "I thought you had a bond of common interest."

"We had," was the reply. "But it is more than ten years since Henry Jekyll became too fanciful for me. He began to go wrong, wrong in mind; and though of course I continue to take an interest in him for old sake's sake, as they say, I see and I have seen devilish little of the man. Such unscientific balderdash," added the doctor, flushing suddenly purple, "would have estranged Damon and Pythias."

This little spirit of temper was somewhat of a relief to Mr. Utterson. "They have only differed on some point of science," he thought; and being a man of no scientific passions (except in the matter of conveyancing), he even added: "It is nothing worse than that!" He gave his friend a few seconds to recover his composure, and then approached the question he had come to put. "Did you ever come across a protégé of his—one Hyde?" he asked.

"Hyde?" repeated Lanyon. "No. Never heard of him. Since my time."

That was the amount of information that the lawyer carried back with him to the great, dark bed on which he tossed *foryshadowing?*

to and fro, until the small hours of the morning began to grow large. It was a night of little ease to his toiling mind, toiling in mere darkness and besieged by questions.

Six o'clock struck on the bells of the church that was so conveniently near to Mr. Utterson's dwelling, and still he was digging at the problem. Hitherto it had touched him on the intellectual side alone; but now his imagination also was engaged, or rather enslaved; and as he lay and tossed in the gross darkness of the night and the curtained room, Mr. Enfield's tale went by before his mind in a scroll of lighted pictures. He would be aware of the great field of lamps of a nocturnal city; then of a figure of a man walking swiftly; then of a child running from the doctor's; and then these met, and that human juggernaut trod the child down and passed on regardless of her screams. Or else he would see a room in a rich house, where his friend lay asleep, dreaming and smiling at his dreams; and then the door of that room would be opened, the curtains of the bed plucked apart, the sleeper recalled, and lo! there would stand by his side a figure to whom power was given, and even at that dead hour, he must rise and do its bidding. The figure in these two phases haunted the lawyer all night; and if at any time he dozed over, it was but to see it glide more stealthily through sleeping houses, or move the more swiftly and still the more swiftly, even to dizziness, through wider labyrinths of lamplighted city, and at every street corner crush a child and leave her screaming. And still the figure had no face by which he might know it; even in his dreams, it had no face, or one that baffled him and melted before his eyes; and thus it was that there sprang up and grew apace in the lawyer's mind a singularly strong, almost an inordinate, curiosity to behold the features of the real Mr. Hyde. If he could but once set eyes on him, he thought the mystery would lighten and perhaps roll altogether away, as was the

121

habit of mysterious things when well examined. He might see a reason for his friend's strange preference or bondage (call it which you please) and even for the startling clause of the will. At least it would be a face worth seeing: the face of a man who was without bowels of mercy: a face which had but to show itself to raise up, in the mind of the unimpressionable Enfield, a spirit of enduring hatred.

From that time forward, Mr. Utterson began to haunt the door in the by-street of shops. In the morning before office hours, at noon when business was plenty, and time scarce, at night under the face of the fogged city moon, by all lights and at all hours of solitude or concourse, the lawyer was to be found on his chosen post. |0|

"If he be Mr. Hyde," he had thought, "I shall be Mr. Seek."

And at last his patience was rewarded. It was a fine dry night; frost in the air; the streets as clean as a ballroom floor; the lamps unshaken by any wind, drawing a regular pattern of light and shadow. By ten o'clock, when the shops were closed, the by-street was very solitary and, in spite of the low growl of London from all round, very silent. Small sounds carried far; domestic sounds out of the houses were clearly audible on either side of the roadway; and the rumour of the approach of any passenger preceded him by a long time. Mr. Utterson had been some minutes at his post, when he was aware of an odd, light footstep drawing near. In the course of his nightly patrols, he had long grown accustomed to the quaint effect with which the footfalls of a single person, while he is still a great way off, suddenly spring out distinct from the vast hum and clatter of the city. Yet his attention had never before been so sharply and decisively arrested; and it was with a strong, superstitious prevision of success that he withdrew into the entry of the court.

The steps drew swiftly nearer, and swelled out suddenly

louder as they turned the end of the street. The lawyer, looking forth from the entry, could soon see what manner of man
he had to deal with. He was small and very plainly dressed,
and the look of him, even at that distance, went somehow
strongly against the watcher's inclination. But he made
straight for the door, crossing the roadway to save time; and as
he came, he drew a key from his pocket like one approaching
home.

Mr. Utterson stepped out and touched him on the shoulder
as he passed. "Mr. Hyde, I think?"

Mr. Hyde shrank back with a hissing intake of the breath.
But his fear was only momentary, and though he did not look
the lawyer in the face, he answered coolly enough: "That is
my name. What do you want?"

"I see you are going in," returned the lawyer. "I am an old
friend of Dr. Jekyll's—Mr. Utterson of Gaunt Street—you
must have heard of my name; and meeting you so conveniently, I thought you might admit me." way to apprach it

"You will not find Dr. Jekyll; he is from home," replied Mr.
Hyde, blowing in the key. And then suddenly, but still without looking up, "How did you know me?" he asked.

"On your side," said Mr. Utterson, "will you do me a
favour?"

"With pleasure," replied the other. "What shall it be?"

"Will you let me see your face?" asked the lawyer.

Mr. Hyde appeared to hesitate, and then, as if upon some
sudden reflection, fronted about with an air of defiance; and
the pair stared at each other pretty fixedly for a few seconds. "Now I shall know you again," said Mr. Utterson. "It
may be useful."

"Yes," returned Mr. Hyde, "it is as well we have met; and
à propos, you should have my address." And he gave a number
of a street in Soho.

123

"Good God!" thought Mr. Utterson, "can he, too, have been thinking of the will?" But he kept his feelings to himself and only grunted in acknowledgment of the address.

"And now," said the other, "how did you know me?"

"By description," was the reply.

"Whose description?"

"We have common friends," said Mr. Utterson.

"Common friends?" echoed Mr. Hyde, a little hoarsely. "Who are they?"

"Jekyll, for instance," said the lawyer.

"He never told you," cried Mr. Hyde, with a flush of anger. "I did not think you would have lied."

"Come," said Mr. Utterson, "that is not fitting language."

The other snarled aloud into a savage laugh; and the next moment, with extraordinary quickness, he had unlocked the door and disappeared into the house.

The lawyer stood awhile when Mr. Hyde had left him, the picture of disquietude. Then he began slowly to mount the street, pausing every step or two and putting his hand to his brow like a man in mental perplexity. The problem he was thus debating as he walked, was one of a class that is rarely solved. Mr. Hyde was pale and dwarfish, he gave an impression of deformity without any nameable malforma-tion, he had a displeasing smile, he had borne himself to the lawyer with a sort of murderous mixture of timidity and boldness, and he spoke with a husky, whispering, and some-what broken voice; all these were points against him, but not all of these together could explain the hitherto unknown disgust, loathing, and fear with which Mr. Utterson regarded him. "There must be something else," said the perplexed gentleman. "There *is* something more, if I could find a name for it. God bless me, the man seems hardly human! Some-thing troglodytic, shall we say? or can it be the old story of

124

Dr. Fell?* or is it the mere radiance of a foul soul that thus transpires through, and transfigures, its clay continent? The last, I think; for, O my poor old Harry Jekyll, if ever I read Satan's signature upon a face, it is on that of your new friend."

Round the corner from the by-street, there was a square of ancient, handsome houses, now for the most part decayed from their high estate and let in flats and chambers to all sorts and conditions of men; map-engravers, architects, shady lawyers, and the agents of obscure enterprises. One house, however, second from the corner, was still occupied entire; and at the door of this, which wore a great air of wealth and comfort, though it was now plunged in darkness except for the fanlight, Mr. Utterson stopped and knocked. A well-dressed, elderly servant opened the door. *lift house before*

"Is Dr. Jekyll at home, Poole?" asked the lawyer.

"I will see, Mr. Utterson," said Poole, admitting the visitor, as he spoke, into a large, low-roofed, comfortable hall, paved with flags, warmed (after the fashion of a country house) by a bright, open fire, and furnished with costly cabinets of oak. "Will you wait here by the fire, sir? or shall I give you a light in the dining room?"

"Here, thank you," said the lawyer, and he drew near and leaned on the tall fender. This hall, in which he was now left alone, was a pet fancy of his friend the doctor's; and Utterson himself was wont to speak of it as the pleasantest room in London. But tonight there was a shudder in his blood; the face of Hyde sat heavy on his memory; he felt (what was rare with him) a nausea and distaste for life; and in the gloom of his spirits, he seemed to read a menace in the flickering of the

Mr. hyde leaving him suspicions

---

* **Dr. Fell** describes a person who is disliked for no particular reason. The expression comes from the old nursery rhyme.

firelight on the polished cabinets and the uneasy starting of the shadow on the roof. He was ashamed of his relief, when Poole presently returned to announce that Dr. Jekyll was gone out.

"I saw Mr. Hyde go in by the old dissecting-room door, Poole," he said. "Is that right, when Dr. Jekyll is from home?"

"Quite right, Mr. Utterson, sir," replied the servant. "Mr. Hyde has a key."

"Your master seems to repose a great deal of trust in that young man, Poole," resumed the other musingly.

"Yes, sir, he do indeed," said Poole. "We have all orders to obey him."

"I do not think I ever met Mr. Hyde?" asked Utterson.

"O, dear no, sir. He never dines here," replied the butler. "Indeed we see very little of him on this side of the house; he mostly comes and goes by the laboratory."

"Well, good night, Poole."

"Good night, Mr. Utterson."

And the lawyer set out homeward with a very heavy heart. "Poor Harry Jekyll," he thought, "my mind misgives me he is in deep waters! He was wild when he was young; a long while ago to be sure; but in the law of God, there is no statute of limitations. Ay, it must be that; the ghost of some old sin, the cancer of some concealed disgrace: punishment coming, *pede claudo*,* years after memory has forgotten and self-love condoned the fault." And the lawyer, scared by the thought, brooded awhile on his own past, groping in all the corners of memory, lest by chance some Jack-in-the-Box of an old iniquity should leap to light there. His past was fairly blameless; few men could read the rolls of their life with less apprehen-

---

* **pede claudo.** With a limp.

sion; yet he was humbled to the dust by the many ill things he had done, and raised up again into a sober and fearful gratitude by the many he had come so near to doing, yet avoided. And then by a return on his former subject, he conceived a spark of hope. "This Master Hyde, if he were studied," thought he, "must have secrets of his own; black secrets, by the look of him; secrets compared to which poor Jekyll's worst would be like sunshine. Things cannot continue as they are. It turns me cold to think of this creature stealing like a thief to Harry's bedside; poor Harry, what a wakening! And the danger of it; for if this Hyde suspects the existence of the will, he may grow impatient to inherit. Ay, I must put my shoulder to the wheel—if Jekyll will but let me," he added, "if Jekyll will only let me." For once more he saw before his mind's eye, as clear as transparency, the strange clauses of the will.

Mr. U b/c involvd Mr. U b/c he knows his bff's will is insane his safe CHAPTER 3 *stalks MR. Hyde too see why the estate was left to him*

DR. JEKYLL WAS QUITE AT EASE
relaxed

A fortnight later, by excellent good fortune, the doctor gave one of his pleasant dinners to some five or six old cronies, all intelligent, reputable men and all judges of good wine; and Mr. Utterson so contrived that he remained behind after the others had departed. This was no new arrangement, but a thing that had befallen many scores of time. Where Utterson was liked, he was liked well. Hosts loved to detain the dry lawyer, when the light-hearted and loose-tongued had already their foot on the threshold; they liked to sit awhile in his unobtrusive company, practising for solitude, sobering their minds in the man's rich silence after the expense and strain of gaiety. To this rule, Dr. Jekyll was no exception; and as he now sat on the opposite side of the fire—a large, well-made, smooth-faced man of fifty, with something of a slyish cast perhaps, but every mark of capacity and kindness—you could see by his looks that he cherished for Mr. Utterson a sincere and warm affection.

"I have been wanting to speak to you, Jekyll," began the latter. "You know that will of yours?"

A close observer might have gathered that the topic was distasteful; but the doctor carried it off gaily. "My poor Utterson," said he, "you are unfortunate in such a client. I never saw a man so distressed as you were by my will; unless it were that hide-bound pedant, Lanyon, at what he called my scientific heresies. O, I know he's a good fellow—you needn't frown—an excellent fellow, and I always mean to see more of him; but a hide-bound pedant for all that; an ignorant, blatant pedant. I was never more disappointed in any man than Lanyon."

"You know I never approved of it," pursued Utterson, ruthlessly disregarding the fresh topic.

"My will? Yes, certainly, I know that," said the doctor, a trifle sharply. "You have told me so."

"Well, I tell you so again," continued the lawyer. "I have been learning something of young Hyde."

The large handsome face of Dr. Jekyll grew pale to the very lips, and there came a blackness about his eyes. "I do not care to hear more," said he. "This is a matter I thought we had agreed to drop."

"What I heard was abominable," said Utterson.

"It can make no change. You do not understand my position," returned the doctor, with a certain incoherency of manner. "I am painfully situated, Utterson; my position is a very strange—a very strange one. It is one of those affairs that cannot be mended by talking."

"Jekyll," said Utterson, "you know me: I am a man to be

trusted. Make a clean breast of this in confidence; and I make no doubt I can get you out of it."

"My good Utterson," said the doctor, "this is very good of you, this is downright good of you, and I cannot find words to thank you in. I believe you fully; I would trust you before any man alive, ay, before myself, if I could make the choice; but indeed it isn't what you fancy; it is not as bad as that; and just to put your good heart at rest, I will tell you one thing: the moment I choose, I can be rid of Mr. Hyde. I give you my hand upon that; and I thank you again and again; and I will just add one little word, Utterson, that I'm sure you'll take in good part: this is a private matter, and I beg of you to let it sleep."

Utterson reflected a little, looking in the fire.

"I have no doubt you are perfectly right," he said at last, getting to his feet.

"Well, but since we have touched upon this business, and for the last time I hope," continued the doctor, "there is one point I should like you to understand. I have really a very great interest in poor Hyde. I know you have seen him; he told me so; and I fear he was rude. But I do sincerely take a great, a very great interest in that young man; and if I am taken away, Utterson, I wish you to promise me that you will bear with him and get his rights for him. I think you would, if you knew all; and it would be a weight off my mind if you would promise."

"I can't pretend that I shall ever like him," said the lawyer.

"I don't ask that," pleaded Jekyll, laying his hand upon the other's arm; "I only ask for justice; I only ask you to help him for my sake, when I am no longer here."

Utterson heaved an irrepressible sigh. "Well," said he, "I promise."

CHAPTER 4

THE CAREW MURDER CASE

Nearly a year later, in the month of October, 18—, London was startled by a crime of singular ferocity and rendered all the more notable by the high position of the victim. The details were few and startling. A maid servant living alone in a house not far from the river had gone upstairs to bed about eleven. Although a fog rolled over the city in the small hours, the early part of the night was cloudless, and the lane, which the maid's window overlooked, was brilliantly lit by the full moon. It seems she was romantically given, for she sat down upon her box, which stood immediately under the window, and fell into a dream of musing. Never (she used to say, with streaming tears, when she narrated that experience), never had she felt more at peace with all men or thought more kindly of the world. And as she so sat she became aware of an aged beautiful gentleman with white hair, drawing near along the lane; and advancing to meet him, another and very small gentleman, to whom at first she paid less attention. When they had come within speech (which was just under the maid's eyes) the older man bowed and accosted the other with a very pretty manner of politeness. It did not seem as if the subject of his address were of great importance; indeed, from his pointing, it sometimes appeared as if he were only inquiring his way; but the moon shone on his face as he spoke, and the girl was pleased to watch it, it seemed to breathe such an innocent and old-world kindness of disposition, yet with something high too, as of a well-founded self-content. Presently her eye wandered to the other, and she was surprised to recognise in him a certain Mr. Hyde, who had once visited her master and for whom she had conceived a dislike. He had in his hand a heavy cane, with which he was trifling; but he answered never a word, and

130

seemed to listen with an ill-contained impatience. And then all of a sudden he broke out in a great flame of anger, stamping with his foot, brandishing the cane, and carrying on (as the maid described it) like a madman. The old gentleman took a step back, with the air of one very much surprised and a trifle hurt; and at that Mr. Hyde broke out of all bounds and clubbed him to the earth. And next moment, with ape-like fury, he was trampling his victim under foot and hailing down a storm of blows, under which the bones were audibly shattered and the body jumped upon the roadway. At the horror of these sights and sounds, the maid fainted.

It was two o'clock when she came to herself and called for the police. The murderer was gone long ago; but there lay his victim in the middle of the lane, incredibly mangled. The stick with which the deed had been done, although it was of some rare and very tough and heavy wood, had broken in the middle under the stress of this insensate cruelty; and one splintered half had rolled in the neighbouring gutter—the other, without doubt, had been carried away by the murderer. A purse and gold watch were found upon the victim: but no cards or papers, except a sealed and stamped envelope, which he had been probably carrying to the post, and which bore the name and address of Mr. Utterson.

This was brought to the lawyer the next morning, before he was out of bed; and he had no sooner seen it, and been told the circumstances, than he shot out a solemn lip. "I shall say nothing till I have seen the body," said he; "this may be very serious. Have the kindness to wait while I dress." And with the same grave countenance he hurried through his breakfast and drove to the police station, whither the body had been carried. As soon as he came into the cell, he nodded.

"Yes," said he, "I recognise him. I am sorry to say that this is Sir Danvers Carew."

"Good God, sir," exclaimed the officer, "is it possible?" And the next moment his eye lighted up with professional ambition. "This will make a deal of noise," he said. "And perhaps you can help us to the man." And he briefly narrated what the maid had seen, and showed the broken stick.

Mr. Utterson had already quailed at the name of Hyde; but when the stick was laid before him, he could doubt no longer; broken and battered as it was, he recognised it for one that he had himself presented many years before to Henry Jekyll.

"Is this Mr. Hyde a person of small stature?" he inquired.

"Particularly small and particularly wicked-looking, is what the maid calls him," said the officer.

Mr. Utterson reflected; and then, raising his head, "If you will come with me in my cab," he said, "I think I can take you to his house."

It was by this time about nine in the morning, and the first fog of the season. A great chocolate-coloured pall lowered over heaven, but the wind was continually charging and routing these embattled vapours; so that as the cab crawled from street to street, Mr. Utterson beheld a marvelous number of degrees and hues of twilight; for here it would be dark like the back-end of evening; and there would be a glow of a rich, lurid brown, like the light of some strange conflagration; and here, for a moment, the fog would be quite broken up, and a haggard shaft of daylight would glance in between the swirling wreaths. The dismal quarter of Soho seen under these changing glimpses, with its muddy ways, and slatternly passengers, and its lamps, which had never been extinguished or had been kindled afresh to combat this mournful reinvasion of darkness, seemed, in the lawyer's eyes, like a district of some city in a nightmare. The thoughts of his mind, besides, were of the gloomiest dye; and when he glanced at the companion of his drive, he was conscious of some touch of that

132

terror of the law and the law's officers, which may at times assail the most honest.

As the cab drew up before the address indicated, the fog lifted a little and showed him a dingy street, a gin palace, a low French eating house, a shop for the retail of penny numbers and twopenny salads, many ragged children huddled in the doorways, and many women of many different nationalities passing out, key in hand, to have a morning glass; and the next moment the fog settled down again upon that part, as brown as umber, and cut him off from his blackguardly surroundings. This was the home of Henry Jekyll's favourite; of a man who was heir to a quarter of a million sterling.

An ivory-faced and silvery-haired old woman opened the door. She had an evil face, smoothed by hypocrisy: but her manners were excellent. Yes, she said, this was Mr. Hyde's, but he was not at home; he had been in that night very late, but he had gone away again in less than an hour; there was nothing strange in that; his habits were very irregular, and he was often absent; for instance, it was nearly two months since she had seen him till yesterday.

"Very well, then, we wish to see his rooms," said the lawyer, and when the woman began to declare it was impossible, "I had better tell you who this person is," he added. "This is Inspector Newcomen of Scotland Yard."

A flash of odious joy appeared upon the woman's face. "Ah!" said she, "he is in trouble! What has he done?"

Mr. Utterson and the inspector exchanged glances. "He don't seem a very popular character," observed the latter. "And now, my good woman, just let me and this gentleman have a look about us."

In the whole extent of the house, which but for the old woman remained otherwise empty, Mr. Hyde had only used a couple of rooms; but these were furnished with luxury and

133

good taste. A closet was filled with wine; the plate was of silver, the napery elegant; a good picture hung upon the walls, a gift (as Utterson supposed) from Henry Jekyll, who was much of a connoisseur; and the carpets were of many plies and agreeable in colour. At this moment, however, the rooms bore every mark of having been recently and hurriedly ransacked; clothes lay about the floor, with their pockets inside out; lock-fast drawers stood open; and on the hearth there lay a pile of grey ashes, as though many papers had been burned. From these embers the inspector disinterred the butt end of a green cheque book, which had resisted the action of the fire; the other half of the stick was found behind the door; and as this clinched his suspicions, the officer declared himself delighted. A visit to the bank, where several thousand pounds were found to be lying to the murderer's credit, completed his gratification.

"You may depend upon it, sir," he told Mr. Utterson: "I have him in my hand. He must have lost his head, or he never would have left the stock or, above all, burned the cheque book. Why, money's life to the man. We have nothing to do but wait for him at the bank, and get out the handbills."

This last, however, was not so easy of accomplishment; for Mr. Hyde had numbered few familiars—even the master of the servant maid had only seen him twice; his family could nowhere be traced; he had never been photographed; and the few who could describe him differed widely, as common observers will. Only on one point were they agreed; and that was the haunting sense of unexpressed deformity with which the fugitive impressed his beholders.

CHAPTER 5

INCIDENT OF THE LETTER

It was late in the afternoon when Mr. Utterson found his way to Dr. Jekyll's door, where he was at once admitted by Poole, and carried down by the kitchen offices and across a yard which had once been a garden, to the building which was indifferently known as the laboratory or dissecting rooms. The doctor had bought the house from the heirs of a celebrated surgeon; and his own tastes being rather chemical than anatomical, had changed the destination of the block at the bottom of the garden. It was the first time that the lawyer had been received in that part of his friend's quarters; and he eyed the dingy, windowless structure with curiosity, and gazed round with a distasteful sense of strangeness as he crossed the theatre, once crowded with eager students and now lying gaunt and silent, the tables laden with chemical apparatus, the floor strewn with crates and littered with packing straw, and the light falling dimly through the foggy cupola. At the further end, a flight of stairs mounted to a door covered with red baize; and through this, Mr. Utterson was at last received into the doctor's cabinet. It was a large room fitted round with glass presses, furnished, among other things, with a cheval-glass and a business table, and looking out upon the court by three dusty windows barred with iron. The fire burned in the grate; a lamp was set lighted on the chimney shelf, for even in the houses the fog began to lie thickly; and there, close up to the warmth, sat Dr. Jekyll, looking deadly sick. He did not rise to meet his visitor, but held out a cold hand and bade him welcome in a changed voice.

"And now," said Mr. Utterson, as soon as Poole had left them, "you have heard the news?"

The doctor shuddered. "They were crying it in the square," he said. "I heard them in my dining room."

"One word," said the lawyer. "Carew was my client, but so are you, and I want to know what I am doing. You have not been mad enough to hide this fellow?"

"Utterson, I swear to God," cried the doctor, "I swear to God I will never set eyes on him again. I bind my honour to you that I am done with him in this world. It is all at an end. And indeed he does not want my help; you do not know him as I do; he is safe, he is quite safe; mark my words, he will never more be heard of."

The lawyer listened gloomily; he did not like his friend's feverish manner. "You seem pretty sure of him," said he; "and for your sake, I hope you may be right. If it came to a trial, your name might appear." *angvj*

"I am quite sure of him," replied Jekyll; "I have grounds for certainty that I cannot share with anyone. But there is one thing on which you may advise me. I have—I have received a letter; and I am at a loss whether I should show it to the police. I should like to leave it in your hands, Utterson; you would judge wisely, I am sure; I have so great a trust in you."

"You fear, I suppose, that it might lead to his detection?" asked the lawyer.

"No," said the other. "I cannot say that I care what becomes of Hyde; I am quite done with him. I was thinking of my own character, which this hateful business has rather exposed."

Utterson ruminated awhile; he was surprised at his friend's selfishness, and yet relieved by it. "Well," said he, at last, "let me see the letter."

The letter was written in an odd, upright hand and signed "Edward Hyde": and it signified, briefly enough, that the writer's benefactor, Dr. Jekyll, whom he had long so unworthi-ly repaid for a thousand generosities, need labour under no alarm for his safety, as he had means of escape on which he placed a sure dependence. The lawyer liked this letter well enough; it put a better colour on the intimacy than he had looked for; and he blamed himself for some of his past suspicions.

"Have you the envelope?" he asked.

"I burned it," replied Jekyll, "before I thought what I was about. But it bore no postmark. The note was handed in."

"Shall I keep this and sleep upon it?" asked Utterson.

"I wish you to judge for me entirely," was the reply. "I have lost confidence in myself."

"Well, I shall consider," returned the lawyer. "And now one word more: it was Hyde who dictated the terms in your will about that disappearance?"

The doctor seemed seized with a qualm of faintness; he shut his mouth tight and nodded.

"I knew it," said Utterson. "He meant to murder you. You had a fine escape."

"I have had what is far more to the purpose," returned the doctor solemnly: "I have had a lesson—O God, Utterson, what a lesson I have had!" And he covered his face for a moment with his hands.

On his way out, the lawyer stopped and had a word or two with Poole. "By the bye," said he, "there was a letter handed in today: what was the messenger like?" But Poole was positive nothing had come except by post; "and only circulars by that," he added.

This news sent off the visitor with his fears renewed. Plainly the letter had come by the laboratory door; possibly, indeed, it had been written in the cabinet; and if that were so, it must be differently judged, and handled with the more caution. The newsboys, as he went, were crying themselves hoarse along the footways: "Special edition. Shocking murder of an M.P."* That was the funeral oration of one friend and client; and he could not help a certain apprehension lest the good name of another should be sucked down in the eddy of the scandal. It was, at least, a ticklish decision that he had to make; and self-reliant as he was by habit, he began to cherish a longing for advice. It was not to be had directly; but perhaps, he thought, it might be fished for.

Presently after, he sat on one side of his own hearth, with Mr. Guest, his head clerk, upon the other, and midway between, at a nicely calculated distance from the fire, a bottle of a particular old wine that had long dwelt unsunned in the foundations of his house. The fog still slept on the wing above the drowned city, where the lamps glimmered like carbuncles; and through the muffle and smother of these fallen clouds, the procession of the town's life was still rolling in through the great arteries with a sound as of a mighty wind. But the room was gay with firelight. In the bottle the acids were long ago resolved; the imperial dye had softened with time, as the colour grows richer in stained windows; and the glow of hot autumn afternoons on hillside vineyards was ready to be set free and to disperse the fogs of London. Insensibly the lawyer melted. There was no man from whom he kept fewer secrets than Mr. Guest; and he was not always sure that he kept as many as he meant. Guest had often been on business to the doctor's; he knew Poole; he could scarce have failed to hear of Mr. Hyde's familiarity about the house; he might draw conclusions: was it not as well, then, that he should see a letter which put that mystery to rights? and above all since Guest, being a great student and critic of handwriting, would

---

* M.P. Member of Parliament. Parliament is the legislative body of Great Britain, equivalent to Congress in the United States.

consider the step natural and obliging? The clerk, besides, was a man of counsel; he could scarce read so strange a document without dropping a remark; and by that remark Mr. Utterson might shape his future course.

"This is a sad business about Sir Danvers," he said.

"Yes, sir, indeed. It has elicited a great deal of public feeling," returned Guest. "The man, of course, was mad."

"I should like to hear your views on that," replied Utterson. "I have a document here in his handwriting; it is between ourselves, for I scarce know what to do about it; it is an ugly business at the best. But there it is; quite in your way: a murderer's autograph."

Guest's eyes brightened, and he sat down at once and studied it with passion. "No sir," he said: "not mad; but it is an odd hand."

"And by all accounts a very odd writer," added the lawyer.

Just then the servant entered with a note.

"Is that from Dr. Jekyll, sir?" inquired the clerk. "I thought I knew the writing. Anything private, Mr. Utterson?"

"Only an invitation to dinner. Why? Do you want to see it?"

"One moment. I thank you, sir"; and the clerk laid the two sheets of paper alongside and sedulously compared their contents. "Thank you, sir," he said at last, returning both; "it's a very interesting autograph."

There was a pause, during which Mr. Utterson struggled with himself. "Why did you compare them, Guest?" he inquired suddenly.

"Well, sir," returned the clerk, "there's a rather singular resemblance; the two hands are in many points identical: only differently sloped."

"Rather quaint," said Utterson.

"It is, as you say, rather quaint," returned Guest.

"I wouldn't speak of this note, you know," said the master.

"No, sir," said the clerk. "I understand."

But no sooner was Mr. Utterson alone that night, than he locked the note into his safe, where it reposed from that time forward. "What!" he thought. "Henry Jekyll forge for a murderer!" And his blood ran cold in his veins.

CHAPTER 6

REMARKABLE INCIDENT OF DR. LANYON

Time ran on; thousands of pounds were offered in reward, for the death of Sir Danvers was resented as a public injury; but Mr. Hyde had disappeared out of the ken of the police as though he had never existed. Much of his past was unearthed, indeed, and all disreputable: tales came out of the man's cruelty, at once so callous and violent; of his vile life, of his strange associates, of the hatred that seemed to have surrounded his career; but of his present whereabouts, not a whisper. From the time he had left the house in Soho on the morning of the murder, he was simply blotted out; and gradually, as time drew on, Mr. Utterson began to recover from the hotness of his alarm, and to grow more at quiet with himself. The death of Sir Danvers was, to his way of thinking, more than paid for by the disappearance of Mr. Hyde. Now that that evil influence had been withdrawn, a new life began for Dr. Jekyll. He came out of his seclusion, renewed relations with his friends, became once more their familiar guest and entertainer; and whilst he had always been known for charities, he was now no less distinguished for religion. He was busy, he was much in the open air, he did good; his face seemed to open and brighten, as if with an inward consciousness of service; and for more than two months, the doctor was at peace.

140

On the 8th of January Utterson had dined at the doctor's with a small party; Lanyon had been there; and the face of the host had looked from one to the other as in the old days when the trio were inseparable friends. On the 12th, and again on the 14th, the door was shut against the lawyer. "The doctor was confined to the house," Poole said, "and saw no one." On the 15th, he tried again, and was again refused; and having now been used for the last two months to see his friend almost daily, he found this return of solitude to weigh upon his spirits. The fifth night he had in Guest to dine with him; and the sixth he betook himself to Dr. Lanyon's.

There at least he was not denied admittance; but when he came in, he was shocked at the change which had taken place in the doctor's appearance. He had his death-warrant written legibly upon his face. The rosy man had grown pale; his flesh had fallen away; he was visibly balder and older; and yet it was not so much these tokens of a swift physical decay that arrested the lawyer's notice, as a look in the eye and quality of manner that seemed to testify to some deep-seated terror of the mind. It was unlikely that the doctor should fear death; and yet that was what Utterson was tempted to suspect. "Yes," he thought; "he is a doctor, he must know his own state and that his days are counted; and the knowledge is more than he can bear." And yet when Utterson remarked on his ill-looks, it was with an air of great firmness that Lanyon declared himself a doomed man.

"I have had a shock," he said, "and I shall never recover. It is a question of weeks. Well, life has been pleasant; I liked it; yes, sir, I used to like it. I sometimes think if we knew all, we should be more glad to get away." dead

"Jekyll is ill, too," observed Utterson. "Have you seen him?"

But Lanyon's face changed, and he held up a trembling hand. "I wish to see or hear no more of Dr. Jekyll," he said in a loud, unsteady voice. "I am quite done with that person; and I beg that you will spare me any allusion to one whom I regard as dead."

"Tut-tut," said Mr. Utterson; and then after a considerable pause, "Can't I do anything?" he inquired. "We are three very old friends, Lanyon; we shall not live to make others."

"Nothing can be done," returned Lanyon; "ask himself."

"He will not see me," said the lawyer.

"I am not surprised at that," was the reply. "Some day, Utterson, after I am dead, you may perhaps come to learn the right and wrong of this. I cannot tell you. And in the meantime, if you can sit and talk with me of other things, for God's sake, stay and do so; but if you cannot keep clear of this accursed topic, then in God's name, go, for I cannot bear it."

As soon as he got home, Utterson sat down and wrote to Jekyll, complaining of his exclusion from the house, and asking the cause of this unhappy break with Lanyon; and the next day brought him a long answer, often very pathetically worded, and sometimes darkly mysterious in drift. The quarrel with Lanyon was incurable. "I do not blame our old friend," Jekyll wrote, "but I share his view that we must never meet. I mean from henceforth to lead a life of extreme seclusion; you must not be surprised, nor must you doubt my friendship, if my door is often shut even to you. You must suffer me to go my own dark way. I have brought on myself a punishment and a danger that I cannot name. If I am the chief of sinners, I am the chief of sufferers also. I could not think that this earth contained a place for sufferings and terrors so unmanning; and you can do but one thing, Utterson, to lighten this destiny, and that is to respect my silence." Utterson was amazed; the dark influence of Hyde had been withdrawn, the doctor had returned to his old tasks and amities; a week ago, the prospect had smiled with every promise of a cheerful and an honoured age; and now in a moment, friendship, and peace of mind, and the whole tenor of his life were wrecked. So great and unprepared a change pointed to madness; but in view of Lanyon's manner and words, there must lie for it some deeper ground.

A week afterwards Dr. Lanyon took to his bed, and in something less than a fortnight he was dead. The night after the funeral, at which he had been sadly affected, Utterson locked the door of his business room, and sitting there by the light of a melancholy candle, drew out and set before him an envelope addressed by the hand and sealed with the seal of his dead friend. "PRIVATE: for the hands of G. J. Utterson ALONE, and in case of his predecease *to be destroyed unread*," so it was emphatically superscribed; and the lawyer dreaded to behold the contents. "I have buried one friend today," he thought: "what if this should cost me another?" And then he condemned the fear as a disloyalty, and broke the seal. Within there was another enclosure, likewise sealed, and marked upon the cover as "not to be opened till the death or disappearance of Dr. Henry Jekyll." Utterson could not trust his eyes. Yes, it was disappearance; here again, as in the mad will which he had long ago restored to its author, here again were the idea of a disappearance and the name of Henry Jekyll bracketed. But in the will, that idea had sprung from the sinister suggestion of the man Hyde; it was set there with a purpose all too plain and horrible. Written by the hand of Lanyon, what should it mean? A great curiosity came on the trustee, to disregard the prohibition and dive at once to the bottom of these mysteries; but professional honour and faith to his dead friend were stringent obligations; and the packet slept in the inmost corner of his private safe.

It is one thing to mortify curiosity, another to conquer it; and it may be doubted if, from that day forth, Utterson

desired the society of his surviving friend with the same eagerness. He thought of him kindly; but his thoughts were disqui-
eted and fearful. He went to call indeed; but he was perhaps
relieved to be denied admittance; perhaps, in his heart, he
preferred to speak with Poole upon the doorstep and surrounded by the air and sounds of the open city, rather than to
be admitted into that house of voluntary bondage, and to sit
and speak with its inscrutable recluse. Poole had, indeed, no
very pleasant news to communicate. The doctor, it appeared,
now more than ever confined himself to the cabinet over the
laboratory, where he would sometimes even sleep; he was out
of spirits, he had grown very silent, he did not read; it seemed
as if he had something on his mind. Utterson became so used
to the unvarying character of these reports, that he fell off
little by little in the frequency of his visits.

CHAPTER 7

INCIDENT AT THE WINDOW

It chanced on Sunday, when Mr. Utterson was on his usual
walk with Mr. Enfield, that their way lay once again through
the by-street; and that when they came in front of the door,
both stopped to gaze on it.

"Well," said Enfield, "that story's at an end at least. We
shall never see more of Mr. Hyde."

"I hope not," said Utterson. "Did I ever tell you that I once
saw him, and shared your feeling of repulsion?"

"It was impossible to do the one without the other,"
returned Enfield. "And by the way, what an ass you must have
thought me, not to know that was a back way to Dr. Jekyll's!
It was partly your own fault that I found it out, even when
I did."

"So you found it out, did you?" said Utterson. "But if that be so, we may step into the court and take a look at the windows. To tell you the truth, I am uneasy about poor Jekyll; and even outside, I feel as if the presence of a friend might do him good."

The court was very cool and a little damp, and full of premature twilight, although the sky, high up overhead, was still bright with sunset. The middle one of the three windows was halfway open; and sitting close beside it, taking the air with an infinite sadness of mien, like some disconsolate prisoner, Utterson saw Dr. Jekyll.

"What! Jekyll!" he cried. "I trust you are better."

"I am very low, Utterson," replied the doctor drearily, "very low. It will not last long, thank God."

"You stay too much indoors," said the lawyer. "You should be out, whipping up the circulation like Mr. Enfield and me. (This is my cousin—Mr. Enfield—Dr. Jekyll.) Come now; get your hat and take a quick turn with us."

"You are very good," sighed the other. "I should like to very much; but no, no, no, it is quite impossible; I dare not. But indeed, Utterson, I am very glad to see you; this is really a great pleasure; I would ask you and Mr. Enfield up, but the place is really not fit."

"Why then," said the lawyer, good-naturedly, "the best thing we can do is to stay down here and speak with you from where we are."

"That is just what I was about to venture to propose," returned the doctor with a smile. But the words were hardly uttered, before the smile was struck out of his face and succeeded by an expression of such abject terror and despair, as froze the very blood of the two gentlemen below. They saw it but for a glimpse, for the window was instantly thrust down; but that glimpse had been sufficient, and they turned and left

145

the court without a word. In silence, too, they traversed the by-street; and it was not until they had come into a neighbouring thoroughfare, where even upon a Sunday there were still some stirrings of life, that Mr. Utterson at last turned and looked at his companion. They were both pale; and there was an answering horror in their eyes.

"God forgive us, God forgive us," said Mr. Utterson.

But Mr. Enfield only nodded his head very seriously, and walked on once more in silence.

CHAPTER 8

THE LAST NIGHT

Mr. Utterson was sitting by his fireside one evening after dinner, when he was surprised to receive a visit from Poole.

"Bless me, Poole, what brings you here?" he cried; and then taking a second look at him, "What ails you?" he added; "is the doctor ill?"

"Mr. Utterson," said the man, "there is something wrong."

"Take a seat, and here is a glass of wine for you," said the lawyer. "Now, take your time, and tell me plainly what you want."

"You know the doctor's ways, sir," replied Poole, "and how he shuts himself up. Well, he's shut up again in the cabinet; and I don't like it, sir—I wish I may die if I like it. Mr. Utterson, sir, I'm afraid."

"Now, my good man," said the lawyer, "be explicit. What are you afraid of?"

"I've been afraid for about a week," returned Poole, doggedly disregarding the question, "and I can bear it no more."

The man's appearance amply bore out his words; his manner was altered for the worse; and except for the moment when he had first announced his terror, he had not once looked the lawyer in the face. Even now, he sat with the glass of wine untasted on his knee, and his eyes directed to a corner of the floor. "I can bear it no more," he repeated.

"Come," said the lawyer, "I see you have some good reason, Poole; I see there is something seriously amiss. Try to tell me what it is."

"I think there's been foul play," said Poole, hoarsely.

"Foul play!" cried the lawyer, a good deal frightened and rather inclined to be irritated in consequence. "What foul play! What does the man mean?"

"I daren't say, sir," was the answer; "but will you come along with me and see for yourself?"

Mr. Utterson's only answer was to rise and get his hat and greatcoat; but he observed with wonder the greatness of the relief that appeared upon the butler's face, and perhaps with no less, that the wine was still untasted when he set it down to follow.

It was a wild, cold, seasonable night of March, with a pale moon, lying on her back as though the wind had tilted her, and a flying wrack* of the most diaphanous and lawny texture. The wind made talking difficult, and flecked the blood into the face. It seemed to have swept the streets unusually bare of passengers, besides; for Mr. Utterson thought he had never seen that part of London so deserted. He could have wished it otherwise; never in his life had he been conscious of so sharp a wish to see and touch his fellow-creatures; for struggle as he might, there was borne in upon his mind a crushing anticipation of calamity. The square, when they got there, was full of wind and dust, and the thin trees in the

---

* **wrack.** A mass of thin clouds.

garden were lashing themselves along the railing. Poole, who had kept all the way a pace or two ahead, now pulled up in the middle of the pavement, and in spite of the biting weather, took off his hat and mopped his brow with a red pocket-handkerchief. But for all the hurry of his coming, these were not the dews of exertion that he wiped away, but the moisture of some strangling anguish; for his face was white and his voice, when he spoke, harsh and broken.

"Well, sir," he said, "here we are, and God grant there be nothing wrong."

"Amen, Poole," said the lawyer.

Thereupon the servant knocked in a very guarded manner; the door was opened on the chain; and a voice asked from within, "Is that you, Poole?"

"It's all right," said Poole. "Open the door."

The hall, when they entered it, was brightly lighted up; the fire was built high; and about the hearth the whole of the servants, men and women, stood huddled together like a flock of sheep. At the sight of Mr. Utterson, the housemaid broke into hysterical whimpering; and the cook, crying out "Bless God! it's Mr. Utterson," ran forward as if to take him in her arms.

"What, what? Are you all here?" said the lawyer peevishly. "Very irregular, very unseemly; your master would be far from pleased."

"They're all afraid," said Poole.

Blank silence followed, no one protesting; only the maid lifted up her voice and now wept loudly.

"Hold your tongue!" Poole said to her, with a ferocity of accent that testified to his own jangled nerves; and indeed when the girl had so suddenly raised the note of her lamentation, they had all started and turned towards the inner door with faces of dreadful expectation. "And now," continued the butler, addressing the knife-boy, "reach me a candle, and we'll get this through hands at once." And then he begged Mr. Utterson to follow him, and led the way to the back garden.

"Now, sir," said he, "you come as gently as you can. I want you to hear, and I don't want you to be heard. And see here, sir, if by any chance he was to ask you in, don't go."

Mr. Utterson's nerves, at this unlooked-for termination, gave a jerk that nearly threw him from his balance; but he recollected his courage and followed the butler into the laboratory building and through the surgical theatre, with its lumber of crates and bottles, to the foot of the stair. Here Poole motioned him to stand on one side and listen; while he himself, setting down the candle and making a great and obvious call on his resolution, mounted the steps and knocked with a somewhat uncertain hand on the red baize of the cabinet door.

"Mr. Utterson, sir, asking to see you," he called; and even as he did so, once more violently signed to the lawyer to give ear.

A voice answered from within: "Tell him I cannot see anyone," it said complainingly.

"Thank you, sir," said Poole, with a note of something like triumph in his voice; and taking up his candle, he led Mr. Utterson back across the yard and into the great kitchen, where the fire was out and the beetles were leaping on the floor.

"Sir," he said, looking Mr. Utterson in the eyes, "was that my master's voice?"

"It seems much changed," replied the lawyer, very pale, but giving look for look.

"Changed? Well, yes, I think so," said the butler. "Have I been twenty years in this man's house, to be deceived about his voice? No, sir; master's made away with; he was made away with eight days ago, when we heard him cry out upon the name of God; and *who's* in there instead of him, and *why* it stays there, is a thing that cries to Heaven, Mr. Utterson!"

"This is a very strange tale, Poole; this is rather a wild tale, my man," said Mr. Utterson, biting his finger. "Suppose it were as you suppose, supposing Dr. Jekyll to have been—well, murdered, what could induce the murderer to stay? That won't hold water; it doesn't commend itself to reason."

"Well, Mr. Utterson, you are a hard man to satisfy, but I'll do it yet," said Poole. "All this last week (you must know) him, or it, whatever it is that lives in that cabinet, has been crying night and day for some sort of medicine and cannot get it to his mind. It was sometimes his way—the master's, that is—to write his orders on a sheet of paper and throw it on the stair. We've had nothing else this week back; nothing but papers, and a closed door, and the very meals left there to be smuggled in when nobody was looking. Well, sir, every day, ay, and twice and thrice in the same day, there have been orders and complaints, and I have been sent flying to all the wholesale chemists in town. Every time I brought the stuff back, there would be another paper telling me to return it, because it was not pure, and another order to a different firm. This drug is wanted bitter bad, sir, whatever for."

"Have you any of these papers?" asked Mr. Utterson.

Poole felt in his pocket and handed out a crumpled note, which the lawyer, bending nearer to the candle, carefully examined. Its contents ran thus: "Dr. Jekyll presents his compliments to Messrs. Maw. He assures them that their last sample is impure and quite useless for his present purpose. In the year 18—, Dr. J. purchased a somewhat large quantity from Messrs. M. He now begs them to search with most sedulous care, and should any of the same quality be left, to forward it to him at once. Expense is no consideration. The importance of this to Dr. J. can hardly be exaggerated."

So far the letter had run composedly enough, but here with a sudden splutter of the pen, the writer's emotion had broken loose. "For God's sake," he added, "find me some of the old."

"This is a strange note," said Mr. Utterson; and then sharply, "How do you come to have it open?"

"The man at Maw's was main angry, sir, and he threw it back at me like so much dirt," returned Poole.

"This is unquestionably the doctor's hand, do you know?" resumed the lawyer.

"I thought it looked like it," said the servant rather sulkily; and then, with another voice, "But what matters hand of write?" he said. "I've seen him!"

"Seen him?" repeated Mr. Utterson. "Well?"

"That's it!" said Poole. "It was this way. I came suddenly into the theatre from the garden. It seems he had slipped out to look for this drug or whatever it is; for the cabinet door was open, and there he was at the far end of the room digging among the crates. He looked up when I came in, gave a kind of cry, and whipped upstairs into the cabinet. It was but for one minute that I saw him, but the hair stood upon my head like quills. Sir, if that was my master, why had he a mask upon his face? If it was my master, why did he cry out like a rat, and run from me? I have served him long enough. And then . . ." The man paused and passed his hand over his face.

"These are all very strange circumstances," said Mr. Utterson, "but I think I begin to see daylight. Your master, Poole, is plainly seized with one of those maladies that both torture and deform the sufferer; hence, for aught I know, the alteration of his voice; hence the mask and the avoidance of his friends; hence his eagerness to find this drug, by means of which the poor soul retains some hope of ultimate recovery— God grant that he be not deceived! There is my explanation; it is sad enough, Poole, ay, and appalling to consider; but it is

151

plain and natural, hangs well together, and delivers us from all exorbitant alarms."

"Sir," said the butler, turning to a sort of mottled pallor, "that thing was not my master, and there's the truth. My master"—here he looked round him and began to whisper—"is a tall, fine build of a man, and this was more of a dwarf." Utterson attempted to protest. "O, sir," cried Poole, "do you think I do not know my master after twenty years? Do you think I do not know where his head comes to in the cabinet door, where I saw him every morning of my life? No, sir, that thing in the mask was never Dr. Jekyll—God knows what it was, but it was never Dr. Jekyll; and it is the belief of my heart that there was murder done."

"Poole," replied the lawyer, "if you say that, it will become my duty to make certain. Much as I desire to spare your master's feelings, much as I am puzzled by this note which seems to prove him to be still alive, I shall consider it my duty to break in that door."

"Ah, Mr. Utterson, that's talking!" cried the butler.

"And now comes the second question," resumed Utterson: "Who is going to do it?"

"Why, you and me, sir," was the undaunted reply.

"That's very well said," returned the lawyer; "and whatever comes of it, I shall make it my business to see you are no loser."

"There is an axe in the theatre," continued Poole; "and you might take the kitchen poker for yourself."

The lawyer took that rude but weighty instrument into his hand, and balanced it. "Do you know, Poole," he said, looking up, "that you and I are about to place ourselves in a position of some peril?"

"You may say so, sir, indeed," returned the butler.

"It is well, then, that we should be frank," said the other. "We both think more than we have said; let us make a clean breast. This masked figure that you saw, did you recognise it?"

"Well, sir, it went so quick, and the creature was so doubled up, that I could hardly swear to that," was the answer. "But if you mean, was it Mr. Hyde?—why, yes, I think it was! You see, it was much of the same bigness; and it had the same quick, light way with it; and then who else could have got in by the laboratory door? You have not forgot, sir, that at the time of the murder he had still the key with him? But that's not all. I don't know, Mr. Utterson, if you ever met this Mr. Hyde?"

"Yes," said the lawyer, "I once spoke with him."

"Then you must know as well as the rest of us that there was something queer about that gentleman—something that gave a man a turn—I don't know rightly how to say it, sir, beyond this: that you felt in your marrow kind of cold and thin."

"I own I felt something of what you describe," said Mr. Utterson.

"Quite so, sir," returned Poole. "Well, when that masked thing like a monkey jumped from among the chemicals and whipped into the cabinet, it went down my spine like ice. O, I know it's not evidence, Mr. Utterson; I'm book-learned enough for that; but a man has his feelings, and I give you my bible-word it was Mr. Hyde!"

"Ay, ay," said the lawyer. "My fears incline to the same point. Evil, I fear, founded—evil was sure to come—of that connection. Ay truly, I believe you; I believe poor Harry is killed; and I believe his murderer (for what purpose, God alone can tell) is still lurking in his victim's room. Well, let our name be vengeance. Call Bradshaw."

The footman came at the summons, very white and nervous.

"Pull yourself together, Bradshaw," said the lawyer. "This suspense, I know, is telling upon all of you; but it is now our intention to make an end of it. Poole, here, and I are going to force our way into the cabinet. If all is well, my shoulders are broad enough to bear the blame. Meanwhile, lest anything should really be amiss, or any malefactor seek to escape by the back, you and the boy must go round the corner with a pair of good sticks and take your post at the laboratory door. We give you ten minutes, to get to your stations."

As Bradshaw left, the lawyer looked at his watch. "And now, Poole, let us get to ours," he said; and taking the poker under his arm, led the way into the yard. The scud had banked over the moon, and it was now quite dark. The wind, which only broke in puffs and draughts into that deep well of building, tossed the light of the candle to and fro about their steps, until they came into the shelter of the theatre, where they sat down silently to wait. London hummed solemnly all around; but nearer at hand, the stillness was only broken by the sounds of a footfall moving to and fro along the cabinet floor.

"So it will walk all day, sir," whispered Poole; "ay, and the better part of the night. Only when a new sample comes from the chemist, there's a bit of a break. Ah, it's an ill conscience that's such an enemy to rest! Ah, sir, there's blood foully shed in every step of it! But hark again, a little closer—put your heart in your ears, Mr. Utterson, and tell me, is that the doctor's foot?"

The steps fell lightly and oddly, with a certain swing, for all they went so slowly; it was different indeed from the heavy creaking tread of Henry Jekyll. Utterson sighed. "Is there never anything else?" he asked.

Poole nodded. "Once," he said. "Once I heard it weeping!"

"Weeping? how that?" said the lawyer, conscious of a sudden chill of horror.

"Weeping like a woman or a lost soul," said the butler. "I came away with that upon my heart, that I could have wept too."

But now the ten minutes drew to an end. Poole disinterred the axe from under a stack of packing straw; the candle was set upon the nearest table to light them to the attack; and they drew near with bated breath to where the patient foot was still going up and down, up and down, in the quiet of the night. "Jekyll," cried Utterson, with a loud voice, "I demand to see you." He paused a moment, but there came no reply. "I give you fair warning, our suspicions are aroused, and I must and shall see you," he resumed; "if not by fair means, then by foul—if not of your consent, then by brute force!"

"Utterson," said the voice, "for God's sake, have mercy!"

"Ah, that's not Jekyll's voice—it's Hyde's!" cried Utterson. "Down with the door, Poole!"

Poole swung the axe over his shoulder; the blow shook the building, and the red baize door leaped against the lock and hinges. A dismal screech, as of mere animal terror, rang from the cabinet. Up went the axe again, and again the panels crashed and the frame bounded; four times the blow fell; but the wood was tough and the fittings were of excellent workmanship; and it was not until the fifth that the lock burst and the wreck of the door fell inwards on the carpet.

The besiegers, appalled by their own riot and the stillness that had succeeded, stood back a little and peered in. There lay the cabinet before their eyes in the quiet lamplight, a good fire glowing and chattering on the hearth, the kettle singing its thin strain, a drawer or two open, papers neatly set forth on the business table, and nearer the fire, the things laid out for tea; the quietest room, you would have said, and, but for the glazed presses full of chemicals, the most commonplace that night in London.

Right in the midst there lay the body of a man sorely contorted and still twiching. They drew near on tiptoe, turned it on its back and beheld the face of Edward Hyde. He was dressed in clothes far too large for him, clothes of the doctor's bigness; the cords of his face still moved with a semblance of life, but life was quite gone; and by the crushed phial in the hand and the strong smell of kernels that hung upon the air, Utterson knew that he was looking on the body of a self-destroyer.

"We have come too late," he said sternly, "whether to save or punish. Hyde is gone to his account; and it only remains for us to find the body of your master."

The far greater proportion of the building was occupied by the theatre, which filled almost the whole ground storey and was lighted from above, and by the cabinet, which formed an upper storey at one end and looked upon the court. A corridor joined the theatre to the door on the by-street; and with this the cabinet communicated separately by a second flight of stairs. There were besides a few dark closets and a spacious cellar. All these they now thoroughly examined. Each closet needed but a glance, for all were empty, and all, by the dust that fell from their doors, had stood long unopened. The cellar, indeed, was filled with crazy lumber, mostly dating from the times of the surgeon who was Jekyll's predecessor; but even as they opened the door they were advertised of the uselessness of further search, by the fall of a perfect mat of cobweb which had for years sealed up the entrance. Nowhere was there any trace of Henry Jekyll, dead or alive.

Poole stamped on the flags of the corridor. "He must be buried here," he said, hearkening to the sound.

"Or he may have fled," said Utterson, and he turned to examine the door in the by-street. It was locked; and lying nearby on the flags, they found the key, already stained with rust.

"This does not look like use," observed the lawyer.

"Use!" echoed Poole. "Do you not see, sir, it is broken? much as if a man had stamped on it."

"Ay," continued Utterson, "and the fractures, too, are rusty." The two men looked at each other with a scare. "This is beyond me, Poole," said the lawyer. "Let us go back to the cabinet."

They mounted the stair in silence, and still with an occasional awestruck glance at the dead body, proceeded more thoroughly to examine the contents of the cabinet. At one table, there were traces of chemical work, various measured heaps of some white salt being laid on glass saucers, as though for an experiment in which the unhappy man had been prevented.

"That is the same drug that I was always bringing him," said Poole; and even as he spoke, the kettle with a startling noise boiled over.

This brought them to the fireside, where the easy chair was drawn cosily up, and the tea things stood ready to the sitter's elbow, the very sugar in the cup. There were several books on a shelf; one lay beside the tea things open, and Utterson was amazed to find it a copy of a pious work, for which Jekyll had several times expressed a great esteem, annotated, in his own hand, with startling blasphemies.

Next, in the course of their review of the chamber, the searchers came to the cheval-glass, into whose depths they looked with an involuntary horror. But it was so turned as to show them nothing but the rosy glow playing on the roof, the fire sparkling in a hundred repetitions along the glazed front

157

of the presses, and their own pale and fearful countenances stooping to look in.

"This glass has seen some strange things, sir," whispered Poole.

"And surely none stranger than itself," echoed the lawyer in the same tones. "For what did Jekyll"—he caught himself up at the word with a start, and then conquering the weakness—"what could Jekyll want with it?" he said.

"You may say that!" said Poole.

Next they turned to the business table. On the desk, among the neat array of papers, a large envelope was uppermost, and bore, in the doctor's hand, the name of Mr. Utterson. The lawyer unsealed it, and several enclosures fell to the floor. The first was a will drawn in the same eccentric terms as the one which he had returned six months before, to serve as a testament in case of death and as a deed of gift in case of disappearance; but in place of the name of Edward Hyde, the lawyer, with indescribable amazement, read the name of Gabriel John Utterson. He looked at Poole, and then back at the paper, and last of all at the dead malefactor stretched upon the carpet.

"My head goes round," he said. "He has been all these days in possession; he had no cause to like me; he must have raged to see himself displaced; and he has not destroyed this document."

He caught up the next paper; it was a brief note in the doctor's hand and dated at the top. "O Poole!" the lawyer cried, "he was alive and here this day. He cannot have been disposed of in so short a space; he must be still alive, he must have fled! And then, why fled? and how? and in that case, can we venture to declare this suicide? O, we must be careful. I foresee that we may yet involve your master in some dire catastrophe."

"Why don't you read it, sir?" asked Poole.

"Because I fear," replied the lawyer solemnly. "God grant I have no cause for it!" And with that he brought the paper to his eyes and read as follows:

My dear Utterson,

When this shall fall into your hands, I shall have disappeared, under what circumstances I have not the penetration to foresee, but my instinct and all the circumstances of my nameless situation tell me that the end is sure and must be early. Go then, and first read the narrative which Lanyon warned me he was to place in your hands; and if you care to hear more, turn to the confession of

Your unworthy and unhappy friend,

HENRY JEKYLL

"There was a third enclosure?" asked Utterson.

"Here, sir," said Poole, and gave into his hands a considerable packet sealed in several places.

The lawyer put it in his pocket. "I would say nothing of this paper. If your master has fled or is dead, we may at least save his credit. It is now ten; I must go home and read these documents in quiet; but I shall be back before midnight, when we shall send for the police."

They went out, locking the door of the theatre behind them; and Utterson, once more leaving the servants gathered about the fire in the hall, trudged back to his office to read the two narratives in which this mystery was now to be explained.

CHAPTER 9

DR. LANYON'S NARRATIVE

On the ninth of January, now four days ago, I received by the evening delivery a registered envelope, addressed in the hand of my colleague and old school companion, Henry Jekyll. I was a good deal surprised by this; for we were by no means in the habit of correspondence; I had seen the man, dined with him, indeed, the night before; and I could imagine nothing in our intercourse that should justify formality of registration. The contents increased my wonder; for this is how the letter ran:

10th December, 18—.

Dear Lanyon,

You are one of my oldest friends; and although we may have differed at times on scientific questions, I cannot remember, at least on my side, any break in our affection. There was never a day when, if you had said to me, "Jekyll, my life, my honour, my reason, depend upon you," I would not have sacrificed my left hand to help you. Lanyon, my life, my honour, my reason, are all at your mercy; if you fail me tonight, I am lost. You might suppose, after this preface, that I am going to ask you for something dishonourable to grant. Judge for yourself.

I want you to postpone all other engagements for tonight—ay, even if you were summoned to the bedside of an emperor; to take a cab, unless your carriage should be actually at the door; and with this letter in your hand for consultation, to drive straight to my house. Poole, my butler, has his orders; you will find him waiting your

1. drive to my house
2. pull all the contents

arrival with a locksmith. The door of my cabinet is then to be forced: and you are to go in alone; to open the glazed press (letter E) on the left hand, breaking the lock if it be shut; and to draw out, *with all its contents as they stand,* the fourth drawer from the top or (which is the same thing) the third from the bottom. In my extreme distress of mind, I have a morbid fear of misdirecting you; but even if I am in error, you may know the right drawer by its contents: some powders, a phial, and a paper book. This drawer I beg of you to carry back with you to Cavendish Square exactly as it stands.

That is the first part of the service: now for the second. You should be back, if you set out at once on the receipt of this, long before midnight; but I will leave you that amount of margin, not only in the fear of one of those obstacles that can neither be prevented nor foreseen, but because an hour when your servants are in bed is to be preferred for what will then remain to do. At midnight, then, I have to ask you to be alone in your consulting room, to admit with your own hand into the house a man who will present himself in my name, and to place in his hands the drawer that you will have brought with you from my cabinet. Then you will have played your part and earned my gratitude completely. Five minutes afterwards, if you insist upon an explanation, you will have understood that these arrangements are of capital importance; and that by the neglect of one of them, fantastic as they must appear, you might have charged your conscience with my death or the shipwreck of my reason.

Confident as I am that you will not trifle with this appeal, my heart sinks and my hand trembles at the bare thought of such a possibility. Think of me at this hour,

in a strange place, labouring under a blackness of distress
that no fancy can exaggerate, and yet well aware that, if
you will but punctually serve me, my troubles will roll
away like a story that is told. Serve me, my dear Lanyon,
and save

Your friend,

H. J.

P. S.—I had already sealed this up when a fresh terror
struck upon my soul. It is possible that the post-office
may fail me, and this letter not come into your hands
until tomorrow morning. In that case, dear Lanyon, do
my errand when it shall be most convenient for you in
the course of the day; and once more expect my messenger at midnight. It may then already be too late; and if
that night passes without event, you will know that you
have seen the last of Henry Jekyll.

Upon the reading of this letter, I made sure my colleague
was insane; but till that was proved beyond the possibility of
doubt, I felt bound to do as he requested. The less I understood of this farrago, the less I was in a position to judge of its
importance; and an appeal so worded could not be set aside
without a grave responsibility. I rose accordingly from table,
got into a hansom, and drove straight to Jekyll's house. The
butler was awaiting my arrival; he had received by the same
post as mine a registered letter of instruction, and had sent at
once for a locksmith and a carpenter. The tradesmen came
while we were yet speaking; and we moved in a body to old Dr.
Denman's surgical theatre, from which (as you are doubtless
aware) Jekyll's private cabinet is most conveniently entered.
The door was very strong, the lock excellent; the carpenter

avowed he would have great trouble and have to do much damage, if force were to be used; and the locksmith was near despair. But this last was a handy fellow, and after two hours' work, the door stood open. The press marked E was unlocked; and I took out the drawer, had it filled up with straw and tied in a sheet, and returned with it to Cavendish Square.

Here I proceeded to examine its contents. The powders were neatly enough made up, but not with the nicety of the dispensing chemist; so that it was plain they were of Jekyll's private manufacture: and when I opened one of the wrappers I found what seemed to me a simple crystalline salt of a white colour. The phial, to which I next turned my attention, might have been about half full of a blood-red liquor, which was highly pungent to the sense of smell and seemed to me to contain phosphorus and some volatile ether. At the other ingredients I could make no guess. The book was an ordinary version book and contained little but a series of dates. These covered a period of many years, but I observed that the entries ceased nearly a year ago and quite abruptly. Here and there a brief remark was appended to a date, usually no more than a single word: "double" occurring perhaps six times in a total of several hundred entries; and once very early in the list and followed by several marks of exclamation, "total failure!!!" All this, though it whetted my curiosity, told me little that was definite. Here were a phial of some tincture, a paper of some salt, and the record of a series of experiments that had led (like too many of Jekyll's investigations) to no end of practical usefulness. How could the presence of these articles in my house affect either the honour, the sanity, or the life of my flighty colleague? If his messenger could go to one place, why could he not go to another? And even granting some impediment, why was this gentleman to be received by me in secret? The more I reflected the more convinced I grew that I was

163

dealing with a case of cerebral disease; and though I dismissed my servants to bed, I loaded an old revolver, that I might be found in some posture of self-defence.

Twelve o'clock had scarce rung out over London, ere the knocker sounded very gently on the door. I went myself at the summons, and found a small man crouching against the pillars of the portico.

"Are you come from Dr. Jekyll?" I asked.

He told me "yes" by a constrained gesture; and when I had bidden him enter, he did not obey me without a searching backward glance into the darkness of the square. There was a policeman not far off, advancing with his bull's eye* open; and at the sight, I thought my visitor started and made greater haste.

These particulars struck me, I confess, disagreeably; and as I followed him into the bright light of the consulting room, I kept my hand ready on my weapon. Here, at last, I had a chance of clearly seeing him. I had never set eyes on him before, so much was certain. He was small, as I have said; I was struck besides with the shocking expression of his face, with his remarkable combination of great muscular activity and great apparent debility of constitution, and—last but not least—with the odd, subjective disturbance caused by his neighbourhood. This bore some resemblance to incipient rigour, and was accompanied by a marked sinking of the pulse. At the time, I set it down to some idiosyncratic, personal distaste; and merely wondered at the acuteness of the symptoms; but I have since had reason to believe the cause to lie much deeper in the nature of man, and to turn on some nobler hinge than the principle of hatred.

---

* bull's eye. A lantern.

This person (who had thus, from the first moment of his entrance, struck in me what I can only describe as a disgustful curiosity) was dressed in a fashion that would have made an ordinary person laughable; his clothes, that is to say, although they were of rich and sober fabric, were enormously too large for him in every measurement—the trousers hanging on his legs and rolled up to keep them from the ground, the waist of the coat below his haunches, and the collar sprawling wide upon his shoulders. Strange to relate, this ludicrous accoutrement was far from moving me to laughter. Rather, as there was something abnormal and misbegotten in the very essence of the creature that now faced me—something seizing, surprising, and revolting—this fresh disparity seemed but to fit in with and to reinforce it; so that to my interest in the man's nature and character, there was added a curiosity as to his origin, his life, his fortune and status in the world.

These observations, though they have taken so great a space to be set down in, were yet the work of a few seconds. My visitor was, indeed, on fire with sombre excitement.

"Have you got it?" he cried. "Have you got it?" And so lively was his impatience that he even laid his hand upon my arm and sought to shake me.

I put him back, conscious at his touch of a certain icy pang along my blood. "Come, sir," said I. "You forget that I have not yet the pleasure of your acquaintance. Be seated, if you please." And I showed him an example, and sat down myself in my customary seat and with as fair an imitation of my ordinary manner to a patient, as the lateness of the hour, the nature of my preoccupations, and the horror I had of my visitor, would suffer me to muster.

"I beg your pardon, Dr. Lanyon," he replied civilly enough. "What you say is very well founded; and my impatience has shown its heels to my politeness. I come here at the instance of your colleague, Dr. Henry Jekyll, on a piece of business of some moment; and I understood . . ." He paused and put his hand to his throat, and I could see, in spite of his collected manner, that he was wrestling against the approaches of the hysteria—"I understood, a drawer . . ."

But here I took pity on my visitor's suspense, and some perhaps on my own growing curiosity.

"There it is, sir," said I, pointing to the drawer, where it lay on the floor behind a table and still covered with the sheet.

He sprang to it, and then paused, and laid his hand upon his heart: I could hear his teeth grate with the convulsive action of his jaws; and his face was so ghastly to see that I grew alarmed both for his life and reason.

"Compose yourself," said I.

He turned a dreadful smile to me, and as if with the decision of despair, plucked away the sheet. At sight of the contents, he uttered one loud sob of such immense relief that I sat petrified. And the next moment, in a voice that was already fairly well under control, "Have you a graduated glass?" he asked.

I rose from my place with something of an effort and gave him what he asked.

He thanked me with a smiling nod, measured out a few minims of the red tincture and added one of the powders. The mixture, which was at first of a reddish hue, began, in proportion as the crystals melted, to brighten in colour, to effervesce audibly, and to throw off small fumes of vapour. Suddenly and at the same moment, the ebullition ceased and the compound changed to a dark purple, which faded again more slowly to a watery green. My visitor, who had watched these metamorphoses with a keen eye, smiled, set down the glass upon the table, and then turned and looked upon me with an air of scrutiny.

166

"And now," said he, "to settle what remains. Will you be wise? will you be guided? will you suffer me to take this glass in my hand and to go forth from your house without further parley? or has the greed of curiosity too much command of you? Think before you answer, for it shall be done as you decide. As you decide, you shall be left as you were before, and neither richer nor wiser, unless the sense of service rendered to a man in mortal distress may be counted as a kind of riches of the soul. Or, if you shall so prefer to choose, a new province of knowledge and new avenues to fame and power shall be laid open to you, here, in this room, upon the instant; and your sight shall be blasted by a prodigy to stagger the unbelief of Satan."

"Sir," said I, affecting a coolness that I was far from truly possessing, "you speak enigmas, and you will perhaps not wonder that I hear you with no very strong impression of belief. But I have gone too far in the way of inexplicable services to pause before I see the end."

"It is well," replied my visitor. "Lanyon, you remember your vows: what follows is under the seal of our profession. And now, you who have so long been bound to the most narrow and material views, you who have denied the virtue of transcendental medicine, you who have derided your superiors—behold!"

He put the glass to his lips and drank at one gulp. A cry followed; he reeled, staggered, clutched at the table and held on, staring with injected eyes, gasping with open mouth; and as I looked there came, I thought, a change—he seemed to swell—his face became suddenly black and the features seemed to melt and alter—and the next moment, I had sprung to my feet and leaped back against the wall, my arm raised to shield me from the prodigy, my mind submerged in terror.

167

"O God!" I screamed, and "O God!" again and again; for there before my eyes—pale and shaken, and half fainting, and groping before him with his hands, like a man restored from the death—there stood Henry Jekyll!

What he told me in the next hour, I cannot bring my mind to set on paper. I saw what I saw, I heard what I heard, and my soul sickened at it; and yet now when that sight has faded from my eyes, I ask myself if I believe it, and I cannot answer. My life is shaken to its roots; sleep has left me; the deadliest terror sits by me at all hours of the day and night; and I feel that my days are numbered, and that I must die; and yet I shall die incredulous. As for the moral turpitude that man unveiled to me, even with tears of penitence, I cannot, even in memory, dwell on it without a start of horror. I will say but one thing, Utterson, and that (if you can bring your mind to credit it) will be more than enough. The creature who crept into my house that night was, on Jekyll's own confession, known by the name of Hyde and hunted for in every corner of the land as the murderer of Carew.

HASTIE LANYON

CHAPTER 10

HENRY JEKYLL'S FULL STATEMENT OF THE CASE

I was born in the year 18— to a large fortune, endowed besides with excellent parts, inclined by nature to industry, fond of the respect of the wise and good among my fellow-men, and thus, as might have been supposed, with every guarantee of an honourable and distinguished future. And indeed the worst of my faults was a certain impatient gaiety of disposition, such as has made the happiness of many, but such as I found it hard to reconcile with my imperious desire to carry my head high, and wear a more than commonly grave countenance before the public. Hence it came about that I concealed my pleasures; and that when I reached years of reflection, and began to look round me and take stock of my progress and position in the world, I stood already committed to a profound duplicity of life. Many a man would have even blazoned such irregularities as I was guilty of; but from the high views that I had set before me, I regarded and hid them →Hyde with an almost morbid sense of shame. It was thus rather the exacting nature of my aspirations than any particular degra-dation in my faults, that made me what I was, and, with even a deeper trench than in the majority of men, severed in me those provinces of good and ill which divide and compound man's dual nature. In this case, I was driven to reflect deeply and inveterately on that hard law of life, which lies at the root of religion and is one of the most plentiful springs of distress. Though so profound a double-dealer, I was in no sense a hypocrite; both sides of me were in dead earnest; I was no more myself when I laid aside restraint and plunged in shame, than when I laboured, in the eye of day, at the furtherance of knowledge or the relief of sorrow and suffering. And it chanced that the direction of my scientific studies, which led wholly towards the mystic and the transcendental, reacted and shed a strong light on this consciousness of the perennial war among my members. With every day, and from both sides of my intelligence, the moral and the intellectual, I thus drew steadily nearer to that truth, by whose partial discovery I have been doomed to such a dreadful shipwreck: that man is not truly one, but truly two. I say two, because the state of my own knowledge does not pass beyond that point. Others will follow, others will outstrip me on the same lines; and I hazard the guess that man will be ultimately known for a mere polity of multifarious, incongruous, and independent denizens. I, for my part, from the nature of my life, advanced infallibly in one direction and in one direction only. It was on the moral side, and in my own person, that I learned to recognise the thorough and primitive duality of man; I saw that, of the two natures that contended in the field of my consciousness, even if I could rightly be said to be either, it was only because I was radically both; and from an early date, even before the course of my scientific discoveries had begun to suggest the most naked possibility of such a miracle, I had learned to dwell with pleasure, as a beloved daydream, on the thought of the separation of these elements. If each, I told myself, could be housed in separate identities, life would be relieved of all that was unbearable; the unjust might go his way, delivered from the aspirations and remorse of his more upright twin; and the just could walk steadfastly and securely on his upward path, doing the good things in which he found his pleasure, and no longer exposed to disgrace and penitence by the hands of this extraneous evil. It was the curse of mankind that these incongruous faggots* were thus bound together—that in the agonised womb of consciousness, these polar twins should be continuously struggling. How, then, were they dissociated?

I was so far in my reflections when, as I have said, a side light began to shine upon the subject from the laboratory table. I began to perceive more deeply than it has ever yet been stated, the trembling immateriality, the mistlike transience, of this seemingly so solid body in which we walk attired. Certain agents I found to have the power to shake and pluck back that fleshly vestment, even as a wind might toss the curtains of a pavilion. For two good reasons, I will not

---

* **faggot.** A bundle of sticks.

enter deeply into this scientific branch of my confession. First, because I have been made to learn that the doom and burthen of our life is bound forever on man's shoulders, and when the attempt is made to cast it off, it but returns upon us with more unfamiliar and more awful pressure. Second, because, as my narrative will make, alas! too evident, my discoveries were incomplete. Enough, then, that I not only recognised my natural body from the mere aura and effulgence of certain of the powers that made up my spirit, but managed to compound a drug by which these powers should be dethroned from their supremacy, and a second form and countenance substituted, none the less natural to me because they were the expression and bore the stamp of lower elements in my soul.

I hesitated long before I put this theory to the test of practice. I knew well that I risked death; for any drug that so potently controlled and shook the very fortress of identity, might, by the least scruple of an overdose or at the least inopportunity in the moment of exhibition, utterly blot out that immaterial tabernacle which I looked to it to change. But the temptation of a discovery so singular and profound at last overcame the suggestions of alarm. I had long since prepared my tincture; I purchased at once, from a firm of wholesale chemists, a large quantity of a particular salt which I knew, from my experiments, to be the last ingredient required; and late one accursed night, I compounded the elements, watched them boil and smoke together in the glass, and when the ebullition had subsided, with a strong glow of courage, drank off the potion.

The most racking pangs succeeded: a grinding in the bones, deadly nausea, and a horror of the spirit that cannot be exceeded at the hour of birth or death. Then these agonies began swiftly to subside, and I came to myself as if out of a great sickness. There was something strange in my sensations, something indescribably new and, from its very novelty, incredibly sweet. I felt younger, lighter, happier in body; within I was conscious of a heady recklessness, a current of disordered sensual images running like a millrace in my fancy, a solution of the bonds of obligation, an unknown but not an innocent freedom of the soul. I knew myself, at the first breath of this new life, to be more wicked, tenfold more wicked, sold a slave to my original evil; and the thought, in that moment, braced and delighted me like wine. I stretched out my hands, exulting in the freshness of these sensations; and in the act, I was suddenly aware that I had lost in stature.

There was no mirror, at that date, in my room; that which stands beside me as I write was brought there later on and for the very purpose of these transformations. The night, however, was far gone into the morning—the morning, black as it was, was nearly ripe for the conception of the day—the inmates of my house were locked in the most rigorous hours of slumber; and I determined, flushed as I was with hope and triumph, to venture in my new shape as far as to my bed-room. I crossed the yard, wherein the constellations looked down upon me, I could have thought, with wonder, the first creature of that sort that their unsleeping vigilance had yet disclosed to them; I stole through the corridors, a stranger in my own house; and coming to my room, I saw for the first time the appearance of Edward Hyde.

I must here speak by theory alone, saying not that which I know, but that which I suppose to be most probable. The evil side of my nature, to which I had now transferred the stamp-ing efficacy, was less robust and less developed than the good which I had just deposed. Again, in the course of my life, which had been, after all, nine tenths a life of effort, virtue, and control, it had been much less exercised and much less exhausted. And hence, as I think, it came about that Edward

Hyde was so much smaller, slighter, and younger than Henry Jekyll. Even as good shone upon the countenance of the one, evil was written broadly and plainly on the face of the other. Evil besides (which I must still believe to be the lethal side of man) had left on that body an imprint of deformity and decay. And yet when I looked upon that ugly idol in the glass, I was conscious of no repugnance, rather of a leap of welcome. This, too, was myself. It seemed natural and human. In my eyes it bore a livelier image of the spirit, it seemed more express and single, than the imperfect and divided countenance I had been hitherto accustomed to call mine. And in so far I was doubtless right. I have observed that when I wore the semblance of Edward Hyde, none could come near to me at first without a visible misgiving of the flesh. This, as I take it, was because all human beings, as we meet them, are commingled out of good and evil: and Edward Hyde, alone in the ranks of mankind, was pure evil.

I lingered but a moment at the mirror: the second and conclusive experiment had yet to be attempted; it yet remained to be seen if I had lost my identity beyond redemption and must flee before daylight from a house that was no longer mine; and hurrying back to my cabinet, I once more prepared and drank the cup, once more suffered the pangs of dissolution, and came to myself once more with the character, the stature, and the face of Henry Jekyll.

That night I had come to the fatal crossroads. Had I approached my discovery in a more noble spirit, had I risked the experiment while under the empire of generous or pious aspirations, all must have been otherwise, and from these agonies of death and birth, I had come forth an angel instead of a fiend. The drug had no discriminating action; it was neither diabolical nor divine; it but shook the doors of the prisonhouse of my disposition; and like the captives of

Philippi, that which stood within ran forth. At that time my virtue slumbered; my evil, kept awake by ambition, was alert and swift to seize the occasion; and the thing that was projected was Edward Hyde. Hence, although I had now two characters as well as two appearances, one was wholly evil, and the other was still the old Henry Jekyll, that incongruous compound of whose reformation and improvement I had already learned to despair. The movement was thus wholly toward the worse.

Even at that time, I had not conquered my aversions to the dryness of a life of study. I would still be merrily disposed at times; and as my pleasures were (to say the least) undignified, and I was not only well known and highly considered, but growing towards the elderly man, this incoherency of my life was daily growing more unwelcome. It was on this side that my new power tempted me until I fell in slavery. I had but to drink the cup, to doff at once the body of the noted professor, and to assume, like a thick cloak, that of Edward Hyde. I smiled at the notion; it seemed to me at the time to be humourous; and I made my preparations with the most studious care. I took and furnished that house in Soho, to which Hyde was tracked by the police; and engaged as a housekeeper a creature whom I knew well to be silent and unscrupulous. On the other side, I announced to my servants that a Mr. Hyde (whom I described) was to have full liberty and power about my house in the square; and to parry mishaps, I even called and made myself a familiar object, in my second character. I next drew up that will to which you so much objected; so that if anything befell me in the person of Dr. Jekyll, I could enter on that of Edward Hyde without pecuniary loss. And thus fortified, as I supposed, on every side, I began to profit by the strange immunities of my position.

Men have before hired bravos to transact their crimes, while their own person and reputation sat under shelter. I was the first that ever did so for his pleasures. I was the first that could plod in the public eye with a load of genial respectability, and in a moment, like a schoolboy, strip off these lendings and spring headlong into the sea of liberty. But for me, in my impenetrable mantle, the safety was complete. Think of it—I did not even exist! Let me but escape into my laboratory door, give me but a second or two to mix and swallow the draught that I had always standing ready; and whatever he had done, Edward Hyde would pass away like the stain of breath upon a mirror, and there in his stead, quietly at home, trimming the midnight lamp in his study, a man who could afford to laugh at suspicion, would be Henry Jekyll.

The pleasures which I made haste to seek in my disguise were, as I have said, undignified; I would scarce use a harder term. But in the hands of Edward Hyde, they soon began to turn toward the monstrous. When I would come back from these excursions, I was often plunged into a kind of wonder at my vicarious depravity. This familiar that I called out of my own soul, and sent forth alone to do his good pleasure, was a being inherently malign and villainous; his every act and thought centered on self; drinking pleasure with bestial avidity from any degree of torture to another; relentless like a man of stone. Henry Jekyll stood at times aghast before the acts of Edward Hyde; but the situation was apart from ordinary laws, and insidiously relaxed the grasp of conscience. It was Hyde, after all, and Hyde alone, that was guilty. Jekyll was no worse; he woke again to his good qualities seemingly unimpaired; he would even make haste, where it was possible, to undo the evil done by Hyde. And thus his conscience slumbered.

Into the details of the infamy at which I thus connived (for even now I can scarce grant that I committed it) I have no

design of entering; I mean but to point out the warnings and
the successive steps with which my chastisement approached.
I met with one accident which, as it brought on no consequence, I shall no more than mention. An act of cruelty to a
child aroused against me the anger of a passerby, whom I
recognised the other day in the person of your kinsman; the
doctor and the child's family joined him; there were moments
when I feared for my life; and at last, in order to pacify their
too just resentment, Edward Hyde had to bring them to the
door, and pay them in a cheque drawn in the name of Henry
Jekyll. But this danger was easily eliminated from the future,
by opening an account at another bank in the name of Edward
Hyde himself; and when, by sloping my own hand backward,
I had supplied my double with a signature, I thought I sat
beyond the reach of fate.

Some two months before the murder of Sir Danvers, I had
been out for one of my adventures, had returned at a late hour,
and woke the next day in bed with somewhat odd sensations.
It was in vain I looked about me; in vain I saw the decent furniture and tall proportions of my room in the square; in vain
that I recognised the pattern of the bed curtains and the
design of the mahogany frame; something still kept insisting
that I was not where I was, that I had not wakened where I
seemed to be, but in the little room in Soho where I was
accustomed to sleep in the body of Edward Hyde. I smiled to
myself, and, in my psychological way, began lazily to inquire
into the elements of this illusion, occasionally, even as I did so,
dropping back into a comfortable morning doze. I was still so
engaged when, in one of my more wakeful moments, my eyes
fell upon my hand. Now the hand of Henry Jekyll (as you
have often remarked) was professional in shape and size: it was
large, firm, white, and comely. But the hand which I now saw,
clearly enough, in the yellow light of a mid-London morning,

lying half shut on the bedclothes, was lean, corded, knuckly, of a dusky pallor and thickly shaded with a swart growth of hair. It was the hand of Edward Hyde.

I must have stared upon it for near half a minute, sunk as I was in the mere stupidity of wonder, before terror woke up in my breast as sudden and startling as the crash of cymbals; and bounding from my bed, I rushed to the mirror. At the sight that met my eyes, my blood was changed into something exquisitely thin and icy. Yes, I had gone to bed Henry Jekyll, I had awakened Edward Hyde. How was this to be explained? I asked myself; and then, with another bound of terror—how was it to be remedied? It was well on in the morning; the servants were up; all my drugs were in the cabinet—a long journey down two pairs of stairs, through the back passage, across the open court and through the anatomical theatre, from where I was then standing horror-struck. It might indeed be possible to cover my face; but of what use was that, when I was unable to conceal the alteration in my stature? And then with an overpowering sweetness of relief, it came back upon my mind that the servants were already used to the coming and going of my second self. I had soon dressed, as well as I was able, in clothes of my own size; had soon passed through the house, where Bradshaw stared and drew back at seeing Mr. Hyde at such an hour and in such a strange array; and ten minutes later, Dr. Jekyll had returned to his own shape and was sitting down, with a darkened brow, to make a feint of breakfasting.

Small indeed was my appetite. This inexplicable incident, this reversal of my previous experience, seemed, like the Babylonian finger on the wall, to be spelling out the letters of my judgment; and I began to reflect more seriously than ever before on the issues and possibilities of my double existence. That part of me which I had the power of projecting, had lately been much exercised and nourished; it had seemed to me of late as though the body of Edward Hyde had grown in stature, as though (when I wore that form) I were conscious of a more generous tide of blood; and I began to spy a danger that, if this were much prolonged, the balance of my nature might be permanently overthrown, the power of voluntary change be forfeited, and the character of Edward Hyde become irrevocably mine. The power of the drug had not been always equally displayed. Once, very early in my career, it had totally failed me; since then I had been obliged on more than one occasion to double, and once, with infinite risk of death, to treble the amount; and these rare uncertainties had cast hitherto the sole shadow on my contentment. Now, however, and in the light of that morning's accident, I was led to remark that whereas, in the beginning, the difficulty had been to throw off the body of Jekyll, it had of late gradually but decidedly transferred itself to the other side. All things therefore seemed to point to this; that I was slowly losing hold of my original and better self, and becoming slowly incorporated with my second and worse.

Between these two, I now felt I had to choose. My two natures had memory in common, but all other faculties were most unequally shared between them. Jekyll (who was composite) now with the most sensitive apprehensions, now with a greedy gusto, projected and shared in the pleasures and adventures of Hyde; but Hyde was indifferent to Jekyll, or but remembered him as the mountain bandit remembers the cavern in which he conceals himself from pursuit. Jekyll had more than a father's interest; Hyde had more than a son's indifference. To cast in my lot with Jekyll, was to die to those appetites which I had long secretly indulged and had of late begun to pamper. To cast it in with Hyde, was to die to a thousand interests and aspirations, and to become, at a blow and forever, despised and friendless. The bargain might appear unequal; but there was still another consideration in the scales; for while Jekyll would suffer smartingly in the fires of abstinence, Hyde would be not even conscious of all that he had lost. Strange as my circumstances were, the terms of this debate are as old and commonplace as man; much the same inducements and alarms cast the die for any tempted and trembling sinner; and it fell out with me, as it falls with so vast a majority of my fellows, that I chose the better part and was found wanting in the strength to keep to it.

Yes, I preferred the elderly and discontented doctor, surrounded by friends and cherishing honest hopes; and bade a resolute farewell to the liberty, the comparative youth, the light step, leaping impulses, and secret pleasures, that I had enjoyed in the disguise of Hyde. I made this choice perhaps with some unconscious reservation, for I neither gave up the house in Soho, nor destroyed the clothes of Edward Hyde, which still lay ready in my cabinet. For two months, however, I was true to my determination; for two months, I led a life of such severity as I had never before attained to, and enjoyed the compensations of an approving conscience. But time began at last to obliterate the freshness of my alarm; the praises of conscience began to grow into a thing of course; I began to be tortured with throes and longings, as of Hyde struggling after freedom; and at last, in an hour of moral weakness, I once again compounded and swallowed the transforming draught.

I do not suppose that, when a drunkard reasons with himself upon his vice, he is once out of five hundred times affected by the dangers that he runs through his brutish, physical insensibility; neither had I, long as I had considered my position, made enough allowance for the complete moral insensibility and insensate readiness to evil, which were the

179

leading characters of Edward Hyde. Yet it was by these that I was punished. My devil had been long caged; he came out roaring. I was conscious, even when I took the draught, of a more unbridled, a more furious propensity to ill. It must have been this, I suppose, that stirred in my soul that tempest of impatience with which I listened to the civilities of my unhappy victim; I declare, at least, before God, no man morally sane could have been guilty of that crime upon so pitiful a provocation; and that I struck in no more reasonable spirit than that in which a sick child may break a plaything. But I had voluntarily stripped myself of all those balancing instincts by which even the worst of us continues to walk with some degree of steadiness among temptations; and in my case, to be tempted, however slightly, was to fall.

Instantly the spirit of hell awoke in me and raged. With a transport of glee, I mauled the unresisting body, tasting delight from every blow; and it was not till weariness had begun to succeed, that I was suddenly, in the top fit of my delirium, struck through the heart by a cold thrill of terror. A mist dispersed; I saw my life to be forfeit; and fled from the scene of these excesses, at once glorying and trembling, my lust of evil gratified and stimulated, my love of life screwed to the topmost peg. I ran to the house in Soho, and (to make assurance doubly sure) destroyed my papers; thence I set out through the lamplit streets, in the same divided ecstasy of mind, gloating on my crime, light-headedly devising others in the future, and yet still hastening and still hearkening in my wake for the steps of the avenger. Hyde had a song upon his lips as he compounded the draught, and as he drank it, pledged the dead man. The pangs of transformation had not done tearing him, before Henry Jekyll, with streaming tears of gratitude and remorse, had fallen upon his knees and lifted his clasped hands to God. The veil of self-indulgence was rent from head to foot. I saw my life as a whole: I followed it up from the days of childhood, when I had walked with my father's hand, and through the self-denying toils of my professional life, to arrive again and again, with the same sense of unreality, at the damned horrors of the evening. I could have screamed aloud; I sought with tears and prayers to smother down the crowd of hideous images and sounds with which my memory swarmed against me; and still, between the petitions, the ugly face of my iniquity stared into my soul. As the acuteness of this remorse began to die away, it was succeeded by a sense of joy. The problem of my conduct was solved. Hyde was thenceforth impossible; whether I would or not, I was now confined to the better part of my existence; and O, how I rejoiced to think of it! with what willing humility I embraced anew the restrictions of natural life! with what sincere renunciation I locked the door by which I had so often gone and come, and ground the key under my heel!

The next day came the news that the murder had been overlooked, that the guilt of Hyde was patent to the world, and that the victim was a man high in public estimation. It was not only a crime, it had been a tragic folly. I think I was glad to know it; I think I was glad to have my better impulses thus buttressed and guarded by the terrors of the scaffold. Jekyll was now my city of refuge; let but Hyde peep out an instant, and the hands of all men would be raised to take and slay him.

I resolved in my future conduct to redeem the past; and I can say with honesty that my resolve was fruitful of some good. You know yourself how earnestly, in the last months of the last year, I laboured to relieve suffering; you know that much was done for others, and that the days passed quietly, almost happily for myself. Nor can I truly say that I wearied of this beneficent and innocent life; I think instead that I

181

daily enjoyed it more completely; but I was still cursed with my duality of purpose; and as the first edge of my penitence wore off, the lower side of me, so long indulged, so recently chained down, began to growl for licence. Not that I dreamed of resuscitating Hyde; the bare idea of that would startle me to frenzy: no, it was in my own person that I was once more tempted to trifle with my conscience; and it was as an ordinary secret sinner that I at last fell before the assaults of temptation.

There comes an end to all things; the most capacious measure is filled at last; and this brief condescension to my evil finally destroyed the balance of my soul. And yet I was not alarmed; the fall seemed natural, like a return to the old days before I had made my discovery. It was a fine, clear, January day, wet under foot where the frost had melted, but cloudless overhead; and the Regent's Park was full of winter chirrupings and sweet with spring odours. I sat in the sun on a bench; the animal within me licking the chops of memory; the spiritual side a little drowsed, promising subsequent penitence, but not yet moved to begin. After all, I reflected, I was like my neighbours; and then I smiled, comparing myself with other men, comparing my active good will with the lazy cruelty of their neglect. And at the very moment of that vainglorious thought, a qualm came over me, a horrid nausea and the most deadly shuddering. These passed away, and left me faint; and then as in its turn faintness subsided, I began to be aware of a change in the temper of my thoughts, a greater boldness, a contempt of danger, a solution of the bonds of obligation. I looked down; my clothes hung formlessly on my shrunken limbs; the hand that lay on my knee was corded and hairy. I was once more Edward Hyde. A moment before I had been safe of all men's respect, wealthy, beloved—the cloth laying for me in the dining room at home; and now I was the common quarry of mankind, hunted, houseless, a known murderer, thrall to the gallows.

My reason wavered, but it did not fail me utterly. I have more than once observed that, in my second character, my faculties seemed sharpened to a point and my spirits more tensely elastic; thus it came about that, where Jekyll perhaps might have succumbed, Hyde rose to the importance of the moment. My drugs were in one of the presses of my cabinet; how was I to reach them? That was the problem that (crushing my temples in my hands) I set myself to solve. The laboratory door I had closed. If I sought to enter by the house, my own servants would consign me to the gallows. I saw I must employ another hand, and thought of Lanyon. How was he to be reached? how persuaded? Supposing that I escaped capture in the streets, how was I to make my way into his presence? and how should I, an unknown and displeasing visitor, prevail on the famous physician to rifle the study of his colleague, Dr. Jekyll? Then I remembered that of my original character, one part remained to me: I could write my own hand; and once I had conceived that kindling spark, the way that I must follow became lighted up from end to end.

Thereupon, I arranged my clothes as best I could, and summoning a passing hansom, drove to a hotel in Portland Street, the name of which I chanced to remember. At my appearance (which was indeed comical enough, however tragic a fate these garments covered) the driver could not conceal his mirth. I gnashed my teeth upon him with a gust of devilish fury; and the smile withered from his face—happily for him—yet more happily for myself, for in another instant I had certainly dragged him from his perch. At the inn, as I entered, I looked about me with so black a countenance as made the attendants tremble; not a look did they exchange in my presence; but obsequiously took my orders, led me to a private room, and brought me wherewithal to write. Hyde in danger of his life was a creature new to me; shaken with inordinate anger, strung to the pitch of murder, lusting to inflict pain. Yet the creature was astute; mastered his fury with a great effort of the will; composed his two important letters, one to Lanyon and one to Poole; and that he might receive actual evidence of their being posted, sent them out with directions that they should be registered. Thenceforward, he sat all day over the fire in the private room, gnawing his nails; there he dined, sitting alone with his fears, the waiter visibly quailing before his eye; and thence, when the night was fully come, he set forth in the corner of a closed cab, and was driven to and fro about the streets of the city. He, I say—I cannot say, I. That child of Hell had nothing human; nothing lived in him but fear and hatred. And when at last, thinking the driver had begun to grow suspicious, he discharged the cab and ventured on foot, attired in his misfitting clothes, an object marked out for observation, into the midst of the nocturnal passengers, these two base passions raged within him like a tempest. He walked fast, hunted by his fears, chattering to himself, skulking through the less frequented thoroughfares, counting the minutes that still divided him from midnight. Once a woman spoke to him, offering, I think, a box of lights. He smote her in the face, and she fled.

When I came to myself at Lanyon's, the horror of my old friend perhaps affected me somewhat: I do not know; it was at least but a drop in the sea to the abhorrence with which I looked back upon these hours. A change had come over me. It was no longer the fear of the gallows, it was the horror of being Hyde that racked me. I received Lanyon's condemnation partly in a dream; it was partly in a dream that I came home to my own house and got into bed. I slept after the prostration of the day, with a stringent and profound slumber which not even the nightmares that wrung me could avail to break. I awoke in the morning shaken, weakened, but refreshed. I still hated and feared the thought of the brute that slept within me, and I had not of course forgotten the appalling dangers of the day before; but I was once more at home, in my own house and close to my drugs; and gratitude for my escape shone so strong in my soul that it almost rivalled the brightness of hope.

I was stepping leisurely across the court after breakfast, drinking the chill of the air with pleasure, when I was seized again with those indescribable sensations that heralded the change; and I had but the time to gain the shelter of my cabinet, before I was once again raging and freezing with the passions of Hyde. It took on this occasion a double dose to recall me to myself; and alas! six hours after, as I sat looking sadly in the fire, the pangs returned, and the drug had to be readministered. In short, from that day forth it seemed only by a great effort as of gymnastics, and only under the immediate stimulation of the drug, that I was able to wear the countenance of Jekyll. At all hours of the day and night, I would be taken with the premonitory shudder; above all, if I slept, or even dozed for a moment in my chair, it was always as Hyde that I awakened. Under the strain of this continually impending doom and by the sleeplessness to which I now condemned myself, ay, even beyond what I had thought possible to man, I became, in my own person, a creature eaten up and emptied by fever, languidly weak both in body and mind, and solely occupied by one thought: the horror of my other self. But when I slept, or when the virtue of the medicine wore off, I would leap almost without transition (for the pangs of transformation grew daily less marked) into the possession of a fancy brimming with images of terror, a soul boiling with causeless hatreds, and a body that seemed not strong enough

185

to contain the raging energies of life. The powers of Hyde seemed to have grown with the sickliness of Jekyll. And certainly the hate that now divided them was equal on each side. With Jekyll, it was a thing of vital instinct. He had now seen the full deformity of that creature that shared with him some of the phenomena of consciousness, and was co-heir with him to death: and beyond these links of community, which in themselves made the most poignant part of his distress, he thought of Hyde, for all his energy of life, as of something not only hellish but inorganic. This was the shocking thing; that the slime of the pit seemed to utter cries and voices; that the amorphous dust gesticulated and sinned; that what was dead, and had no shape, should usurp the offices of life. And this again, that that insurgent horror was knit to him closer than a wife, closer than an eye; lay caged in his flesh, where he heard it mutter and felt it struggle to be born; and at every hour of weakness, and in the confidence of slumber, prevailed against him, and deposed him out of life. The hatred of Hyde for Jekyll was of a different order. His terror of the gallows drove him continually to commit temporary suicide, and return to his subordinate station of a part instead of a person; but he loathed the necessity, he loathed the despondency into which Jekyll was now fallen, and he resented the dislike with which he was himself regarded. Hence the ape-like tricks that he would play me, scrawling in my own hand blasphemies on the pages of my books, burning the letters and destroying the portrait of my father; and indeed, had it not been for his fear of death, he would long ago have ruined himself in order to involve me in the ruin. But his love of life is wonderful; I go further: I, who sicken and freeze at the mere thought of him, when I recall the abjection and passion of this attachment, and when I know how he fears my power to cut him off by suicide, I find it in my heart to pity him.

It is useless, and the time awfully fails me, to prolong this description; no one has ever suffered such torments, let that suffice; and yet even to these, habit brought—no, not allevi-ation—but a certain callousness of soul, a certain acquies-cence of despair; and my punishment might have gone on for years, but for the last calamity which has now fallen, and which has finally severed me from my own face and nature. My provision of the salt, which had never been renewed since the date of the first experiment, began to run low. I sent out for a fresh supply and mixed the draught; the ebullition fol-lowed, and the first change of colour, not the second; I drank it and it was without efficiency. You will learn from Poole how I have had London ransacked; it was in vain; and I am now persuaded that my first supply was impure, and that it was that unknown impurity which lent efficacy to the draught.

About a week has passed, and I am now finishing this statement under the influence of the last of the old powders. This, then, is the last time, short of a miracle, that Henry Jekyll can think his own thoughts or see his own face (now how sadly altered!) in the glass. Nor must I delay too long to bring my writing to an end; for if my narrative has hitherto escaped destruction, it has been by a combination of great prudence and great good luck. Should the throes of change take me in the act of writing it, Hyde will tear it in pieces; but if some time shall have elapsed after I have laid it by, his wonderful selfishness and circumscription to the moment will probably save it once again from the action of his ape-like spite. And indeed the doom that is closing on us both has already changed and crushed him. Half an hour from now, when I shall again and forever reindue that hated personality, I know how I shall sit shuddering and weeping in my chair, or continue, with the most strained and fearstruck ecstasy of listening, to pace up and down this room (my last earthly

THE STRANGE CASE OF DR. JEKYLL AND MR. HYDE

refuge) and give ear to every sound of menace. Will Hyde die upon the scaffold? or will he find courage to release himself at the last moment? God knows; I am careless; this is my true hour of death, and what is to follow concerns another than myself. Here then, as I lay down the pen and proceed to seal up my confession, I bring the life of that unhappy Henry Jekyll to an end.

THE LITTLE COUSINS

Peter Taylor

To the annual Veiled Prophet's Ball children were not cordially invited. High up in the balcony, along with servants and poor relations, they were tolerated. Their presence was even sometimes suffered in the lower tiers and, under certain circumstances, even down in the boxes. But, generally speaking, children were expected to enjoy the Prophet's parade the night before and be content to go to bed without complaint on the night of the Ball. This was twenty-five years ago, of course. There is no telling what the practices are out there in St. Louis now. Children have it much better everywhere nowadays. Perhaps they flock to the Veiled Prophet's Ball by the hundred, and even go to the Statler Hotel for breakfast afterward.

But I can't help hoping they don't. I hope they are denied something. Else what do they have that's tangible to hold against the grownups? My sister and I were denied *everything*. She more than I, since a boy naturally didn't want so much— or so much of what it was St. Louis seemed to offer us.

189

Having less to complain of myself, however, I undertook to suffer a good many things for Corinna. And she suffered a few for me. We were motherless, and very close to each other at times.

What I suffered for Corinna I suffered in silence. But the grand thing about Corinna was that she could always find the right words for my feelings as well as her own. The outrage I felt, for example, at our being always taken down to Sportsman's Park to see the Browns play and never the Cardinals left me grimly inarticulate. But Corinna would say for me that it seemed "such an empty glory" to have box seats at the Browns' games. "Any fool had rather sit in the bleachers and watch the Cardinals," she said, "than have the very best box seats to see a Browns' game." She phrased things beautifully. At our house we had always to serve Dr Pep instead of Coca-Cola. Of this Corinna said, "It makes us seem so provincial." But we both knew that with a father like ours we just had to endure these embarrassments. According to Corinna, Daddy was "blind to the disadvantage he put us at"—disadvantage, that is, with our friends at Mary Institute and Country Day. What's more, she had divined at an early age what it was that blinded Daddy: It was always some friend or other of his who owned or manufactured the product imposed on us. We even had Bessie Calhoun because of one of his friends—Bessie, from Selma, Alabama, instead of some stylish, white foreign governess who might be teaching us French or German. "Except for Bessie," Corinna said, "we would be bilingual, like the Altvaders and the Tomlinsons."

The year Corinna and I were finally taken to the Ball, the project was kept a secret from us until the last moment—or practically. I came in from school at five-thirty, and Corinna had got home two hours before that, as usual. At the side door, which Bessie made us use on all days but Sunday in order to save "her floors," Corinna was waiting for me with narrow eyes and pursed lips. "You and I are going to the VP tonight," she said, "but they couldn't permit us the pleasures of anticipation. Isn't that typical?" The news had been broken to her when she came in from school and told Bessie she was going down the block to play. Corinna was already twelve at this time, and though at school she would never deign to associate with girls in the lower grades, out of school she spent most of her time playing with the younger children in our block. The little girls adored her, and I used to watch her sometimes, mothering them and supervising their games. She never seemed happier than then, and she often spoke of the younger children as her "little cousins." This, I suppose, was in fond allusion to all the tales we had listened to from Daddy, and from Bessie, too, about the horde of first, second, and third cousins they each had grown up among—Daddy in Kentucky, Bessie in Alabama. At any rate, when Bessie told her she had to stay in and do her homework that afternoon, Corinna wasn't satisfied until she had wrung the reason out of her, and then, of course, she was indignant.

"*Why* didn't you tell me before, Bessie?" she said. "Two other girls in my class were lording it over everybody else today because *they're* going."

"That's it," said Bessie. "I didn't want you lording it over everybody you saw today. That's not the way I'm bringing you up. And I didn't want you being flighty about your lessons."

Corinna knew that Daddy must have told her not to tell us. Or she knew at least that Bessie had got his approval. Yet Bessie always pretended to do everything absolutely on her own authority. And this made life more difficult. This made us forget that she was merely someone hired to take charge of us. It made us try to reason with her about things, made us pretend to be sick sometimes in order to break down her resistance, made us nag at her continually for all kinds of privileges. Bessie's utter disregard for what we considered justice and reason was something else that made us forget who she was, and she never showed any fear of our telling on her or going over her head. Her favorite answer to our "whys" was "Because I said so" or "Because I said to." And if one of us gobbled up his dessert and begged for a share of the other's, Bessie was as apt as not to make the other one share. She was illogical, and she was inconsistent. When we were disobedient, she would hand out terrible punishments—dessertless days and movieless weekends—but then sometimes she would forget, or weaken of her own accord at the last moment. You could not tell about her.

There was her brutal frankness, too. Though she was as blind as Daddy to any need of ours to have our egos bolstered—such as by serving our friends the right drink—and as blind as he to our deep moral and intellectual failings—failings that we ourselves were aware of and often confessed to each other—still she never failed to notice the least sign of vanity in either of us. Corinna was beginning to worry about her looks, and when she asked Bessie whether she thought she would grow up to be as beautiful as a certain Mary Elizabeth Caswell, Bessie said, "Your legs are too thin. You'll have to do a lot of filling out before you can talk about that." I was proud of my drawing ability, and I tried to get Bessie to say she thought I might grow up to be an artist. "Do you like nature?" she said, and I had to admit what she already knew: Flowers and trees had little attraction for me. Bessie only shook her head and gave me a doubting look.

Yet when I was sick in bed with mumps or measles she would often read my palm, and, among other glories, she saw that I would be a great musician. I objected that the singing teacher at school said I couldn't even carry a tune. "What does *he* know about how you may change if you keep trying? I know how little teachers know." It was when we were sick that we discovered Bessie's real talents and saw how indulgent she could be when she had a mind to. This made us sick a good deal; and pretended illness was one of our moral failings that Bessie was blind to. I never knew her to doubt a headache or a stomachache or even "a funny feeling all over." When we were sick, she played cards with us, told our fortunes, read to us.

She read to us a lot even when we were well. She had taught school in Alabama before she came north and went into service, but it wasn't the kind of stories we were used to in St. Louis schools that she read to us. She read "Unc' Edinburg's Drowndin' " and "No Haid Pawn," and her favorites were the *Post* stories by Octavus Roy Cohen. When she read us those stories, she would sometimes throw back her head and laugh and slap her thigh the way she never did about anything else. We loved hearing her read, but we didn't ourselves think the stories were so funny. "Never mind," said Bessie. " *You* don't have to think they're funny."

In conversation Bessie had only two real subjects, and one of them was Mary Elizabeth Caswell. Mary Elizabeth was the bane of Corinna's existence. Bessie had brought up Mary Elizabeth to the age of thirteen. When our mother died, Mr. Caswell had sent Bessie over to us—supposedly for only a few days. I was five at the time and Corinna was eight. Mr. Caswell came to our house on several occasions during those first days and had long conferences with Bessie; it was finally decided between them that she would stay with us. Probably Mr. Caswell felt that Daddy's need was greater than his own. Though Mary Elizabeth was motherless, too, it was already known that Mr. Caswell was going to marry again within a few months. Besides, not only was Mary Elizabeth a big girl then, but her mother had been of an old family in the city and there was an abundance of aunts and other female relatives to guide her. And so *we* got Bessie, with the result that Corinna had to "spend her life," as she said, listening to unfavorable comparisons of herself to Mary Elizabeth.

Bessie's other subject was her own family down in Alabama and, more particularly, her half sister, Lilly Belle Patton. Lilly Belle was a saint. Bessie assured us that Lilly Belle was nothing like her, had none of her bad temper and selfish ways, was always doing for others and asked nothing for herself. Lilly Belle was the finest-looking, the smartest, and the best-natured of all Bessie's mama's eleven children. Yet she hadn't insisted on going through high school, the way Bessie had, and she hadn't married. Bessie not only went through school and took to teaching afterward but the money she made teaching she spent foolishly—not on her mama, who was pretty greedy about money anyway, but on first one husband and then another. But Lilly Belle was content to stay at home and help Mama, who was certainly never much help to herself. Lilly Belle took in washing and looked after her little half brothers and sisters, of which Bessie was next to youngest, and even "adopted-like" two orphaned cousins. She was a hard church worker, a beautiful seamstress and laundress, she was the best cook in the whole town of Selma, she kept a garden that was the envy of everyone.

Corinna and I never tired of hearing about Lilly Belle, but for Corinna the most interesting part always was Lilly Belle's courtship. Lilly Belle never felt she could go off and marry while the younger children were still at home to be looked after, and by the time the younger ones were up and gone ("gone to the bad, most of them") Mama was too old to leave at home alone. But Lilly Belle had a faithful suitor, who had been waiting for her through all the years. He was, in fact, still waiting, and Lilly Belle wasn't even engaged to him. Sometimes Bessie had letters from a neighbor friend telling her she ought to make Lilly Belle have pity on Mr. Barker. It seems that on summer evenings he and Lilly Belle kept company sitting together on her front porch. Neighbors would hear their voices over there, and sometimes they would hear Mr. Barker break down and cry as he begged her "at least to get engaged" to him. But Lilly Belle knew what was right; she had taken a vow not even to get *engaged* while Mama lived. Sometimes, too, there would be a letter that Lilly Belle had asked the neighbor friend to write Bessie, warning her that Mama was "low sick." Bessie always "reckoned" Mama was really going this time. And Corinna would be on tenterhooks about it for days. She would try to linger in the mornings till the postman came, and she would rush home from school in the afternoon to see if there was any news. "If Mama goes this time," she would ask, "will Lilly Belle really get engaged to Mr. Barker?" And Bessie would reply, "Of course she will. She hasn't kept him waiting for nothing."

The unfavorable comparisons that Bessie made between herself and Lilly Belle were much more severe than those she made between Corinna and Mary Elizabeth. Yet, quite naturally, Corinna was able to think of Lilly Belle as a heroine of pure romance, whereas she saw Mary Elizabeth as a "pampered, spoiled, stuck-up thing." The worst of it was, Corinna was subject to wearing hand-me-downs from Mary Elizabeth. There was no need for it, of course, but Mr. Caswell and Daddy were that close. Or perhaps Bessie Calhoun was still *that* close to the Caswell family. The dresses would just appear in Corinna's closet and be allowed to hang there for her to ignore until she could resist them no longer. Once she had taken them down and begun wearing them, they became her favorite dresses. She may have managed to forget who it was they had belonged to. Or, without admitting it to me and perhaps to herself, she may have remembered how lovely Mary Elizabeth had looked in them; because Corinna had never lacked opportunity for observing Mary Elizabeth Caswell firsthand. The older girl and Corinna were in the same school together until Corinna was ten. After that, Mary Elizabeth went off to finishing school for two years, but even so she was home for all the holidays, and she and her father and the step-mother would be at our house for meals or we would be at their house. Daddy, during these two years, had begun going about with a very stylish-looking young widow, who was a close friend of Mr. Caswell's second wife. Corinna and I knew this lady then as Mrs. Richards. It was not to be long before she would become our stepmother—a fact that deserves men-tion only because it explains why our family and the Caswells were now thrown together still more than formerly.

Bessie Calhoun had a clear recollection of every mark Mary Elizabeth ever received in the lower grades at Mary Institute. "Because of Mary Elizabeth," said Corinna, "I have to live in mortal dread of not making the honor roll." At an early age, Mary Elizabeth could cook and sew in a way that promised to rival the arts of Lilly Belle. This information cost Corinna many precious hours that might have been spent with her "little cousins." And because Mary Elizabeth had had a little pansy garden of her own, Corinna was sent "grubbing in the earth" every spring. On the other hand, Mary Elizabeth was almost certainly not the reader that Corinna was, or not the reader of novels—the old best sellers on the shelves of what had been our mother's sitting room. One day Corinna inquired after Mary Elizabeth's reading habits. Bessie didn't answer right away—something unusual for her. "At your age that child read the Bible, honey." Corinna opened her mouth in astonishment and then she closed it again without saying

196

anything. This was one time when both she and I doubted Bessie's veracity, but Corinna let it pass. There was a limit to what she would undertake. She never raised the question again.

We knew perfectly well why we were being taken to the Veiled Prophet's Ball. This was the year that Mary Elizabeth Caswell was going to be presented. As a matter of fact, Corinna had nagged Daddy about it one Sunday afternoon in the early fall. Since Mary Elizabeth was to be one of the debutantes this year, didn't he think Bessie might take us to watch from the balcony? ("Mary Elizabeth ought to be good for *something* to us," she had said to me in private beforehand.) But Daddy replied, "Don't be silly. You couldn't either of you stay awake that late. You can come downtown and watch the parade from my office the night before. One school night out will be enough." And, of course, we did go down and watch the parade. In fact, we went downtown for dinner with Daddy and Mrs. Richards, and the Caswells and some other grownups joined us at the office afterward. They all had a party, with drinks and hors d'oeuvres, while we tossed confetti out the window and watched the floats go by. I hadn't even realized that Mary Elizabeth wasn't present until Mrs. Caswell came over to the window where we were and said, "Mary Elizabeth's out with some of her own crowd, Corinna. But she told me to give you her love and say she would be thinking about you tomorrow night. She's dying for you to see her dress."

Suddenly Corinna leaned so far out the window that I thought she was sure to fall, and I grabbed hold of her.

"Stop it, stupid," she hissed. "Here comes the Prophet's float. The parade's nearly over."

Just below us was passing the last of the countless tableaux representing life in French colonial times and in the days of the Louisiana Territory. We had seen Lewis and Clark, Marquette and Joliet, Indians, fur traders, French peasant girls, river bullies from the days of the keelboat and the pirogue. The parade had begun, for some reason, with Jean Lafitte in the Old Absinthe House at New Orleans, and the final tableau was of Thomas Jefferson signing the Louisiana Purchase. Beyond Jefferson, in his oversized wig and silk knee breeches, I could see the Prophet's float approaching. But I knew that for me the best part of the parade was already over. After so many Indians and fur traders, after the French explorers, after the pirates, the Prophet, with his veil-hidden face and all his Eastern finery, was bound to seem an anticlimax. I stood beside Corinna, hardly watching the royal float go by. As she continued to lean far out over the window ledge, I quietly took hold of the sash of her dress and, without her knowing it, held on to it tightly as long as we remained at the window.

The night of the Ball, we had an early dinner without Daddy. He came in and went up to dress while we were still at the table. After dinner, he sent for us to come to his room, where he said that he wanted us to behave ourselves that night "as never before." He was going out to dinner with the Caswells and Mrs. Richards and some other friends, but he would send the car and chauffeur to fetch us to the Colosseum. He didn't tell us that Bessie wasn't going to accompany us or that we would be sitting with him in one of the boxes downstairs.

And Bessie herself withheld this information till the very last. When it was finally divulged, we had already been so dazzled by another piece of news that the evening before us and these unexpected arrangements seemed of little consequence. When we were both dressed, we went into the sewing room, where Bessie always sat in the evening, to have her look us over.

"How do I look?" Corinna asked.

"You look fine," said Bessie. Then she saw Corinna eyeing herself in the mirror stand, and she added, "But no better than you should."

Corinna went up on her tiptoes and said, "I ought to have on heels."

"Behave yourself tonight, Corinna," Bessie said. "And see that *he* does." She didn't look at me, even. Then leaning back in her chair she said, "I've got something to tell both of you."

"What?" said Corinna.

"I want you to behave yourself next week, too."

"Oh, I thought it was something," said Corinna.

"It *is* something. They've sent for me down home. I'll be gone on the train before you get home tonight."

Corinna stared at Bessie in the mirror. "It's Mama?" she asked, breathless. "*Tell* me, Bessie!"

Bessie nodded. "She's dead. She's been dead for two days. I've just been waiting around here to get tonight over."

Corinna observed a moment of silence. She knew that Mama had been "no pleasure to herself or anybody else" for several years now. Further, she knew that she had never heard Bessie say one good word for her mama, and that no commiseration was expected. But still, the respectful silence would be appreciated and would assure her getting answers to the questions she was bound to ask presently. She sat down on a wooden stool by the mirror and placed her feet, in their patent leather slippers, close together. She sat there smoothing the black velvet skirt over her knees. "Lilly Belle?" she said. "Is she engaged to Mr. Barker yet?"

Bessie nodded again. "She already has Mr. Barker's ring on her finger."

Now it was safe for Corinna to look up. "Will it be a long engagement?" she asked, still restraining herself somewhat.

199

"I'm going to stay over for the wedding Sunday week."

Corinna sprang to her feet. "Bessie!" she said. "Let me lend you my Brownie so you can bring us some pictures!"

Bessie shook her head. "Never mind about that. Lilly Belle's not going to get herself married to Mr. Barker without some high-type photographer there."

"Bessie, I wish I could go with you! Remember *every*thing."

"When did I forget anything, Corinna? Is there anything I haven't told you about Lilly Belle before this? I'll tell you one thing now. She's going to marry in her mourning, with a black veil to the floor."

Corinna sat down on the stool again, obviously stunned—more by the striking picture in her mind than by the impropriety. But presently she did ask, "Will that be quite proper, though, Bessie?"

"Of course it's proper, if black becomes you like it does Lilly Belle."

Corinna fixed her gaze on the wastebasket in the far corner of the room. "Do you think—" she began, speaking in a tone at once admiring and suspicious. "Do you think maybe she's kept Mr. Barker waiting just so she could marry in black?"

"How can you ask that, Corinna? Do you suppose Lilly Belle's as vain as *you* are?" Then she got up from her chair and said, "It's time for you-all to start downstairs. That car will be here."

It was only after we were out in the upstairs hall that we realized she wasn't going with us. At first, Corinna said she would refuse to go without her. It would be much more fun just to stay at home and talk, she said. "Yes," said Bessie heavily. "I can just see us sending word to your daddy and Mrs. Richards that you've decided to stay home and talk to Bessie."

"Then you'll *have* to come with us," Corinna said. "How can we go by ourselves?"

"Yes, 'have' to come with you," Bessie said. "Can't you just see me in my six-dollar silk sitting down there in the box with you-all and the Caswells." That was the first we knew of where we would be sitting.

We heard Mrs. Richards's voice downstairs; she had convinced Daddy that he couldn't merely have the chauffeur pick us up and have us arrive at the Colosseum by ourselves. And so there Daddy and Mrs. Richards were, waiting for us at the foot of the stairs. As Bessie helped Corinna into her Sunday coat, she said in an undertone, "Behave yourself, Corinna. Don't act silly. Remember this isn't just something gay tonight. I suspect you'll see folks crying. You know, it'll be like a wedding or funeral. There'll be something sad about seeing Mary Elizabeth and all of those other debutantes walking out in their white dresses."

Then we started down, with Bessie still watching from the head of the stairs and Daddy and Mrs. Richards waiting below.

Only a scene as strange and brilliant as that in the Colosseum could have made Corinna forget Lilly Belle altogether. But perhaps the pleasures of anticipation made her begin forgetting in the car. Or it might have been the sight of Mrs. Richards in her furs at the foot of the stairs. I had noticed before that night that with Mrs. Richards Corinna could be counted on to act more grown up than she did with anyone else. As we rode through town to the Colosseum, she and Mrs. Richards conversed, it seemed to me, with wonderful ease. Mrs. Richards had been a Special Maid at the Veiled Prophet's Court when she was a debutante some fifteen years before. She described the excitement of it as though it had been only yesterday—how you waited behind the curtains to hear the herald call out your name, and then how you heard, or imagined you heard, the gasps of surprise from the throngs whose admiring eyes would presently be focused on you as you walked, trembling, the length of the Colosseum, and knelt before the Prophet to be crowned, and then took your place on the dais.

For me, the Colosseum was like the most unreal of dreams. Before that night it had meant to me a wide sawdust arena with metal girders overhead and surrounded by gloomy, often half-empty tiers of seats. It was where I was taken to watch the annual horse show, the radio show, and the Boy Scout Jamboree. Now it had been transformed, by untold yards of bunting and by acres of white canvas on the floor, into a quite cheerful, if rather bathroomy-looking, ballroom. At one end were the thrones of the Prophet and his Queen-to-be, on a raised dais underneath a tasseled canopy, and they were flanked on either side by tiers of folding chairs provided for members of the Court. At the other end were the immense and immaculate white portieres through which the entrances of all persons of the first importance would be made.

After a drill by the Prophet's Guard of Bengal Lancers, the Prophet himself, attired in splendid medieval-Oriental garments and with his face veiled, made his duly ceremonious entrance. I was so bedazzled by the drill of the Prophet's guards and then by the arrival of the pirates and fur traders and Indians I had seen on the floats the night before that I hardly noticed when the Matrons of Honor began filing past our front-row box. These ladies, perhaps forty of them, circled the whole arena and at last took the places reserved for them on the Prophet's left. Even when the debutantes themselves, in white dresses and long white gloves, began to file by, I found it hard not just to sit there peering between them for glimpses of the people in costumes, who now occupied their places in the Court.

It was Corinna who brought me down to earth and remind-ed me of where my attention ought to be directed. She didn't do it intentionally, with a nudge or a cross whisper, but by her erratic behavior. She was sitting on the edge of her chair and leaning halfway across my lap trying to see the faces of the debutantes, who were now emerging from a small gateway on our side of the arena. I felt that she ought to wait and see them when they passed before our box.

"Stop," I said, trying to push her from in front of me.

"Oh, hush," she said, not budging.

She and I were in the very front row, and I glanced over my shoulder to see if Daddy had noticed her behavior. I discov-ered that he, along with everybody else in the box, was beam-ing at her. I was glad they couldn't see her face, or couldn't see it as well as I could, or at any rate didn't know what her nar-rowed-eyes-and-pursed-lips expression meant. Everything sud-denly became clear to me. I knew what all the adults' smiling indulgence meant. Mary Elizabeth Caswell was going to have a place of honor in the Prophet's Court, and they expected Corinna to be thrilled by this. But I knew what tortures Corinna was suffering. Probably she was wishing I had let her fall out of that window last night. For, after this, how could she hope to measure up to Mary Elizabeth? It was hopeless. Now I began watching the faces of the girls as intently as she.

When the last debutante had passed us, Mrs. Richards leaned forward, smiling, and said to Corinna, "I didn't see Mary Elizabeth, did you?" And somehow, probably just because it *was* Mrs. Richards, Corinna managed to give her a very knowing, grown-up smile. When she turned around and faced the arena, she sat staring straight ahead with a glazed look.

After this came the separate entrances of the four Special Maids, each summoned individually to the Court of Love and

Beauty by the Prophet's herald, each making her entrance between the great portieres and walking the length of the arena with measured steps and drawing after her a wide satin train. How I prayed each time that the next would be Mary Elizabeth! But already I knew that Mary Elizabeth would be nothing less than the Queen. Corinna knew it, too. By the time that awful announcement came, Corinna was even able to turn and smile at Mr. and Mrs. Caswell.

"His Mysterious Majesty, the Veiled Prophet, commands me to summon to his Court of Love and Beauty to reign as Queen for one year . . . Miss Mary Elizabeth Caswell." That was all. The Queen's subjects came to their feet. Between the white portieres Mary Elizabeth appeared, arrayed in her white silk coronation gown, its bodice and its wide skirts embroidered all over with pearls and sparkling beads; her slender arms held gracefully, if just a little too stiffly, away from her body and encased in pure white kid so perfectly and smoothly fitted that only the occasional trembling of Mary Elizabeth's hands could suggest there were real hands and arms beneath; and her hair, her head of golden blond hair, fairly shimmering under the brilliant lights that now shone down on her from somewhere up among the panoplied steel girders. The orchestra, perched in a lofty spot directly above the portieres, began to play. To the strains of "Pomp and Circumstance," Mary Elizabeth moved across our vision, with four liveried pages holding up the expanse of her bejeweled train—moved across the white canvas floor of the Colosseum toward her throne.

When the brief coronation ceremony was finished, the Prophet took his Queen's hand and led her out onto the floor for their dance. After only a few measures, the guards broke their formation, each of them going to seek the hand of one of the debutantes as a dancing partner. The Ball had officially commenced.

Very soon, Daddy and Mrs. Richards went out on the floor, with the Caswells, to congratulate the Queen and to join in dancing themselves. Corinna and I were urged to come along, but I rejected the idea even quicker than Corinna did. We would wait in the box and find a chance to congratulate Mary Elizabeth later.

In almost no time, the floor was crowded with dancers. All but those who sat in the balcony were free to participate. Corinna and I sat with our elbows on the rail of the box, staring into the crowd. It was curious to see the Prophet's guards dancing in their heavy shoes, and it was most curious to me to see in how many instances there was a person in costume dancing with someone in ordinary evening clothes. I was seeking among the dancers for Mary Elizabeth and the Prophet.

It was Corinna, of course, who spied Mary Elizabeth first. "There she is," she said in a perfectly flat voice, indicating where with a tilt of her head, being very careful not to point. "She's not dancing with the Prophet anymore."

And then I saw her out there, not twenty feet from us, dancing with a dark-haired young man in white tie and tails. Just as I caught my first glimpse of her, another young man tapped this one on the shoulder, and she changed partners. She was, as Corinna might have phrased it, the cynosure of all eyes.

Corinna was on her feet. She cupped her hands to her mouth and shouted, "Lilly Belle's engaged!"

Mary Elizabeth couldn't hear her above the music. But she stopped dancing and started toward us, leading her partner by the hand. The other dancers respectfully made way for her. When she had come about half the distance, Corinna called out again, "Lilly Belle's engaged!"

"No!" Mary Elizabeth called back, and her voice and her radiant countenance expressed astonishment and delight. "Is it Mr. Barker?"

205

"None other!" said Corinna in her most grown-up tone. Mary Elizabeth was hurrying toward us now, and I beheld the spectacle of Corinna and Mary Elizabeth Caswell throwing their arms about each other. In that moment all was forgiven—all those splendid accomplishments, and all those unfavorable comparisons: forgiven forever. That which had separated them for so long had now united them.

"But Bessie didn't tell me!" Mary Elizabeth was saying. "She was by, this very morning, to have a close-up look at my dress."

"It's gorgeous," said Corinna.

"Isn't it!" And now another embrace.

"She told me just before I left the house," said Corinna. (Told *me*, not *us*? Before *I*, not *we*, left the house? How selfish that sounded.) "The wedding's Sunday week. And Lilly Belle's going to marry in her mourning veil!"

"Oh no! Stop it!" cried Mary Elizabeth, and she and Corinna shrieked with laughter.

"Bessie's taking the train to Alabama late tonight," Corinna said when she had got her breath again.

"Oh, that wonderful Bessie!" said Mary Elizabeth.

"Isn't she splendid!"

"Have you seen her?"

"Seen her?"

"Up there," said Mary Elizabeth, pointing to the balcony opposite us. "I spotted her a while ago and waved to her."

"Why, she didn't tell me she was coming!" said Corinna. "Isn't that typical?"

The two girls tried to locate Bessie again but soon gave it up. Next, I heard Mary Elizabeth introducing us to her partner, referring to us as her two "little cousins," and realized that Bessie must have talked to her about us. She went on to say how brilliant Corinna was in school and how well I could draw and what "perfect lambs" we both were.

206

I didn't stop searching for Bessie when they did, and I didn't hear what they were saying any longer. My eyes traveled up one row of the balcony and down the next, searching for Bessie's green silk dress. The crowd up there was thinning out; the poor relations and the children and the servants were going home. Bessie had likely hurried off to catch her train. Already I felt that I might never see Bessie Calhoun again.

But I kept looking for her until I could bear my lonely thoughts no longer. I put my arms on the railing before me, hid my face in them, and commenced to sob.

Instantly all attention was turned toward me, but I wouldn't look up or answer questions. In a matter of seconds Daddy and Mrs. Richards arrived.

"What is it, honey?" I heard Mrs. Richards say.

"He's just tired," Daddy said. "He's not used to being up so late. This is what it means, bringing children to something like this."

Then I was led to a seat at the rear of the box, where I wouldn't be so conspicuous. The Caswells had returned, too, now. I heard Mrs. Caswell say, "Poor little fellow," and this evoked fresh tears and deeper sobs.

"What is it, Son?" Daddy said. "You must try to tell me."

Finally I knew I had to say something—something that would sound reasonable to him. I swallowed hard and lifted my face and found Daddy. I don't know whether or not I knew what I was going to say before I said it. What I said was "Bessie's mama is dead."

"How did you know that, Son?" Daddy asked.

"She told me just before I was leaving the house tonight," I said. Then I hid my face and tried to begin crying again, but I couldn't.

"How awful of her!" I heard Mrs. Richards say, threateningly. "How really unspeakably awful!"

I sat with my face in my hands. After a moment I felt someone's arm go around my shoulder. I didn't know or care whose it was. Probably it was my father's though it may have been Mrs. Richards's, or even Corinna's. Whosever it was, it didn't have the feel I wanted, and I purposely kept my face hidden until it had been removed.

The Idealist

Frank O'Connor

I don't know how it is about education, but it never seemed to do anything for me but get me into trouble.

Adventure stories weren't so bad, but as a kid I was very serious and preferred realism to romance. School stories were what I liked best, and, judged by our standards, these were romantic enough for anyone. The schools were English, so I suppose you couldn't expect anything else. They were always called "the venerable pile," and there was usually a ghost in them; they were built in a square that was called "the quad," and, according to the pictures, they were all clock towers, spires, and pinnacles, like the lunatic asylum with us. The fellows in the stories were all good climbers and got in and out of school at night on ropes made of knotted sheets. They dressed queerly; they wore long trousers, short, black jackets, and top hats. Whenever they did anything wrong they were given "lines" in Latin. When it was a bad case, they were flogged and never showed any sign of pain; only the bad fellows, and they always said: "Ow! Ow!"

Most of them were grand chaps who always stuck together and were great at football and cricket. They never told lies and wouldn't talk to anyone who did. If they were caught out and asked a point-blank question, they always told the truth, unless someone else was with them, and then even if they were to be expelled for it they wouldn't give his name, even if he was a thief, which, as a matter of fact, he frequently was. It was surprising in such good schools, with fathers who never gave less than five quid, the number of thieves there were. The fellows in our school hardly ever stole, though they only got a penny a week, and sometimes not even that, as when their fathers were on the booze and their mothers had to go to the pawn.

I worked hard at the football and cricket, though of course we never had a proper football and the cricket we played was with a hurley stick against a wicket chalked on some wall. The officers in the barrack played proper cricket, and on summer evenings I used to go and watch them, like one of the souls in Purgatory watching the joys of Paradise.

Even so, I couldn't help being disgusted at the bad way things were run in our school. Our "venerable pile" was a red brick building without tower or pinnacle a fellow could climb, and no ghost at all; we had no team, so a fellow, no matter how hard he worked, could never play for the school; and, instead of giving you "lines," Latin or any other sort, Murderer Moloney either lifted you by the ears or bashed you with a cane. When he got tired of bashing you on the hands he bashed you on the legs.

But these were only superficial things. What was really wrong was ourselves. The fellows sucked up to the masters and told them all that went on. If they were caught out in anything they tried to put the blame on someone else, even if it meant telling lies. When they were caned they snivelled and

said it wasn't fair; drew back their hands as if they were terri-
fied, so that the cane caught only the tips of their fingers, and
then screamed and stood on one leg, shaking out their fingers
in the hope of getting it counted as one. Finally they roared
that their wrist was broken and crawled back to their desks
with their hands squeezed under their armpits, howling. I
mean you couldn't help feeling ashamed, imagining what
chaps from a decent school would think if they saw it.

My own way to school led me past the barrack gate. In
those peaceful days sentries never minded you going past the
guardroom to have a look at the chaps drilling in the barrack
square; if you came at dinnertime they even called you in and
gave you plumduff and tea. Naturally, with such temptations
I was often late. The only excuse, short of a letter from your
mother, was to say you were at early Mass. The Murderer
would never know whether you were or not, and if he did
anything to you you could easily get him into trouble with
the parish priest. Even as kids we knew who the real boss of
the school was.

But after I started reading those confounded school stories
I was never happy about saying I had been to Mass. It was a
lie, and I knew that the chaps in the stories would have died
sooner than tell it. They were all round me like invisible presences, and I hated to do anything which I felt they might
disapprove of.

One morning I came in very late and rather frightened.

"What kept you till this hour, Delaney?" Murderer
Moloney asked, looking at the clock.

I wanted to say I had been at Mass, but I couldn't. The
invisible presences were all about me.

"I was delayed at the barrack, sir," I replied in panic.

There was a faint titter from the class, and Moloney raised
his brows in mild surprise. He was a big powerful man with

fair hair and blue eyes and a manner that at times was deceptively mild.

"Oh, indeed," he said, politely enough. "And what delayed you?"

"I was watching the soldiers drilling, sir," I said.

The class tittered again. This was a new line entirely for them.

"Oh," Moloney said casually, "I never knew you were such a military man. Hold out your hand!"

Compared with the laughter the slaps were nothing, and besides, I had the example of the invisible presences to sustain me. I did not flinch. I returned to my desk slowly and quietly without snivelling or squeezing my hands, and the Murderer looked after me, raising his brows again as though to indicate that this was a new line for him, too. But the others gaped and whispered as if I were some strange animal. At playtime they gathered about me, full of curiosity and excitement.

"Delaney, why did you say that about the barrack?"

"Because 'twas true," I replied firmly. "I wasn't going to tell him a lie."

"What lie?"

"That I was at Mass."

"Then couldn't you say you had to go on a message?"

"That would be a lie too."

"Cripes, Delaney," they said, "you'd better mind yourself. The Murderer is in an awful wax. He'll massacre you."

I knew that. I knew only too well that the Murderer's professional pride had been deeply wounded, and for the rest of the day I was on my best behaviour. But my best wasn't enough, for I underrated the Murderer's guile. Though he pretended to be reading, he was watching me the whole time.

"Delaney," he said at last without raising his head from the book, "was that you talking?"

" 'Twas, sir," I replied in consternation.

The whole class laughed. They couldn't believe but that I was deliberately trailing my coat, and, of course, the laugh must have convinced him that I was. I suppose if people do tell you lies all day and every day, it soon becomes a sort of perquisite which you resent being deprived of.

"Oh," he said, throwing down his book, "we'll soon stop that."

This time it was a tougher job, because he was really on his mettle. But so was I. I knew this was the testing-point for me, and if only I could keep my head I should provide a model for the whole class. When I had got through the ordeal without moving a muscle, and returned to my desk with my hands by my sides, the invisible presences gave me a great clap. But the visible ones were nearly as annoyed as the Murderer himself. After school half a dozen of them followed me down the schoolyard.

"Go on!" they shouted truculently. "Shaping as usual!"

"I was not shaping."

"You were shaping. You're always showing off. Trying to pretend he didn't hurt you—a blooming crybaby like you!"

"I wasn't trying to pretend," I shouted, even then resisting the temptation to nurse my bruised hands. "Only decent fellows don't cry over every little pain like kids."

"Go on!" they bawled after me. "You ould idiot!" And, as I went down the school lane, still trying to keep what the stories called "a stiff upper lip," and consoling myself with the thought that my torment was over until next morning, I heard their mocking voices after me.

"Loony Larry! Yah, Loony Larry!"

I realized that if I was to keep on terms with the invisible presences I should have to watch my step at school.

So I did, all through that year. But one day an awful thing

happened. I was coming in from the yard, and in the porch outside our schoolroom I saw a fellow called Gorman taking something from a coat on the rack. I always described Gorman to myself as "the black sheep of the school." He was a fellow I disliked and feared: a handsome, sulky, spoiled, and sneering lout. I paid no attention to him because I had escaped for a few moments into my dream-world in which fathers never gave less than fivers and the honour of the school was always saved by some quiet, unassuming fellow like myself—"a dark horse," as the stories called him.

"Who are you looking at?" Gorman asked threateningly.

"I wasn't looking at anyone," I replied with an indignant start.

"I was only getting a pencil out of my coat," he added, clenching his fists.

"Nobody said you weren't," I replied, thinking that this was a very queer subject to start a row about.

"You'd better not, either," he snarled. "You can mind your own business."

"You mind yours!" I retorted, purely for the purpose of saving face. "I never spoke to you at all."

And that, so far as I was concerned, was the end of it.

But after playtime the Murderer, looking exceptionally serious, stood before the class, balancing a pencil in both hands.

"Everyone who left the classroom this morning, stand out!" he called. Then he lowered his head and looked at us from under his brows. "Mind now, I said everyone!"

I stood out with the others, including Gorman. We were all very puzzled.

"Did you take anything from a coat on the rack this morning?" the Murderer asked, laying a heavy, hairy paw on Gorman's shoulder and staring menacingly into his eyes.

"Me, sir?" Gorman exclaimed innocently. "No, sir."

"Did you see anyone else doing it?"

"No, sir."

"You?" he asked another lad, but even before he reached me at all, I realized why Gorman had told the lie and wondered frantically what I should do.

"You?" he asked me, and his big red face was close to mine, his blue eyes were only a few inches away, and the smell of his toilet soap was in my nostrils. My panic made me say the wrong thing as though I had planned it.

"I didn't take anything, sir," I said in a low voice.

"Did you see someone else do it?" he asked, raising his brows and showing quite plainly that he had noticed my evasion. "Have you a tongue in your head?" he shouted suddenly, and the whole class, electrified, stared at me. "You?" he added curtly to the next boy as though he had lost interest in me.

"No, sir."

"Back to your desks, the rest of you!" he ordered. "Delaney, you stay here."

He waited till everyone was seated again before going on.

"Turn out your pockets."

I did, and a half-stifled giggle rose, which the Murderer quelled with a thunderous glance. Even for a small boy I had pockets that were museums in themselves: the purpose of half the things I brought to light I couldn't have explained myself. They were antiques, prehistoric and unlabelled. Among them was a school story borrowed the previous evening from a queer fellow who chewed paper as if it were gum. The Murderer reached out for it, and holding it at arm's length, shook it out with an expression of deepening disgust as he noticed the nibbled corners and margins.

"Oh," he said disdainfully, "so this is how you waste your time! What do you do with this rubbish—eat it?"

" 'Tisn't mine, sir," I said against the laugh that sprang up. "I borrowed it."

"Is that what you did with the money?" he asked quickly, his fat head on one side.

"Money?" I repeated in confusion. "What money?"

"The shilling that was stolen from Flanagan's overcoat this morning."

(Flanagan was a little hunchback whose people coddled him; no one else in the school would have possessed that much money.)

"I never took Flanagan's shilling," I said, beginning to cry, "and you have no right to say I did."

"I have the right to say you're the most impudent and defiant puppy in the school," he replied, his voice hoarse with rage, "and I wouldn't put it past you. What else can anyone expect and you reading this dirty, rotten, filthy rubbish?" And he tore my school story in halves and flung them to the furthest corner of the classroom. "Dirty, filthy, English rubbish! Now, hold out your hand."

This time the invisible presences deserted me. Hearing themselves described in these contemptuous terms, they fled. The Murderer went mad in the way people do whenever they're up against something they don't understand. Even the other fellows were shocked, and, heaven knows, they had little sympathy with me.

"You should put the police on him," they advised me later in the playground. "He lifted the cane over his shoulder. He could get the gaol for that."

"But why didn't you say you didn't see anyone?" asked the eldest, a fellow called Spillane.

"Because I did," I said, beginning to sob all over again at the memory of my wrongs. "I saw Gorman."

"Gorman?" Spillane echoed incredulously. "Was it Gorman took Flanagan's money? And why didn't you say so?"

"Because it wouldn't be right," I sobbed.

"Why wouldn't it be right?"

"Because Gorman should have told the truth himself," I said. "And if this was a proper school he'd be sent to Coventry."

"He'd be sent where?"

"Coventry. No one would ever speak to him again."

"But why would Gorman tell the truth if he took the money?" Spillane asked as you'd speak to a baby. "Jay, Delaney," he added pityingly, "you're getting madder and madder. Now, look at what you're after bringing on yourself!"

Suddenly Gorman came lumbering up, red and angry.

"Delaney," he shouted threateningly, "did you say I took Flanagan's money?"

Gorman, though I of course didn't realize it, was as much at sea as Moloney and the rest. Seeing me take all that punishment rather than give him away, he concluded that I must be more afraid of him than of Moloney, and that the proper thing to do was to make me more so. He couldn't have come at a time when I cared less for him. I didn't even bother to reply but lashed out with all my strength at his brutal face. This was the last thing he expected. He screamed, and his hand came away from his face, all blood. Then he threw off his satchel and came at me, but at the same moment a door opened behind us and a lame teacher called Murphy emerged. We all ran like mad and the fight was forgotten.

It didn't remain forgotten, though. Next morning after prayers the Murderer scowled at me.

"Delaney, were you fighting in the yard after school yesterday?"

For a second or two I didn't reply. I couldn't help feeling that it wasn't worth it. But before the invisible presences fled forever, I made another effort.

"I was, sir," I said, and this time there wasn't even a titter. I was out of my mind. The whole class knew it and was awe-stricken.

"Who were you fighting?"

"I'd sooner not say, sir," I replied, hysteria beginning to well up in me. It was all very well for the invisible presences, but they hadn't to deal with the Murderer.

"Who was he fighting with?" he asked lightly, resting his hands on the desk and studying the ceiling.

"Gorman, sir," replied three or four voices—as easy as that!

"Did Gorman hit him first?"

"No, sir. He hit Gorman first."

"Stand out," he said, taking up the cane. "Now," he added, going up to Gorman, "you take this and hit him. And make sure you hit him hard," he went on, giving Gorman's arm an encouraging squeeze. "He thinks he's a great fellow. You show him now what we think of him."

Gorman came towards me with a broad grin. He thought it a great joke. The class thought it a great joke. They began to roar with laughter. Even the Murderer permitted himself a modest grin at his own cleverness.

"Hold out your hand," he said to me.

I didn't. I began to feel trapped and a little crazy.

"Hold out your hand, I say," he shouted, beginning to lose his temper.

"I will not," I shouted back, losing all control of myself.

"You what?" he cried incredulously, dashing at me round the classroom with his hand raised as though to strike me. "What's that you said, you dirty little thief?"

218

"I'm not a thief, I'm not a thief," I screamed. "And if he comes near me I'll kick the shins off him. You have no right to give him that cane, and you have no right to call me a thief either. If you do it again, I'll go down to the police and then we'll see who the thief is."

"You refused to answer my questions," he roared, and if I had been in my right mind I should have known he had suddenly taken fright; probably the word "police" had frightened him.

"No," I said through my sobs, "and I won't answer them now either. I'm not a spy."

"Oh," he retorted with a sarcastic sniff, "so that's what you call a spy, Mr. Delaney?"

"Yes, and that's what they all are, all the fellows here—dirty spies!—but I'm not going to be a spy for you. You can do your own spying."

"That's enough now, that's enough!" he said, raising his fat hand almost beseechingly. "There's no need to lose control of yourself, my dear young fellow, and there's no need whatever to screech like that. 'Tis most unmanly. Go back to your seat now and I'll talk to you another time."

I obeyed, but I did no work. No one else did much either. The hysteria had spread to the class. I alternated between fits of exultation at my own successful defiance of the Murderer, and panic at the prospect of his revenge; and at each change of mood I put my face in my hands and sobbed again. The Murderer didn't even order me to stop. He didn't so much as look at me.

After that I was the hero of the school for the whole afternoon.

Gorman tried to resume the fight, but Spillane ordered him away contemptuously—a fellow who had taken the master's cane to another had no status. But that wasn't the sort of hero I wanted to be. I preferred something less sensational.

Next morning I was in such a state of panic that I didn't know how I should face school at all. I dawdled, between two minds as to whether or not I should mitch. The silence of the school lane and yard awed me. I had made myself late as well.

"What kept you, Delaney?" the Murderer asked quietly.

I knew it was no good.

"I was at Mass, sir."

"All right. Take your seat."

He seemed a bit surprised. What I had not realized was the incidental advantage of our system over the English one. By this time half a dozen of his pets had brought the Murderer the true story of Flanagan's shilling, and if he didn't feel a monster he probably felt a fool.

But by that time I didn't care. In my school sack I had another story. Not a school story this time, though. School stories were a washout: "Bang! Bang!"—that was the only way to deal with men like the Murderer. "The only good teacher is a dead teacher."

THE TIME MACHINE

H. G. Wells

CHAPTER 1

INTRODUCTION

The Time Traveller (for so it will be convenient to speak of him) was expounding a recondite matter to us. His grey eyes shone and twinkled, and his usually pale face was flushed and animated. The fire burnt brightly, and the soft radiance of the incandescent lights in the lilies of silver caught the bubbles that flashed and passed in our glasses. Our chairs, being his patents, embraced and caressed us rather than submitted to be sat upon, and there was that luxurious after-dinner atmosphere, when thought runs gracefully free of the trammels of precision. And he put it to us in this way—marking the points with a lean forefinger—as we sat and lazily admired his earnestness over this new paradox (as we thought it) and his fecundity.

"You must follow me carefully. I shall have to controvert one or two ideas that are almost universally accepted. The geometry, for instance, they taught you at school is founded on a misconception."

"Is not that rather a large thing to expect us to begin upon?" said Filby, an argumentative person with red hair.

"I do not mean to ask you to accept anything without reasonable ground for it. You will soon admit as much as I need from you. You know of course that a mathematical line, a line of thickness *nil,* has no real existence. They taught you that? Neither has a mathematical plane. These things are mere abstractions."

"That is all right," said the Psychologist.

"Nor, having only length, breadth, and thickness, can a cube have a real existence."

"There I object," said Filby. "Of course a solid body may exist. All real things——"

"So most people think. But wait a moment. Can an *instantaneous* cube exist?"

"Don't follow you," said Filby.

"Can a cube that does not last for any time at all, have a real existence?"

Filby became pensive. "Clearly," the Time Traveller proceeded, "any real body must have extension in *four* directions: it must have Length, Breadth, Thickness, and—Duration. But through a natural infirmity of the flesh, which I will explain to you in a moment, we incline to overlook this fact. There are really four dimensions, three which we call the three planes of Space, and a fourth, Time. There is, however, a tendency to draw an unreal distinction between the former three dimensions and the latter, because it happens that our consciousness moves intermittently in one direction along the latter from the beginning to the end of our lives."

"That," said a very young man, making spasmodic efforts to relight his cigar over the lamp; "that . . . very clear indeed."

"Now, it is very remarkable that this is so extensively overlooked," continued the Time Traveller, with a slight accession of cheerfulness. "Really this is what is meant by the Fourth Dimension, though some people who talk about the Fourth Dimension do not know they mean it. It is only another way of looking at Time. *There is no difference between Time and any of the three dimensions of Space except that our consciousness moves along it.* But some foolish people have got hold of the wrong side of that idea. You have all heard what they have to say about this Fourth Dimension?"

"*I* have not," said the Provincial Mayor.

"It is simply this. That Space, as our mathematicians have it, is spoken of as having three dimensions, which one may call Length, Breadth, and Thickness, and is always definable by reference to three planes, each at right angles to the others. But some philosophical people have been asking why *three* dimensions particularly—why not another direction at right angles to the other three?—and have even tried to construct a Four-Dimensional geometry. Professor Simon Newcomb was expounding this to the New York Mathematical Society only a month or so ago. You know how on a flat surface, which has only two dimensions, we can represent a figure of a three-dimensional solid, and similarly they think that by models of three dimensions they could represent one of four—if they could master the perspective of the thing. See?"

"I think so," murmured the Provincial Mayor; and, knitting his brows, he lapsed into an introspective state, his lips moving as one who repeats mystic words. "Yes, I think I see it now," he said after some time, brightening in a quite transitory manner.

"Well, I do not mind telling you I have been at work upon this geometry of Four Dimensions for some time. Some of my results are curious. For instance, here is a portrait of a man at eight years old, another at fifteen, another at seventeen, another at twenty-three, and so on. All these are evidently sections, as it were, Three-Dimensional representations of his Four-Dimensioned being, which is a fixed and unalterable thing."

"Scientific people," proceeded the Time Traveller, after the pause required for the proper assimilation of this, "know very well that Time is only a kind of Space. Here is a popular scientific diagram, a weather record. This line I trace with my finger shows the movement of the barometer. Yesterday it was so high, yesterday night it fell, then this morning it rose again, and so gently upward to here. Surely the mercury did not trace this line in any of the dimensions of Space generally recognized? But certainly it traced such a line, and that line, therefore, we must conclude was along the Time-Dimension."

"But," said the Medical Man, staring hard at a coal in the fire, "if Time is really only a fourth dimension of Space, why is it, and why has it always been, regarded as something different? And why cannot we move about in Time as we move about in the other dimensions of Space?"

The Time Traveller smiled. "Are you so sure we can move freely in Space? Right and left we can go, backward and forward freely enough, and men always have done so. I admit we move freely in two dimensions. But how about up and down? Gravitation limits us there."

"Not exactly," said the Medical Man. "There are balloons."

"But before the balloons, save for spasmodic jumping and the inequalities of the surface, man had no freedom of vertical movement."

"Still they could move a little up and down," said the Medical Man.

"Easier, far easier down than up."

"And you cannot move at all in Time, you cannot get away from the present moment."

"My dear sir, that is just where you are wrong. That is just where the whole world has gone wrong. We are always getting away from the present moment. Our mental existences, which are immaterial and have no dimensions, are passing along the Time-Dimension with a uniform velocity from the cradle to the grave. Just as we should travel *down* if we began our existence fifty miles above the earth's surface."

"But the great difficulty is this," interrupted the Psychologist. "You *can* move about in all directions of Space, but you cannot move about in Time."

"That is the germ of my great discovery. But you are wrong to say that we cannot move about in Time. For instance, if I am recalling an incident very vividly I go back to the instant of its occurrence: I become absent-minded, as you say. I jump back for a moment. Of course we have no means of staying back for any length of Time, any more than a savage or an animal has of staying six feet above the ground. But a civilized man is better off than the savage in this respect. He can go up against gravitation in a balloon, and why should he not hope that ultimately he may be able to stop or accelerate his drift along the Time-Dimension, or even turn about and travel the other way?"

"Oh, *this*," began Filby, "is all——"

"Why not?" said the Time Traveller.

"It's against reason," said Filby.

"What reason?" said the Time Traveller.

"You can show black is white by argument," said Filby, "but you will never convince me."

"Possibly not," said the Time Traveller. "But now you begin to see the object of my investigations into the geometry of Four Dimensions. Long ago I had a vague inkling of a machine——"

"To travel through Time!" exclaimed the Very Young Man.

225

"That shall travel indifferently in any direction of Space and Time, as the driver determines."

Filby contented himself with laughter.

"But I have experimental verification," said the Time Traveller.

"It would be remarkably convenient for the historian," the Psychologist suggested. "One might travel back and verify the accepted account of the Battle of Hastings, for instance!"

"Don't you think you would attract attention?" said the Medical Man. "Our ancestors had no great tolerance for anachronisms."

"One might get one's Greek from the very lips of Homer and Plato," the Very Young Man thought.

"In which case they would certainly plough you for the Little-go.* The German scholars have improved Greek so much."

"Then there is the future," said the Very Young Man. "Just think! One might invest all one's money, leave it to accumulate at interest, and hurry on ahead!"

"To discover a society," said I, "erected on a strictly communistic basis."

"Of all the wild extravagant theories!" began the Psychologist.

"Yes, so it seemed to me, and so I never talked of it until——"

"Experimental verification!" cried I. "You are going to verify *that*?"

"The experiment!" cried Filby, who was getting brain-weary.

"Let's see your experiment anyhow," said the Psychologist, "though it's all humbug, you know."

---

* **Little-go.** British university slang for the first examination required of a student earning a bachelor's degree.

The Time Traveller smiled round at us. Then, still smiling faintly, and with his hands deep in his trousers pockets, he walked slowly out of the room, and we heard his slippers shuffling down the long passage to his laboratory.

The Psychologist looked at us. "I wonder what he's got?"

"Some sleight-of-hand trick or other," said the Medical Man, and Filby tried to tell us about a conjuror he had seen at Burslem, but before he had finished his preface the Time Traveller came back, and Filby's anecdote collapsed.

CHAPTER 2

THE MACHINE

The thing the Time Traveller held in his hand was a glittering metallic framework, scarcely larger than a small clock, and very delicately made. There was ivory in it, and some transparent crystalline substance. And now I must be explicit, for this that follows—unless his explanation is to be accepted—is an absolutely unaccountable thing. He took one of the small octagonal tables that were scattered about the room, and set it in front of the fire, with two legs on the hearthrug. On this table he placed the mechanism. Then he drew up a chair, and sat down. The only other object on the table was a small shaded lamp, the bright light of which fell full upon the model. There were also perhaps a dozen candles about, two in brass candlesticks upon the mantel and several in sconces, so that the room was brilliantly illuminated. I sat in a low armchair nearest the fire, and I drew this forward so as to be almost between the Time Traveller and the fireplace. Filby sat behind him, looking over his shoulder. The Medical Man and the Provincial Mayor watched him in profile from the right, the Psychologist from the left. The Very Young Man stood behind the Psychologist. We were all on the alert. It appears incredible to me that any kind of trick, however subtly conceived and however adroitly done, could have been played upon us under these conditions.

The Time Traveller looked at us, and then at the mechanism. "Well?" said the Psychologist.

"This little affair," said the Time Traveller, resting his elbows upon the table and pressing his hands together above the apparatus, "is only a model. It is my plan for a machine to travel through time. You will notice that it looks singularly askew, and that there is an odd twinkling appearance about this bar, as though it was in some way unreal." He pointed to the part with his finger. "Also, here is one little white lever, and here is another."

The Medical Man got up out of his chair and peered into the thing. "It's beautifully made," he said.

"It took two years to make," retorted the Time Traveller. Then, when we had all imitated the action of the Medical Man, he said: "Now I want you clearly to understand that this lever, being pressed over, sends the machine gliding into the future, and this other reverses the motion. This saddle represents the seat of a time traveller. Presently I am going to press the lever, and off the machine will go. It will vanish, pass into future time, and disappear. Have a good look at the thing. Look at the table too, and satisfy yourselves there is no trickery. I don't want to waste this model, and then be told I'm a quack."

There was a minute's pause perhaps. The Psychologist seemed about to speak to me, but changed his mind. Then the Time Traveller put forth his finger towards the lever. "No," he said suddenly. "Lend me your hand." And turning to the Psychologist, he took that individual's hand in his own and told him to put out his forefinger. So that it was the

Psychologist himself who sent forth the model Time Machine on its interminable voyage. We all saw the lever turn. I am absolutely certain there was no trickery. There was a breath of wind, and the lamp flame jumped. One of the candles on the mantel was blown out, and the little machine suddenly swung round, became indistinct, was seen as a ghost for a second perhaps, as an eddy of faintly glittering brass and ivory; and it was gone—vanished! Save for the lamp the table was bare.

Everyone was silent for a minute. Then Filby said he was damned.

The Psychologist recovered from his stupor, and suddenly looked under the table. At that the Time Traveller laughed cheerfully. "Well?" he said, with a reminiscence of the Psychologist. Then, getting up, he went to the tobacco jar on the mantel, and with his back to us began to fill his pipe.

We stared at each other. "Look here," said the Medical Man, "are you in earnest about this? Do you seriously believe that that machine has travelled into time?"

"Certainly," said the Time Traveller, stooping to light a spill at the fire. Then he turned, lighting his pipe, to look at the Psychologist's face. (The Psychologist, to show that he was not unhinged, helped himself to a cigar and tried to light it uncut.) "What is more, I have a big machine nearly finished in there"—he indicated the laboratory—"and when that is put together I mean to have a journey on my own account."

"You mean to say that that machine has travelled into the future?" said Filby.

"Into the future or the past—I don't, for certain, know which."

After an interval the Psychologist had an inspiration. "It must have gone into the past if it has gone anywhere," he said.

"Why?" said the Time Traveller.

"Because I presume that it has not moved in space, and if it travelled into the future it would still be here all this time, since it must have travelled through this time."

"But," said I, "if it travelled into the past it would have been visible when we came first into this room; and last Thursday when we were here; and the Thursday before that; and so forth!"

"Serious objections," remarked the Provincial Mayor, with an air of impartiality, turning towards the Time Traveller.

"Not a bit," said the Time Traveller, and, to the Psychologist: "You think. *You* can explain that. It's presentation below the threshold, you know, diluted presentation."

"Of course," said the Psychologist, and reassured us. "That's a simple point in psychology. I should have thought of it. It's plain enough, and helps the paradox delightfully. We cannot see it, nor can we appreciate this machine, any more than we can the spoke of a wheel spinning, or a bullet flying through the air. If it is travelling through time fifty times or a hundred times faster than we are, if it gets through a minute while we get through a second, the impression it creates will of course be only one-fiftieth or one-hundredth of what it would make if it were not travelling in time. That's plain enough." He passed his hand through the space in which the machine had been. "You see?" he said, laughing.

We sat and stared at the vacant table for a minute or so. Then the Time Traveller asked us what we thought of it all.

"It sounds plausible enough tonight," said the Medical Man; "but wait until tomorrow. Wait for the common-sense of the morning."

"Would you like to see the Time Machine itself?" asked the Time Traveller. And therewith, taking the lamp in his hand, he led the way down the long, draughty corridor to his laboratory. I remember vividly the flickering light, his queer, broad head in silhouette, the dance of the shadows, how we all followed him, puzzled but incredulous, and how there in the laboratory we beheld a larger edition of the little mechanism which we had seen vanish from before our eyes. Parts were of nickel, parts of ivory, parts had certainly been filed or sawn out of rock crystal. The thing was generally complete, but the twisted crystalline bars lay unfinished upon the bench beside some sheets of drawings, and I took one up for a better look at it. Quartz it seemed to be.

"Look here," said the Medical Man, "are you perfectly serious? Or is this a trick—like that ghost you showed us last Christmas?"

"Upon that machine," said the Time Traveller, holding the lamp aloft, "I intend to explore time. Is that plain? I was never more serious in my life."

None of us quite knew how to take it.

I caught Filby's eye over the shoulder of the Medical Man, and he winked at me solemnly.

CHAPTER 3

THE TIME TRAVELLER RETURNS

I think that at that time none of us quite believed in the Time Machine. The fact is, the Time Traveller was one of those men who are too clever to be believed: you never felt that you saw all round him; you always suspected some subtle reserve, some ingenuity in ambush, behind his lucid frankness. Had Filby shown the model and explained the matter in the Time Traveller's words, we should have shown *him* far less scepticism. For we should have perceived his motives: a pork-butcher could understand Filby. But the Time Traveller had more than a touch of whim among his elements, and we distrusted him.

Things that would have made the fame of a less clever man seemed tricks in his hands. It is a mistake to do things too easily. The serious people who took him seriously never felt quite sure of his deportment: they were somehow aware that trusting their reputations for judgment with him was like furnishing a nursery with eggshell china. So I don't think any of us said very much about time travelling in the interval between that Thursday and the next, though its odd potentialities ran, no doubt, in most of our minds: its plausibility, that is, its practical incredibleness, the curious possibilities of anachronism and of utter confusion it suggested. For my own part, I was particularly preoccupied with the trick of the model. That I remember discussing with the Medical Man, whom I met on Friday at the Linnaean. He said he had seen a similar thing at Tübingen, and laid considerable stress on the blowing-out of the candle. But how the trick was done he could not explain.

The next Thursday I went again to Richmond—I suppose I was one of the Time Traveller's most constant guests—and, arriving late, found four or five men already assembled in his drawing-room. The Medical Man was standing before the fire with a sheet of paper in one hand and his watch in the other. I looked round for the Time Traveller, and—"It's half-past seven now," said the Medical Man. "I suppose we'd better have dinner?"

"Where's——?" said I, naming our host.

"You've just come? It's rather odd. He's unavoidably detained. He asks me in this note to lead off with dinner at seven if he's not back. Says he'll explain when he comes."

"It seems a pity to let the dinner spoil," said the Editor of a well-known daily paper; and thereupon the Doctor rang the bell.

The Psychologist was the only person besides the Doctor

and myself who had attended the previous dinner. The other men were Blank, the Editor afore-mentioned, a certain journalist, and another—a quiet, shy man with a beard—whom I didn't know, and who, as far as my observation went, never opened his mouth all the evening. There was some speculation at the dinner table about the Time Traveller's absence, and I suggested time travelling, in a half jocular spirit. The Editor wanted that explained to him, and the Psychologist volunteered a wooden account of the "ingenious paradox and trick" we had witnessed that day week. He was in the midst of his exposition when the door from the corridor opened slowly and without noise. I was facing the door, and saw it first. "Hallo!" I said. "At last!" And the door opened wider, and the Time Traveller stood before us. I gave a cry of surprise. "Good heavens! man, what's the matter?" cried the Medical Man, who saw him next. And the whole tableful turned towards the door.

He was in an amazing plight. His coat was dusty and dirty, and smeared with green down the sleeves; his hair disordered, and as it seemed to me greyer—either with dust and dirt or because its colour had actually faded. His face was ghastly pale; his chin had a brown cut on it—a cut half-healed; his expression was haggard and drawn, as by intense suffering. For a moment he hesitated in the doorway, as if he had been dazzled by the light. Then he came into the room. He walked with just such a limp as I have seen in footsore tramps. We stared at him in silence, expecting him to speak.

He said not a word, but came painfully to the table, and made a motion towards the wine. The Editor filled a glass of champagne, and pushed it towards him. He drained it, and it seemed to do him good: for he looked round the table, and the ghost of his old smile flickered across his face. "What on earth have you been up to, man?" said the Doctor. The Time

Traveller did not seem to hear. "Don't let me disturb you," he said, with a certain faltering articulation. "I'm all right." He stopped, held out his glass for more, and took it off at a draught. "That's good," he said. His eyes grew brighter, and a faint colour came into his cheeks. His glance flickered over our faces with a certain dull approval, and then went round the warm and comfortable room. Then he spoke again, still as it were feeling his way among his words. "I'm going to wash and dress, and then I'll come down and explain things. . . . Save me some of that mutton. I'm starving for a bit of meat."

He looked across at the Editor, who was a rare visitor, and hoped he was all right. The Editor began a question. "Tell you presently," said the Time Traveller. "I'm—funny! Be all right in a minute."

He put down his glass, and walked towards the staircase door. Again I remarked his lameness and the soft padding sound of his footfall, and standing up in my place, I saw his feet as he went out. He had nothing on them but a pair of tattered, blood-stained socks. Then the door closed upon him. I had half a mind to follow, till I remembered how he detested any fuss about himself. For a minute, perhaps, my mind was woolgathering. Then, "Remarkable Behaviour of an Eminent Scientist," I heard the Editor say, thinking (after his wont) in headlines. And this brought my attention back to the bright dinner table.

"What's the game?" said the Journalist. "Has he been doing the Amateur Cadger?* I don't follow." I met the eye of the Psychologist, and read my own interpretation in his face. I thought of the Time Traveller limping painfully upstairs. I don't think anyone else had noticed his lameness.

---

* **Cadger.** A beggar.

The first to recover completely from this surprise was the Medical Man, who rang the bell—the Time Traveller hated to have servants waiting at dinner—for a hot plate. At that the Editor turned to his knife and fork with a grunt, and the silent man followed suit. The dinner was resumed. Conversation was exclamatory for a little while, with gaps of wonderment; and then the Editor got fervent in his curiosity. "Does our friend eke out his modest income with a crossing? or has he his Nebuchadnezzar phases?" he inquired. "I feel assured it's this business of the Time Machine," I said, and took up the Psychologist's account of our previous meeting. The new guests were frankly incredulous. The Editor raised objections. "What *was* this time travelling? A man couldn't cover himself with dust by rolling in a paradox, could he?" And then, as the idea came home to him, he resorted to caricature. Hadn't they any clothes-brushes in the Future? The Journalist, too, would not believe at any price, and joined the Editor in the easy work of heaping ridicule on the whole thing. They were both the new kind of journalist—very joyous, irreverent young men. "Our Special Correspondent in the Day after Tomorrow reports," the Journalist was saying—or rather shouting—when the Time Traveller came back. He was dressed in ordinary evening clothes, and nothing save his haggard look remained of the change that had startled me.

"I say," said the Editor, hilariously, "these chaps here say you have been travelling into the middle of next week!! Tell us all about little Rosebery, will you? What will you take for the lot?"

The Time Traveller came to the place reserved for him without a word. He smiled quietly, in his old way. "Where's my mutton?" he said. "What a treat it is to stick a fork into meat again!"

"Story!" cried the Editor.

"Story be damned!" said the Time Traveller. "I want something to eat. I won't say a word until I get some peptone into my arteries. Thanks. And the salt."

"One word," said I. "Have you been time travelling?"

"Yes," said the Time Traveller, with his mouth full, nodding his head.

"I'd give a shilling a line for a verbatim note," said the Editor. The Time Traveller pushed his glass towards the Silent Man and rang it with his fingernail; at which the Silent Man, who had been staring at his face, started convulsively, and poured him wine. The rest of the dinner was uncomfortable. For my own part, sudden questions kept on rising to my lips, and I daresay it was the same with the others. The Journalist tried to relieve the tension by telling anecdotes of Hettie Potter. The Time Traveller devoted his attention to his dinner, and displayed the appetite of a tramp. The Medical Man smoked a cigarette, and watched the Time Traveller through his eyelashes. The Silent Man seemed even more clumsy than usual, and drank champagne with regularity and determination, out of sheer nervousness. At last the Time Traveller pushed his plate away, and looked round us. "I suppose I must apologize," he said. "I was simply starving. I've had a most amazing time." He reached out his hand for a cigar, and cut the end. "But come into the smoking-room. It's too long a story to tell over greasy plates." And ringing the bell in passing, he led the way into the adjoining room.

"You have told Blank, and Dash, and Chose about the machine?" he said to me, leaning back in his easy-chair and naming the three new guests.

"But the thing's a mere paradox," said the Editor.

"I can't argue tonight. I don't mind telling you the story, but I can't argue. I will," he went on, "tell you the story of what has happened to me, if you like, but you must refrain from interruptions. I want to tell it. Badly. Most of it will sound like lying. So be it! It's true—every word of it, all the same. I was in my laboratory at four o'clock, and since then . . . I've lived eight days . . . such days as no human being ever lived before! I'm nearly worn out, but I shan't sleep till I've told this thing over to you. Then I shall go to bed. But no interruptions! It is agreed?"

"Agreed," said the Editor, and the rest of us echoed "Agreed." And with that the Time Traveller began his story as I have set it forth. He sat back in his chair at first, and spoke like a weary man. Afterwards he got more animated. In writing it down I feel with only too much keenness the inadequacy of pen and ink—and, above all, my own inadequacy—to express its quality. You read, I will suppose, attentively enough; but you cannot see the speaker's white, sincere face in the bright circle of the little lamp, nor hear the intonation of his voice. You cannot know how his expression followed the turns of his story! Most of us hearers were in shadow, for the candles in the smoking-room had not been lighted, and only the face of the Journalist and the legs of the Silent Man from the knees downward were illuminated. At first we glanced now and again at each other. After a time we ceased to do that, and looked only at the Time Traveller's face.

CHAPTER 4

TIME TRAVELLING

"I told some of you last Thursday of the principles of the Time Machine, and showed you the actual thing itself, incomplete in the workshop. There it is now, a little travel-worn, truly; and one of the ivory bars is cracked, and a brass rail bent; but the rest of it's sound enough. I expected to finish it on Friday; but on Friday, when the putting together was nearly done, I found that one of the nickel bars was exactly one inch too short, and this I had to get remade; so that the thing was not complete until this morning. It was at ten o'clock today that the first of all Time Machines began its career. I gave it a last tap, tried all the screws again, put one more drop of oil on the quartz rod, and sat myself in the saddle. I suppose a suicide who holds a pistol to his skull feels much the same wonder at what will come next as I felt then. I took the starting lever in one hand and the stopping one in the other, pressed the first, and almost immediately the second. I seemed to reel; I felt a nightmare sensation of falling; and, looking round, I saw the laboratory exactly as before. Had anything happened? For a moment I suspected that my intellect had tricked me. Then I noted the clock. A moment before, as it seemed, it had stood at a minute or so past ten; now it was nearly half-past three!

"I drew a breath, set my teeth, gripped the starting lever with both hands, and went off with a thud. The laboratory got hazy and went dark. Mrs. Watchett came in, and walked, apparently without seeing me, towards the garden door. I suppose it took her a minute or so to traverse the place, but to me she seemed to shoot across the room like a rocket. I pressed the lever over to its extreme position. The night came like the turning out of a lamp, and in another moment came tomorrow. The laboratory grew faint and hazy, then fainter and ever fainter. Tomorrow night came black, then day again, night again, day again, faster and faster still. An eddying murmur filled my ears, and a strange, dumb confusedness descended on my mind.

"I am afraid I cannot convey the peculiar sensations of time travelling. They are excessively unpleasant. There is a feeling exactly like that one has upon a switchback*—of a helpless headlong motion! I felt the same horrible anticipation, too, of an imminent smash. As I put on pace, night followed day like the flapping of a black wing. The dim suggestion of the laboratory seemed presently to fall away from me, and I saw the sun hopping swiftly across the sky, leaping it every minute, and every minute marking a day. I supposed the laboratory had been destroyed and I had come into the open air. I had a dim impression of scaffolding, but I was already going too fast to be conscious of any moving things. The slowest snail that ever crawled dashed by too fast for me. The twinkling succession of darkness and light was excessively painful to the eye. Then, in the intermittent darknesses, I saw the moon spinning swiftly through her quarters from new to full, and had a faint glimpse of the circling stars. Presently, as I went on, still gaining velocity, the palpitation of night and day merged into one continuous greyness; the sky took on a wonderful deepness of blue, a splendid luminous colour like that of early twilight; the jerking sun became a streak of fire, a brilliant arch, in space, the moon a fainter fluctuating band; and I could see nothing of the stars, save now and then a brighter circle flickering in the blue.

"The landscape was misty and vague. I was still on the hillside upon which this house now stands, and the shoulder rose above me grey and dim. I saw trees growing and changing like puffs of vapour, now brown, now green: they grew, spread, shivered, and passed away. I saw huge buildings rise up faint

---

* **switchback.** A roller coaster.

239

and fair, and pass like dreams. The whole surface of the earth seemed changed—melting and flowing under my eyes. The little hands upon the dials that registered my speed raced round faster and faster. Presently I noted that the sun-belt swayed up and down, from solstice to solstice, in a minute or less, and that, consequently, my pace was over a year a minute; and minute by minute the white snow flashed across the world, and vanished, and was followed by the bright, brief green of spring.

"The unpleasant sensations of the start were less poignant now. They merged at last into a kind of hysterical exhilaration. I remarked, indeed, a clumsy swaying of the machine, for which I was unable to account. But my mind was too confused to attend to it, so with a kind of madness growing upon me, I flung myself into futurity. At first I scarce thought of stopping, scarce thought of anything but these new sensations. But presently a fresh series of impressions grew up in my mind—a certain curiosity and therewith a certain dread—until at last they took complete possession of me. What strange developments of humanity, what wonderful advances upon our rudimentary civilization, I thought, might not appear when I came to look nearly into the dim elusive world that raced and fluctuated before my eyes! I saw great and splendid architecture rising about me, more massive than any buildings of our own time, and yet, as it seemed, built of glimmer and mist. I saw a richer green flow up the hillside and remain there without any wintry intermission. Even through the veil of my confusion the earth seemed very fair. And so my mind came round to the business of stopping.

"The peculiar risk lay in the possibility of my finding some substance in the space which I, or the machine, occupied. So long as I travelled at a high velocity through time, this scarcely mattered: I was, so to speak, attenuated—was slipping like a vapour through the interstices of intervening substances! But to come to a stop involved the jamming of myself, molecule by molecule, into whatever lay in my way: meant bringing my atoms into such intimate contact with those of the obstacle that a profound chemical reaction—possibly a far-reaching explosion—would result, and blow myself and my apparatus out of all possible dimensions—into the Unknown. This possibility had occurred to me again and again while I was making the machine; but then I had cheerfully accepted it as an unavoidable risk—one of the risks a man has got to take! Now the risk was inevitable, I no longer saw it in the same cheerful light. The fact is that, insensibly, the absolute strangeness of everything, the sickly jarring and swaying of the machine, above all, the feeling of prolonged falling, had absolutely upset my nerve. I told myself that I could never stop, and with a gust of petulance I resolved to stop forthwith. Like an impatient fool, I lugged over the lever, and incontinently the thing went reeling over, and I was flung headlong through the air.

"There was the sound of a clap of thunder in my ears. I may have been stunned for a moment. A pitiless hail was hissing round me, and I was sitting on soft turf in front of the overset machine. Everything still seemed grey, but presently I remarked that the confusion in my ears was gone. I looked round me. I was on what seemed to be a little lawn in a garden, surrounded by rhododendron bushes, and I noticed that their mauve and purple blossoms were dropping in a shower under the beating of the hailstones. The rebounding, dancing hail hung in a little cloud over the machine, and drove along the ground like smoke. In a moment I was wet to the skin. 'Fine hospitality,' said I, 'to a man who has travelled innumerable years to see you.'

"Presently I thought what a fool I was to get wet. I stood up and looked round me. A colossal figure, carved apparently in some white stone, loomed indistinctly beyond the rhododendrons through the hazy downpour. But all else of the world was invisible.

"My sensations would be hard to describe. As the columns of hail grew thinner, I saw the white figure more distinctly. It was very large, for a silver birch tree touched its shoulder. It was of white marble, in shape something like a winged sphinx, but the wings, instead of being carried vertically at the sides, were spread so that it seemed to hover. The pedestal, it appeared to me, was of bronze, and was thick with verdigris. It chanced that the face was towards me; the sightless eyes seemed to watch me; there was the faint shadow of a smile on the lips. It was greatly weather-worn, and that imparted an unpleasant suggestion of disease. I stood looking at it for a little space—half-a-minute, perhaps, or half-an-hour. It seemed to advance and to recede as the hail drove before it denser or thinner. At last I tore my eyes from it for a moment, and saw that the hail curtain had worn threadbare, and that the sky was lightening with the promise of the sun.

"I looked up again at the crouching white shape, and the full temerity of my voyage came suddenly upon me. What might appear when that hazy curtain was altogether withdrawn? What might not have happened to men? What if cruelty had grown into a common passion? What if in this interval the race had lost its manliness, and had developed into something inhuman, unsympathetic, and overwhelmingly powerful? I might seem some old-world savage animal, only the more dreadful and disgusting for our common likeness—a foul creature to be incontinently slain.

"Already I saw other vast shapes—huge buildings with intricate parapets and tall columns, with a wooded hillside dimly creeping in upon me through the lessening storm. I was seized with a panic fear. I turned frantically to the Time Machine, and strove hard to readjust it. As I did so the shafts of the sun smote through the thunderstorm. The grey down-pour was swept aside and vanished like the trailing garments of a ghost. Above me, in the intense blue of the summer sky, some faint brown shreds of cloud whirled into nothingness. The great buildings about me stood out clear and distinct, shining with the wet of the thunderstorm, and picked out in white by the unmelted hailstones piled along their courses. I felt naked in a strange world. I felt as perhaps a bird may feel in the clear air, knowing the hawk wings above and will swoop. My fear grew to frenzy. I took a breathing space, set my teeth, and again grappled fiercely, wrist and knee, with the machine. It gave under my desperate onset and turned over. It struck my chin violently. One hand on the saddle, the other on the lever, I stood panting heavily in attitude to mount again.

"But with this recovery of a prompt retreat my courage recovered. I looked more curiously and less fearfully at this world of the remote future. In a circular opening, high up in the wall of the nearer house, I saw a group of figures clad in rich soft robes. They had seen me, and their faces were directed towards me.

"Then I heard voices approaching me. Coming through the bushes by the White Sphinx were the heads and shoulders of men running. One of these emerged in a pathway leading straight to the little lawn upon which I stood with my machine. He was a slight creature—perhaps four feet high—clad in a purple tunic, girdled at the waist with a leather belt. Sandals or buskins—I could not clearly distinguish which—were on his feet; his legs were bare to the knees, and his head was bare. Noticing that, I noticed for the first time how warm the air was.

"He struck me as being a very beautiful and graceful creature, but indescribably frail. His flushed face reminded me of the more beautiful kind of consumptive—that hectic beauty of which we used to hear so much. At the sight of him I suddenly regained confidence. I took my hands from the machine.

CHAPTER 5

IN THE GOLDEN AGE

"In another moment we were standing face to face, I and this fragile thing out of futurity. He came straight up to me and laughed into my eyes. The absence from his bearing of any sign of fear struck me at once. Then he turned to the two others who were following him and spoke to them in a strange and very sweet and liquid tongue.

"There were others coming, and presently a little group of perhaps eight or ten of these exquisite creatures were about me. One of them addressed me. It came into my head, oddly enough, that my voice was too harsh and deep for them. So I shook my head and, pointing to my ears, shook it again. He came a step forward, hesitated, and then touched my hand. Then I felt other soft little tentacles upon my back and shoulders. They wanted to make sure I was real. There was nothing in this at all alarming. Indeed, there was something in these pretty little people that inspired confidence—a graceful gentleness, a certain childlike ease. And besides, they looked so frail that I could fancy myself flinging the whole dozen of them about like nine-pins. But I made a sudden motion to warn them when I saw their little pink hands feeling at the Time Machine. Happily then, when it was not too late, I thought of a danger I had hitherto forgotten and, reaching

244

over the bars of the machine, I unscrewed the little levers that would set it in motion, and put these in my pocket. Then I turned again to see what I could do in the way of communication.

"And then, looking more nearly into their features, I saw some further peculiarities in their Dresden china type of prettiness. Their hair, which was uniformly curly, came to a sharp end at the neck and cheek; there was not the faintest suggestion of it on the face, and their ears were singularly minute. The mouths were small, with bright red, rather thin lips, and the little chins ran to a point. The eyes were large and mild; and—this may seem egotism on my part—I fancied even then that there was a certain lack of the interest I might have expected in them.

"As they made no effort to communicate with me, but simply stood round me smiling and speaking in soft cooing notes to each other, I began the conversation. I pointed to the Time Machine and to myself. Then, hesitating for a moment over how to express Time, I pointed to the sun. At once a quaintly pretty little figure in chequered purple and white followed my gesture, and then astonished me by imitating the sound of thunder.

"For a moment I was staggered, though the import of his gesture was plain enough. The question had come into my mind abruptly: were these creatures fools? You may hardly understand how it took me. You see I had always anticipated that the people of the year Eight Hundred and Two Thousand-odd would be incredibly in front of us in knowledge, art, everything. Then one of them suddenly asked me a question that showed him to be on the intellectual level of one of our five-year-old children—asked me, in fact, if I had come from the sun in a thunderstorm! It let loose the judgment I had suspended upon their clothes, their frail light

245

limbs and fragile features. A flow of disappointment rushed across my mind. For a moment I felt that I had built the Time Machine in vain.

"I nodded, pointed to the sun, and gave them such a vivid rendering of a thunderclap as startled them. They all withdrew a pace or so and bowed. Then came one laughing towards me, carrying a chain of beautiful flowers altogether new to me, and put it about my neck. The idea was received with melodious applause; and presently they were all running to and fro for flowers, and laughingly flinging them upon me until I was almost smothered with blossom. You who have never seen the like can scarcely imagine what delicate and wonderful flowers countless years of culture had created. Then someone suggested that their plaything should be exhibited in the nearest building, and so I was led past the sphinx of white marble, which had seemed to watch me all the while with a smile at my astonishment, towards a vast grey edifice of fretted stone. As I went with them the memory of my confident anticipations of a profoundly grave and intellectual posterity came, with irresistible merriment, to my mind.

"The building had a huge entry, and was altogether of colossal dimensions. I was naturally most occupied with the growing crowd of little people, and with the big open portals that yawned before me shadowy and mysterious. My general impression of the world I saw over their heads was of a tangled waste of beautiful bushes and flowers, a long-neglected and yet weedless garden. I saw a number of tall spikes of strange white flowers, measuring a foot perhaps across the spread of the waxen petals. They grew scattered, as if wild, among the variegated shrubs, but, as I say, I did not examine them closely at this time. The Time Machine was left deserted on the turf among the rhododendrons.

246

"The arch of the doorway was richly carved, but naturally I did not observe the carving very narrowly, though I fancied I saw suggestions of old Phoenician decorations as I passed through, and it struck me that they were very badly broken and weather-worn. Several more brightly-clad people met me in the doorway, and so we entered, I dressed in dingy nineteenth-century garments, looking grotesque enough, garlanded with flowers, and surrounded by an eddying mass of bright, soft-coloured robes and shining white limbs, in a melodious whirl of laughter and laughing speech.

"The big doorway opened into a proportionately great hall hung with brown. The roof was in shadow, and the windows, partially glazed with coloured glass and partially unglazed, admitted a tempered light. The floor was made up of huge blocks of some very hard white metal, not plates nor slabs— blocks, and it was so much worn, as I judged by the going to and fro of past generations, as to be deeply channelled along the more frequented ways. Transverse to the length were innumerable tables made of slabs of polished stone, raised, perhaps, a foot from the floor, and upon these were heaps of fruits. Some I recognized as a kind of hypertrophied raspberry and orange, but for the most part they were strange.

"Between the tables was scattered a great number of cushions. Upon these my conductors seated themselves, signing for me to do likewise. With a pretty absence of ceremony they began to eat the fruit with their hands, flinging peel and stalks, and so forth, into the round openings in the sides of the tables. I was not loth to follow their example, for I felt thirsty and hungry. As I did so I surveyed the hall at my leisure.

"And perhaps the thing that struck me most was its dilapidated look. The stained-glass windows, which displayed only a geometrical pattern, were broken in many places, and the curtains that hung across the lower end were thick with dust. And it caught my eye that the corner of the marble table near me was fractured. Nevertheless, the general effect was extremely rich and picturesque. There were, perhaps, a couple of hundred people dining in the hall, and most of them, seated as near to me as they could come, were watching me with interest, their little eyes shining over the fruit they were eating. All were clad in the same soft, and yet strong, silky material.

"Fruit, by the bye, was all their diet. These people of the remote future were strict vegetarians, and while I was with them, in spite of some carnal cravings, I had to be frugivorous also. Indeed, I found afterwards that horses, cattle, sheep, dogs, had followed the Ichthyosaurus into extinction. But the fruits were very delightful; one, in particular, that seemed to be in season all the time I was there—a floury thing in a three-sided husk—was especially good, and I made it my staple. At first I was puzzled by all these strange fruits, and by the strange flowers I saw, but later I began to perceive their import.

"However, I am telling you of my fruit dinner in the distant future now. So soon as my appetite was a little checked, I determined to make a resolute attempt to learn the speech of these new men of mine. Clearly that was the next thing to do. The fruits seemed a convenient thing to begin upon, and holding one of these up I began a series of interrogative sounds and gestures. I had some considerable difficulty in conveying my meaning. At first my efforts met with a stare of surprise or inextinguishable laughter, but presently a fairhaired little creature seemed to grasp my intention and repeated a name. They had to chatter and explain their business at great length to each other, and my first attempts to make their exquisite little sounds of the language caused an immense amount of genuine, if uncivil, amusement. However, I felt like a schoolmaster amidst children, and persisted, and presently I had a score of noun substantives at least at my command; and then I got to demonstrative pronouns, and even the verb 'to eat.' But it was slow work, and the little people soon tired and wanted to get away from my interrogations, so I determined, rather of necessity, to let them give their lessons in little doses when they felt inclined. And very little doses I found they were before long, for I never met people more indolent or more easily fatigued.

CHAPTER 6

THE SUNSET OF MANKIND

"A queer thing I soon discovered about my little hosts, and that was their lack of interest. They would come to me with eager cries of astonishment, like children, but, like children, they would soon stop examining me and wander away after some other toy. The dinner and my conversational beginnings ended, I noted for the first time that almost all those who had surrounded me at first were gone. It is odd, too, how speedily I came to disregard these little people. I went out through the portal into the sunlit world again so soon as my hunger was satisfied. I was continually meeting more of these men of the future, who would follow me a little distance, chatter and laugh about me, and, having smiled and gesticulated in a friendly way, leave me again to my own devices.

"The calm of evening was upon the world as I emerged from the great hall, and the scene was lit by the warm glow of the setting sun. At first things were very confusing. Everything was so entirely different from the world I had known—even the flowers. The big building I had left was situate on the slope of a broad river valley, but the Thames had shifted, perhaps, a mile from its present position. I resolved to mount to the summit of a crest, perhaps a mile and a half away, from which I could get a wider view of this our planet in the year Eight Hundred and Two Thousand Seven Hundred and One, A.D. For that, I should explain, was the date the little dials of my machine recorded.

"As I walked I was watchful for every impression that could possibly help to explain the condition of ruinous splendour in which I found the world—for ruinous it was. A little way up the hill, for instance, was a great heap of granite, bound together by masses of aluminum, a vast labyrinth of precipitous walls and crumbled heaps, amidst which were thick heaps of very beautiful pagoda-like plants—nettles possibly—but wonderfully tinted with brown about the leaves, and incapable of stinging. It was evidently the derelict remains of some vast structure, to what end built I could not determine. It was here that I was destined, at a later date, to have a very strange experience—the first intimation of a still stranger discovery—but of that I will speak in its proper place.

"Looking round, with a sudden thought, from a terrace on which I rested for a while, I realized that there were no small houses to be seen. Apparently, the single house, and possibly even the household, had vanished. Here and there among the greenery were palace-like buildings, but the house and the cottage, which form such characteristic features of our own English landscape, had disappeared.

" 'Communism,' said I to myself.

"And on the heels of that came another thought. I looked at the half-dozen little figures that were following me. Then, in a flash, I perceived that all had the same form of costume, the same soft hairless visage, and the same girlish rotundity of limb. It may seem strange, perhaps, that I had not noticed this before. But everything was so strange. Now, I saw the fact plainly enough. In costume, and in all the differences of texture and bearing that now mark off the sexes from each other, these people of the future were alike. And the children seemed to my eyes to be but the miniatures of their parents. I judged then that the children of that time were extremely precocious, physically at least, and I found afterwards abundant verification of my opinion.

"Seeing the ease and security in which these people were living, I felt that this close resemblance of the sexes was after all what one would expect; for the strength of a man and the softness of a woman, the institution of the family, and the differentiation of occupations are mere militant necessities of an age of physical force. Where population is balanced and abundant, much child-bearing becomes an evil rather than a blessing to the State: where violence comes but rarely and offspring are secure, there is less necessity—indeed there is no necessity—of an efficient family, and the specialization of the sexes with reference to their children's needs disappears. We see some beginnings of this even in our own time, and in this future age it was complete. This, I must remind you, was my speculation at the time. Later, I was to appreciate how far it fell short of the reality.

"While I was musing upon these things, my attention was attracted by a pretty little structure, like a well under a cupola. I thought in a transitory way of the oddness of wells still existing, and then resumed the thread of my speculations. There were no large buildings towards the top of the hill, and as my walking powers were evidently miraculous, I was presently left alone for the first time. With a strange sense of freedom and adventure I pushed on up to the crest.

"There I found a seat of some yellow metal that I did not recognize, corroded in places with a kind of pinkish rust and

251

half-smothered in soft moss, the arm-rests cast and filed into the resemblance of griffins' heads. I sat down on it, and I surveyed the broad view of our old world under the sunset of that long day. It was as sweet and fair a view as I have ever seen. The sun had already gone below the horizon and the west was flaming gold, touched with some horizontal bars of purple and crimson. Below was the valley of the Thames, in which the river lay like a band of burnished steel. I have already spoken of the great palaces dotted about among the variegated greenery, some in ruins and some still occupied. Here and there rose a white or silvery figure in the waste garden of the earth, here and there came the sharp vertical line of some cupola or obelisk. There were no hedges, no signs of proprietary rights, no evidences of agriculture; the whole earth had become a garden.

"So watching, I began to put my interpretation upon the things I had seen, and as it shaped itself to me that evening, my interpretation was something in this way (afterwards I found I had got only a half truth—or only a glimpse of one facet of the truth):

"It seemed to me that I had happened upon humanity upon the wane. The ruddy sunset set me thinking of the sunset of mankind. For the first time I began to realize an odd consequence of the social effort in which we are at present engaged. And yet, come to think, it is a logical consequence enough. Strength is the outcome of need: security sets a premium on feebleness. The work of ameliorating the conditions of life—the true civilizing process that makes life more and more secure—had gone steadily on to a climax. One triumph of a united humanity over Nature had followed another. Things that are now mere dreams had become projects deliberately put in hand and carried forward. And the harvest was what I saw!

"After all, the sanitation and the agriculture of today are still in the rudimentary stage. The science of our time has attacked but a little department of the field of human disease, but, even so, it spreads its operations very steadily and persistently. Our agriculture and horticulture destroy a weed just here and there and cultivate perhaps a score or so of wholesome plants, leaving the greater number to fight out a balance as they can. We improve our favourite plants and animals—and how few they are—gradually by selective breeding; now a new and better peach, now a seedless grape, now a sweeter and larger flower, now a more convenient breed of cattle. We improve them gradually, because our ideals are vague and tentative, and our knowledge is very limited; because Nature, too, is shy and slow in our clumsy hands. Some day all this will be better organized, and still better. That is the drift of the current in spite of the eddies. The whole world will be intelligent, educated, and cooperating; things will move faster and faster towards the subjugation of Nature. In the end, wisely and carefully we shall readjust the balance of animal and vegetable life to suit our human needs.

"This adjustment, I say, must have been done, and done well: done indeed for all time, in the space of Time across which my machine had leapt. The air was free from gnats, the earth from weeds or fungi; everywhere were fruits and sweet and delightful flowers; brilliant butterflies flew hither and thither. The ideal of preventive medicine was attained. Diseases had been stamped out. I saw no evidence of any contagious diseases during all my stay. And I shall have to tell you later that even the process of putrefaction and decay had been profoundly affected by these changes.

"Social triumphs, too, had been effected. I saw mankind housed in splendid shelters, gloriously clothed, and as yet I had found them engaged in no toil. There were no signs of struggle, neither social nor economical struggle. The shop, the advertisement, traffic, all that commerce which constitutes the body of our world, was gone. It was natural on that golden evening that I should jump at the idea of a social paradise. The difficulty of increasing population had been met, I guessed, and population had ceased to increase.

"But with this change in condition come inevitably adaptations to the change. What, unless biological science is a mass of errors, is the cause of human intelligence and vigour? Hardship and freedom: conditions under which the active, strong, and subtle survive and the weaker go to the wall; conditions that put a premium upon the loyal alliance of capable men, upon self-restraint, patience, and decision. And the institution of the family, and the emotions that arise therein, the fierce jealousy, the tenderness for offspring, parental self-devotion, all found their justification and support in the imminent dangers of the young. *Now,* where are these imminent dangers? There is a sentiment arising, and it will grow, against connubial jealousy, against fierce maternity, against passion of all sorts; unnecessary things now, and things that make us uncomfortable, savage survivals, discords in a refined and pleasant life.

"I thought of the physical slightness of the people, their lack of intelligence, and those big abundant ruins, and it strengthened my belief in a perfect conquest of Nature. For after the battle comes Quiet. Humanity had been strong, energetic, and intelligent, and had used all its abundant vitality to alter the conditions under which it lived. And now came the reaction of the altered conditions.

"Under the new conditions of perfect comfort and security, that restless energy, that with us is strength, would become weakness. Even in our own time certain tendencies and desires, once necessary to survival, are a constant source of failure. Physical courage and the love of battle, for instance, are no great help—may even be hindrances—to a civilized man. And in a state of physical balance and security, power, intellectual as well as physical, would be out of place. For countless years I judged there had been no danger of war or solitary violence, no danger from wild beasts, no wasting disease to require strength of constitution, no need of toil. For such a life, what we should call the weak are as well equipped as the strong, are indeed no longer weak. Better equipped indeed they are, for the strong would be fretted by an energy for which there was no outlet. No doubt the exquisite beauty of the buildings I saw was the outcome of the last surgings of the now purposeless energy of mankind before it settled down into perfect harmony with the conditions under which it lived—the flourish of that triumph which began the last great peace. This has ever been the fate of energy in security; it takes to art and to eroticism, and then come languor and decay.

"Even this artistic impetus would at last die away—had almost died in the Time I saw. To adorn themselves with flowers, to dance, to sing in the sunlight; so much was left of the artistic spirit, and no more. Even that would fade in the end into a contented inactivity. We are kept keen on the grindstone of pain and necessity, and, it seemed to me, that here was that hateful grindstone broken at last!

"As I stood there in the gathering dark I thought that in this simple explanation I had mastered the problem of the world—mastered the whole secret of these delicious people. Possibly the checks they had devised for the increase of population had succeeded too well, and their numbers had rather diminished than kept stationary. That would account for the abandoned ruins. Very simple was my explanation, and plausible enough—as most wrong theories are!

255

CHAPTER 7

A SUDDEN SHOCK

"As I stood there musing over this too perfect triumph of man, the full moon, yellow and gibbous, came up out of an overflow of silver light in the northeast. The bright little figures ceased to move about below, a noiseless owl flitted by, and I shivered with the chill of the night. I determined to descend and find where I could sleep.

"I looked for the building I knew. Then my eye travelled along to the figure of the White Sphinx upon the pedestal of bronze, growing distinct as the light of the rising moon grew brighter. I could see the silver birch against it. There was the tangle of rhododendron bushes, black in the pale light, and there was the little lawn. I looked at the lawn again. A queer doubt chilled my complacency. 'No,' I said stoutly to myself, 'that was not the lawn.'

"But it *was* the lawn. For the white leprous face of the sphinx was towards it. Can you imagine what I felt as this conviction came home to me? But you cannot. The Time Machine was gone!

"At once, like a lash across the face, came the possibility of losing my own age, of being left helpless in this strange new world. The bare thought of it was an actual physical sensation. I could feel it grip me at the throat and stop my breathing. In another moment I was in a passion of fear and running with great leaping strides down the slope. Once I fell headlong and cut my face; I lost no time in stanching the blood, but jumped up and ran on, with a warm trickle down my cheek and chin. All the time I ran I was saying to myself, 'They have moved it a little, pushed it under the bushes out of the way.' Nevertheless, I ran with all my might. All the time, with the certainty that sometimes comes with excessive dread, I knew that such assurance was folly, knew instinctively that the machine was removed out of my reach. My breath came with pain. I suppose I covered the whole distance from the hill crest to the little lawn, two miles, perhaps, in ten minutes. And I am not a young man. I cursed aloud, as I ran, at my confident folly in leaving the machine, wasting good breath thereby. I cried aloud, and none answered. Not a creature seemed to be stirring in that moonlit world.

"When I reached the lawn my worst fears were realized. Not a trace of the thing was to be seen. I felt faint and cold when I faced the empty space, among the black tangle of bushes. I ran round it furiously, as if the thing might be hidden in a corner, and then stopped abruptly, with my hands clutching my hair. Above me towered the sphinx, upon the bronze pedestal, white, shining, leprous, in the light of the rising moon. It seemed to smile in mockery of my dismay.

"I might have consoled myself by imagining the little people had put the mechanism in some shelter for me, had I not felt assured of their physical and intellectual inadequacy. That is what dismayed me: the sense of some hitherto unsuspected power, through whose intervention my invention had vanished. Yet, of one thing I felt assured: unless some other age had produced its exact duplicate, the machine could not have moved in time. The attachment of the levers—I will show you the method later—prevented anyone from tampering with it in that way when they were removed. It had moved, and was hid, only in space. But then, where could it be?

"I think I must have had a kind of frenzy. I remember running violently in and out among the moonlit bushes all round the sphinx, and startling some white animal that, in the dim light, I took for a small deer. I remember, too, late that night, beating the bushes with my clenched fists until my knuckles were gashed and bleeding from the broken twigs.

257

Then, sobbing and raving in my anguish of mind, I went down to the great building of stone. The big hall was dark, silent, and deserted. I slipped on the uneven floor, and fell over one of the malachite tables, almost breaking my shin. I lit a match and went on past the dusty curtains, of which I have told you.

"There I found a second great hall covered with cushions, upon which, perhaps, a score or so of the little people were sleeping. I have no doubt they found my second appearance strange enough, coming suddenly out of the quiet darkness with inarticulate noises and the splutter and flare of a match. For they had forgotten about matches. 'Where is my Time Machine?' I began, bawling like an angry child, laying hands upon them and shaking them up together. It must have been very queer to them. Some laughed, most of them looked sorely frightened. When I saw them standing round me, it came into my head that I was doing as foolish a thing as it was possible for me to do under the circumstances, in trying to revive the sensation of fear. For, reasoning from their daylight behaviour, I thought that fear must be forgotten.

"Abruptly, I dashed down the match, and knocking one of the people over in my course, went blundering across the big dining-hall again, out under the moonlight. I heard cries of terror and their little feet running and stumbling this way and that. I do not remember all I did as the moon crept up the sky. I suppose it was the unexpected nature of my loss that maddened me. I felt hopelessly cut off from my own kind—a strange animal in an unknown world. I must have raved to and fro, screaming and crying upon God and Fate. I have a memory of horrible fatigue, as the long night of despair wore away; of looking in this impossible place and that; of groping among moonlit ruins and touching strange creatures in the black shadows; at last, of lying on the ground near the sphinx, and weeping with absolute wretchedness, even anger at the folly of leaving the machine having leaked away with my strength. I had nothing left but misery. Then I slept, and when I woke again it was full day, and a couple of sparrows were hopping round me on the turf within reach of my arm.

"I sat up in the freshness of the morning, trying to remember how I had got there, and why I had such a profound sense of desertion and despair. Then things came clear in my mind. With the plain, reasonable daylight, I could look my circumstances fairly in the face. I saw the wild folly of my frenzy overnight, and I could reason with myself. Suppose the worst? I said. Suppose the machine altogether lost—perhaps destroyed? It behoves me to be calm and patient, to learn the way of the people, to get a clear idea of the method of my loss, and the means of getting materials and tools; so that in the end, perhaps, I may make another. That would be my only hope, a poor hope, perhaps, but better than despair. And, after all, it was a beautiful and curious world.

"But probably the machine had only been taken away. Still, I must be calm and patient, find its hiding-place, and recover it by force or cunning. And with that I scrambled to my feet and looked about me, wondering where I could bathe. I felt weary, stiff, and travel-soiled. The freshness of the morning made me desire an equal freshness. I had exhausted my emotion. Indeed, as I went about my business, I found myself wondering at my intense excitement overnight. I made a careful examination of the ground about the little lawn. I wasted some time in futile questionings, conveyed, as well as I was able, to such of the little people as came by. They all failed to understand my gestures: some were simply stolid; some thought it was a jest, and laughed at me. I had the hardest task in the world to keep my hands off their pretty laughing faces. It was a foolish impulse, but the devil begotten of fear and blind anger was ill curbed and still eager to take advantage of my perplexity. The turf gave better counsel. I found a groove ripped in it, about midway between the pedestal of the sphinx and the marks of my feet where, on arrival, I had struggled with the overturned machine. There were other signs of removal about, with queer narrow footprints like those I could imagine made by a sloth. This directed my closer attention to the pedestal. It was, as I think I have said, of bronze. It was not a mere block, but highly decorated with deep framed panels on either side. I went and rapped at these. The pedestal was hollow. Examining the panels with care, I found them discontinuous with the frames. There were no handles or keyholes, but possibly the panels, if they were doors as I supposed, opened from within. One thing was clear enough to my mind. It took no very great mental effort to infer that my Time Machine was inside that pedestal. But how it got there was a different problem.

"I saw the heads of two orange-clad people coming through the bushes and under some blossom-covered apple-trees towards me. I turned smiling to them, and beckoned them to me. They came, and then, pointing to the bronze pedestal, I tried to intimate my wish to open it. But at my first gesture towards this they behaved very oddly. I don't know how to convey their expression to you. Suppose you were to use a grossly improper gesture to a delicate-minded woman—it is how she would look. They went off as if they had received the last possible insult. I tried a sweet-looking little chap in white next, with exactly the same result. Somehow, his manner made me feel ashamed of myself. But, as you know, I wanted the Time Machine, and I tried him once more. As he turned off, like the others, my temper got the better of me. In three strides I was after him, had him by the loose part of his robe round the neck, and began dragging him towards the sphinx.

Then I saw the horror and repugnance of his face, and all of a sudden I let him go.

"But I was not beaten yet. I banged with my fist at the bronze panels. I thought I heard something stir inside—to be explicit, I thought I heard a sound like a chuckle—but I must have been mistaken. Then I got a big pebble from the river, and came and hammered till I had flattened a coil in the decorations, and the verdigris came off in powdery flakes. The delicate little people must have heard me hammering in gusty outbreaks a mile away on either hand, but nothing came of it. I saw a crowd of them upon the slopes, looking furtively at me. At last, hot and tired, I sat down to watch the place. But I was too restless to watch long; I am too Occidental for a long vigil. I could work at a problem for years, but to wait inactive for twenty-four hours—that is another matter.

"I got up after a time, and began walking aimlessly through the bushes towards the hill again. 'Patience,' said I to myself. 'If you want your machine again you must leave that sphinx alone. If they mean to take your machine away, it's little good your wrecking their bronze panels, and if they don't, you will get it back as soon as you can ask for it. To sit among all those unknown things before a puzzle like that is hopeless. That way lies monomania. Face this world. Learn its ways, watch it, be careful of too hasty guesses at its meaning. In the end you will find clues to it all.' Then suddenly the humour of the situation came into my mind: the thought of the years I had spent in study and toil to get into the future age, and now my passion of anxiety to get out of it. I had made myself the most complicated and the most hopeless trap that ever a man devised. Although it was at my own expense, I could not help myself. I laughed aloud.

"Going through the big palace, it seemed to me that the little people avoided me. It may have been my fancy, or it may have had something to do with my hammering at the gates of bronze. Yet I felt tolerably sure of the avoidance. I was careful, however, to show no concern, and to abstain from any pursuit of them, and in the course of a day or two things got back to the old footing. I made what progress I could in the language, and, in addition, I pushed my explorations here and there. Either I missed some subtle point, or their language was excessively simple—almost exclusively composed of concrete substantives and verbs. There seemed to be few, if any, abstract terms, or little use of figurative language. Their sentences were usually simple and of two words, and I failed to convey or understand any but the simplest propositions. I determined to put the thought of my Time Machine, and the mystery of the bronze doors under the sphinx, as much as possible in a corner of memory, until my growing knowledge would lead me back to them in a natural way. Yet a certain feeling, you may understand, tethered me in a circle of a few miles round the point of my arrival.

CHAPTER 8

EXPLANATION

"So far as I could see, all the world displayed the same exuberant richness as the Thames valley. From every hill I climbed I saw the same abundance of splendid buildings, endlessly varied in material and style; the same clustering thickets of evergreens, the same blossom-laden trees and tree ferns. Here and there water shone like silver, and beyond, the land rose into blue undulating hills, and so faded into the serenity of the sky. A peculiar feature, which presently attracted my attention, was the presence of certain circular wells, several, as it seemed to me, of a very great depth. One lay by the path up the hill which I had followed during my first walk. Like the others, it was rimmed with bronze, curiously wrought, and protected by a little cupola from the rain. Sitting by the side of these wells, and peering down into the shafted darkness, I could see no gleam of water, nor could I start any reflection with a lighted match. But in all of them I heard a certain sound: a thud—thud—thud, like the beating of some big engine; and I discovered, from the flaring of my matches, that a steady current of air set down the shafts. Further, I threw a scrap of paper into the throat of one; and, instead of fluttering slowly down, it was at once sucked swiftly out of sight.

"After a time, too, I came to connect these wells with tall towers standing here and there upon the slopes; for above them there was often just such a flicker in the air as one sees on a hot day above a sun-scorched beach. Putting things together, I reached a strong suggestion of an extensive system of subterranean ventilation, whose true import it was difficult to imagine. I was at first inclined to associate it with the sanitary apparatus of these people. It was an obvious conclusion, but it was absolutely wrong.

"And here I must admit that I learned very little of drains and bells and modes of conveyance, and the like conveniences, during my time in this real future. In some of these visions of Utopias and coming times which I have read, there is a vast amount of detail about buildings, and social arrangements, and so forth. But while such details are easy enough to obtain when the whole world is contained in one's imagination, they are altogether inaccessible to a real traveller amid such realities as I found here. Conceive the tale of London which a negro, fresh from Central Africa, would take back to his tribe! What would he know of railway companies, of social movements, of telephone and telegraph wires, of the Parcels Delivery Company, and postal orders and the like? Yet we, at least, should be willing enough to explain these things to him! And even of what he knew, how much could he make his untravelled friend either apprehend or believe? Then, think how narrow the gap between a negro and a white man of our own times, and how wide the interval between myself and these of the Golden Age! I was sensible of much which was unseen, and which contributed to my comfort; but, save for a general impression of automatic organization, I fear I can convey very little of the difference to your mind.

"In the matter of sepulture, for instance, I could see no signs of crematoria nor anything suggestive of tombs. But it occurred to me that, possibly, there might be cemeteries (or crematoria) somewhere beyond the range of my explorings. This, again, was a question I deliberately put to myself, and my curiosity was at first entirely defeated upon the point. The thing puzzled me, and I was led to make a further remark, which puzzled me still more: that aged and infirm among this people there were none.

"I must confess that my satisfaction with my first theories of an automatic civilization and a decadent humanity did not long endure. Yet I could think of no other. Let me put my difficulties. The several big palaces I had explored were mere living places, great dining-halls and sleeping apartments. I could find no machinery, no appliances of any kind. Yet these people were clothed in pleasant fabrics that must at times need renewal, and their sandals, though undecorated, were fairly complex specimens of metal-work. Somehow such things must be made. And the little people displayed no vestige of a creative tendency. There were no shops, no work-shops, no sign of importations among them. They spent all their time in playing gently, in bathing in the river, in making love in a half-playful fashion, in eating fruit and sleeping. I could not see how things were kept going.

"Then, again, about the Time Machine: something, I knew not what, had taken it into the hollow pedestal of the White Sphinx. *Why?* For the life of me I could not imagine. Those waterless wells, too, those flickering pillars. I felt I lacked a clue. I felt—how shall I put it? Suppose you found an inscription, with sentences here and there in excellent plain English, and, interpolated therewith, others made up of words, of letters even, absolutely unknown to you? Well, on the third day of my visit, that was how the world of Eight Hundred and Two Thousand Seven Hundred and One presented itself to me!

"That day, too, I made a friend—of a sort. It happened that, as I was watching some of the little people bathing in a shallow, one of them was seized with cramp, and began drifting downstream. The main current ran rather swiftly, but not too strongly for even a moderate swimmer. It will give you an idea, therefore, of the strange deficiency in these creatures, when I tell you that none made the slightest attempt to rescue the weakly-crying little thing which was drowning before their eyes. When I realized this, I hurriedly slipped off my clothes, and, wading in at a point lower down, I caught the poor mite, and drew her safe to land. A little rubbing of the limbs soon brought her round, and I had the satisfaction of seeing she was all right before I left her. I had got to such a low estimate of her kind that I did not expect any gratitude from her. In that, however, I was wrong.

"This happened in the morning. In the afternoon I met my little woman, as I believe it was, as I was returning towards my centre from an exploration: and she received me with cries of delight, and presented me with a big garland of flowers—evidently made for me and me alone. The thing took my imagination. Very possibly I had been feeling desolate. At any rate I did my best to display my appreciation of the gift. We were soon seated together in a little stone arbour, engaged in conversation, chiefly of smiles. The creature's friendliness affected me exactly as a child's might have done. We passed each other flowers, and she kissed my hands. I did the same to hers. Then I tried talk, and found that her name was Weena, which, though I don't know what it meant, somehow seemed appropriate enough. That was the beginning of a queer friendship which lasted a week, and ended—as I will tell you!

"She was exactly like a child. She wanted to be with me always. She tried to follow me everywhere, and on my next journey out and about it went to my heart to tire her down, and leave her at last, exhausted and calling after me rather plaintively. But the problems of the world had to be mastered. I had not, I said to myself, come into the future to carry on a miniature flirtation. Yet her distress when I left her was very great, her expostulations at the parting were sometimes frantic, and I think, altogether, I had as much trouble as comfort from her devotion. Nevertheless she was, somehow, a very great comfort. I thought it was mere childish affection that made her cling to me. Until it was too late, I did not clearly know what I had inflicted upon her when I left her. Nor until it was too late did I clearly understand what she was to me. For, by merely seeming fond of me, and showing in her weak futile way that she cared for me, the little doll of a creature presently gave my return to the neighbourhood of the White Sphinx almost the feeling of coming home; and I would watch for her tiny figure of white and gold so soon as I came over the hill.

"It was from her, too, that I learnt that fear had not yet left the world. She was fearless enough in the daylight, and she had the oddest confidence in me; for once, in a foolish moment, I made threatening grimaces at her, and she simply laughed at them. But she dreaded the dark, dreaded shadows, dreaded black things. Darkness to her was the one thing

266

dreadful. It was a singularly passionate emotion, and it set me thinking and observing. I discovered, then, among other things, that these little people gathered into the great houses after dark, and slept in droves. To enter upon them without a light was to put them into a tumult of apprehension. I never found one out of doors, or one sleeping alone within doors, after dark. Yet I was still such a blockhead that I missed the lesson of that fear, and, in spite of Weena's distress, I insisted upon sleeping away from these slumbering multitudes.

"It troubled her greatly, but in the end her odd affection for me triumphed, and for five of the nights of our acquaintance, including the last night of all, she slept with her head pillowed on my arm. But my story slips away from me as I speak of her. It must have been the night before her rescue that I was awakened about dawn. I had been restless, dreaming most disagreeably that I was drowned, and that sea-anemones were feeling over my face with their soft palps. I woke with a start, and with an odd fancy that some greyish animal had just rushed out of the chamber. I tried to get to sleep again, but I felt restless and uncomfortable. It was that dim grey hour when things are just creeping out of darkness, when everything is colourless and clear cut, and yet unreal. I got up, and went down into the great hall, and so out upon the flagstones in front of the palace. I thought I would make a virtue of necessity, and see the sunrise.

"The moon was setting, and the dying moonlight and the first pallor of dawn were mingled in a ghastly half-light. The bushes were inky black, the ground a sombre grey, the sky colourless and cheerless. And up the hill I thought I could see ghosts. There several times, as I scanned the slope, I saw white figures. Twice I fancied I saw a solitary white, ape-like creature running rather quickly up the hill, and once near the ruins I saw a leash of them carrying some dark body. They moved hastily. I did not see what became of them. It seemed that they vanished among the bushes. The dawn was still indistinct, you must understand. I was feeling that chill, uncertain, early-morning feeling you may have known. I doubted my eyes.

"As the eastern sky grew brighter, and the light of the day came on and its vivid colouring returned upon the world once more, I scanned the view keenly. But I saw no vestige of my white figures. They were mere creatures of the half-light. 'They must have been ghosts,' I said; 'I wonder whence they dated.' For a queer notion of Grant Allen's came into my head, and amused me. If each generation die and leave ghosts, he argued, the world at last will get overcrowded with them. On that theory they would have grown innumerable some Eight Hundred Thousand Years hence, and it was no great wonder to see four at once. But the jest was unsatisfying, and I was thinking of these figures all the morning, until Weena's rescue drove them out of my head. I associated them in some indefinite way with the white animal I had startled in my first passionate search for the Time Machine. But Weena was a pleasant substitute. Yet all the same, they were soon destined to take far deadlier possession of my mind.

"I think I have said how much hotter than our own was the weather of this Golden Age. I cannot account for it. It may be that the sun was hotter, or the earth nearer the sun. It is usual to assume that the sun will go on cooling steadily in the future. But people, unfamiliar with such speculations as those of the younger Darwin, forget that the planets must ultimately fall back one by one into the parent body. As these catastrophes occur, the sun will blaze with renewed energy; and it may be that some inner planet had suffered this fate. Whatever the reason, the fact remains that the sun was very much hotter than we know it.

"Well, one very hot morning—my fourth, I think—as I was seeking shelter from the heat and glare in a colossal ruin near the great house where I slept and fed, there happened this strange thing. Clambering among these heaps of masonry, I found a narrow gallery, whose end and side windows were blocked by fallen masses of stone. By contrast with the brilliancy outside, it seemed at first impenetrably dark to me. I entered it groping, for the change from light to blackness made spots of colour swim before me. Suddenly I halted spellbound. A pair of eyes, luminous by reflection against the daylight without, was watching me out of the darkness.

"The old instinctive dread of wild beasts came upon me. I clenched my hands and steadfastly looked into the glaring eyeballs. I was afraid to turn. Then the thought of the absolute security in which humanity appeared to be living came to my mind. And then I remembered that strange terror of the dark. Overcoming my fear to some extent, I advanced a step and spoke. I will admit that my voice was harsh and ill-controlled. I put out my hand and touched something soft. At once the eyes darted sideways, and something white ran past me. I turned with my heart in my mouth, and saw a queer little ape-like figure, its head held down in a peculiar manner, running across the sunlit space behind me. It blundered against a block of granite, staggered aside, and in a moment was hidden in a black shadow beneath another pile of ruined masonry.

"My impression of it is, of course, imperfect; but I know it was a dull white, and had strange large greyish-red eyes; also that there was flaxen hair on its head and down its back. But, as I say, it went too fast for me to see distinctly. I cannot even say whether it ran on all fours, or only with its forearms held very low. After an instant's pause I followed it into the second heap of ruins. I could not find it at first; but, after a time in the profound obscurity, I came upon one of those round well-like openings of which I have told you, half closed by a fallen pillar. A sudden thought came to me. Could this Thing have vanished down the shaft? I lit a match, and, looking down, I saw a small, white, moving creature, with large bright eyes which regarded me steadfastly as it retreated. It made me shudder. It was so like a human spider! It was clambering down the wall, and now I saw for the first time a number of metal foot- and hand-rests forming a kind of ladder down the shaft. Then the light burned my fingers and fell out of my hand, going out as it dropped, and when I had lit another the little monster had disappeared.

"I do not know how long I sat peering down that well. It was not for some time that I could succeed in persuading myself that the thing I had seen was human. But, gradually, the truth dawned on me: that Man had not remained one species, but had differentiated into two distinct animals: that my graceful children of the Upper World were not the sole descendants of our generation, but that this bleached, obscene, nocturnal Thing, which had flashed before me, was also heir to all the ages.

"I thought of the flickering pillars and of my theory of an underground ventilation. I began to suspect their true import. And what, I wondered, was this Lemur doing in my scheme of a perfectly balanced organization? How was it related to the indolent serenity of the beautiful Overworlders? And what was hidden down there, at the foot of that shaft? I sat upon the edge of the well telling myself that, at any rate, there was nothing to fear, and that there I must descend for the solution of my difficulties. And withal I was absolutely afraid to go! As I hesitated, two of the beautiful Upperworld people came running in their amorous sport across the daylight into the shadow. The male pursued the female, flinging flowers at her as he ran.

"They seemed distressed to find me, my arm against the overturned pillar, peering down the well. Apparently it was considered bad form to remark these apertures; for when I pointed to this one, and tried to frame a question about it in their tongue, they were still more visibly distressed and turned away. But they were interested by my matches, and I struck some to amuse them. I tried them again about the well, and again I failed. So presently I left them, meaning to go back to Weena, and see what I could get from her. But my mind was already in revolution; my guesses and impressions were slipping and sliding to a new adjustment. I had now a clue to the import of these wells, to the ventilating towers, to the mystery of the ghosts: to say nothing of a hint at the meaning of the bronze gates and the fate of the Time Machine! And very vaguely there came a suggestion towards the solution of the economic problem that had puzzled me.

"Here was the new view. Plainly, this second species of Man was subterranean. There were three circumstances in particular which made me think that its rare emergence above ground was the outcome of a long-continued underground habit. In the first place, there was the bleached look common in most animals that live largely in the dark—the white fish of the Kentucky caves, for instance. Then, those large eyes, with that capacity for reflecting light, are common features of nocturnal things—witness the owl and the cat. And last of all, that evident confusion in the sunshine, that hasty yet fumbling and awkward flight towards dark shadow, and that peculiar carriage of the head while in the light—all reinforced the theory of an extreme sensitiveness of the retina.

"Beneath my feet then the earth must be tunnelled enormously, and these tunnellings were the habitat of the New

Race. The presence of ventilating-shafts and wells along the hill slopes—everywhere, in fact, except along the river valley—showed how universal were its ramifications. What so natural, then, as to assume that it was in this artificial Underworld that such work as was necessary to the comfort of the daylight race was done? The notion was so plausible that I at once accepted it and went on to assume the *how* of this splitting of the human species. I daresay you will anticipate the shape of my theory, though, for myself, I very soon felt that it fell far short of the truth.

"At first, proceeding from the problems of our own age, it seemed clear as daylight to me that the gradual widening of the present merely temporary and social difference between the Capitalist and the Labourer was the key to the whole position. No doubt it will seem grotesque enough to you—and wildly incredible!—and yet even now there are existing circumstances to point that way. There is a tendency to utilize underground space for the less ornamental purposes of civilization; there is the Metropolitan Railway in London, for instance, there are new electric railways, there are subways, there are underground workrooms and restaurants, and they increase and multiply. Evidently, I thought, this tendency had increased till Industry had gradually lost its birthright in the sky. I mean that it had gone deeper and deeper into larger and ever larger under-ground factories, spending a still-increasing amount of its time therein, till, in the end——! Even now, does not an East End* worker live in such artificial conditions as practically to be cut off from the natural surface of the earth?

"Again, the exclusive tendency of richer people—due, no doubt, to the increasing refinement of their education, and the

---

* **East End.** An industrial, dock, and slum area in London.

widening gulf between them and the rude violence of the poor—is already leading to the closing, in their interest, of considerable portions of the surface of the land. About London, for instance, perhaps half the prettier country is shut in against intrusion. And this same widening gulf—which is due to the length and expense of the higher educational process and the increased facilities for and temptations towards refined habits on the part of the rich—will make that exchange between class and class, that promotion by intermarriage which at present retards the splitting of our species along lines of social stratification, less and less frequent. So, in the end, above ground you must have the Haves, pursuing pleasure and comfort and beauty, and below ground the Have-nots; the Workers getting continually adapted to the conditions of their labour. Once they were there, they would, no doubt, have to pay rent, and not a little of it, for the ventilation of their caverns; and if they refused, they would starve or be suffocated for arrears. Such of them as were so constituted as to be miserable and rebellious would die; and, in the end, the balance being permanent, the survivors would become as well adapted to the conditions of underground life, and as happy in their way, as the Overworld people were to theirs. As it seemed to me, the refined beauty and the etiolated pallor followed naturally enough.

"The great triumph of Humanity I had dreamed of took a different shape in my mind. It had been no such triumph of moral education and general cooperation as I had imagined. Instead, I saw a real aristocracy, armed with a perfected science and working to a logical conclusion the industrial system of today. Its triumph had not been simply a triumph over nature, but a triumph over nature and the fellow-man. This, I must warn you, was my theory at the time. I had no convenient cicerone in the pattern of the Utopian books. My

273

explanation may be absolutely wrong. I still think it is the most plausible one. But even on this supposition the balanced civilization that was at last attained must have long since passed its zenith, and was now far fallen into decay. The too-perfect security of the Overworlders had led them to a slow movement of degeneration, to a general dwindling in size, strength, and intelligence. That I could see clearly enough already. What had happened to the Undergrounders I did not yet suspect; but, from what I had seen of the Morlocks— that, by the bye, was the name by which these creatures were called—I could imagine that the modification of the human type was even far more profound than among the 'Eloi,' the beautiful race that I already knew.

"Then came troublesome doubts. Why had the Morlocks taken my Time Machine? For I felt sure it was they who had taken it. Why, too, if the Eloi were masters, could they not restore the machine to me? And why were they so terribly afraid of the dark? I proceeded, as I have said, to question Weena about this Underworld, but here again I was disappointed. At first she would not understand my questions, and presently she refused to answer them. She shivered as though the topic was unendurable. And when I pressed her, perhaps a little harshly, she burst into tears. They were the only tears, except my own, I ever saw in that Golden Age. When I saw them I ceased abruptly to trouble about the Morlocks, and was only concerned in banishing these signs of her human inheritance from Weena's eyes. And very soon she was smiling and clapping her hands, while I solemnly burnt a match.

The Time Machine

H. G. Wells

CHAPTER 9

THE MORLOCKS

It may seem odd to you, but it was two days before I could follow up the new-found clue in what was manifestly the proper way. I felt a peculiar shrinking from those pallid bodies. They were just the half-bleached colour of the worms and things one sees preserved in spirit in a zoological museum. And they were filthily cold to the touch. Probably my shrinking was largely due to the sympathetic influence of the Eloi, whose disgust of the Morlocks I now began to appreciate.

"The next night I did not sleep well. Probably my health was a little disordered. I was oppressed with perplexity and doubt. Once or twice I had a feeling of intense fear for which I could perceive no definite reason. I remember creeping noiselessly into the great hall where the little people were sleeping in the moonlight—that night Weena was among them—and feeling reassured by their presence. It occurred to me, even then, that in the course of a few days the moon must pass through its last quarter, and the nights grow dark,

when the appearances of these unpleasant creatures from
below, these whitened Lemurs, this new vermin that had
replaced the old, might be more abundant. And on both these
days I had the restless feeling of one who shirks an inevitable
duty. I felt assured that the Time Machine was only to be
recovered by boldly penetrating these mysteries of underground. Yet I could not face the mystery. If only I had had a
companion it would have been different. But I was so horribly alone, and even to clamber down into the darkness of the
well appalled me. I don't know if you will understand my feeling, but I never felt quite safe at my back.

"It was this restlessness, this insecurity, perhaps, that drove
me further and further afield in my exploring expeditions.
Going to the southwestward towards the rising country that
is now called Combe Wood, I observed far off, in the direction of nineteenth-century Banstead, a vast green structure,
different in character from any I had hitherto seen. It was
larger than the largest of the palaces or ruins I knew, and the
façade had an Oriental look: the face of it having the lustre,
as well as the pale-green tint, a kind of bluish-green, of a
certain type of Chinese porcelain. This difference in aspect
suggested a difference in use, and I was minded to push on
and explore. But the day was growing late, and I had come
upon the sight of the place after a long and tiring circuit;
so I resolved to hold over the adventure for the following day,
and I returned to the welcome and the caresses of little
Weena. But next morning I perceived clearly enough that
my curiosity regarding the Palace of Green Porcelain was a
piece of self-deception, to enable me to shirk, by another
day, an experience I dreaded. I resolved I would make the
descent without further waste of time, and started out in the
early morning towards a well near the ruins of granite and
aluminum.

"Little Weena ran with me. She danced beside me to the well, but when she saw me lean over the mouth and look downward, she seemed strangely disconcerted. 'Goodbye, little Weena,' I said, kissing her; and then, putting her down, I began to feel over the parapet for the climbing hooks. Rather hastily, I may as well confess, for I feared my courage might leak away! At first she watched me in amazement. Then she gave a most piteous cry, and, running to me, began to pull at me with her little hands. I think her opposition nerved me rather to proceed. I shook her off, perhaps a little roughly, and in another moment I was in the throat of the well. I saw her agonized face over the parapet, and smiled to reassure her. Then I had to look down at the unstable hooks to which I clung.

"I had to clamber down a shaft of perhaps two hundred yards. The descent was effected by means of metallic bars projecting from the sides of the well, and these being adapted to the needs of a creature much smaller and lighter than myself, I was speedily cramped and fatigued by the descent. And not simply fatigued! One of the bars bent suddenly under my weight, and almost swung me off into the blackness beneath. For a moment I hung by one hand, and after that experience I did not dare to rest again. Though my arms and back were presently acutely painful, I went on clambering down the sheer descent with as quick a motion as possible. Glancing upward, I saw the aperture, a small blue disk, in which a star was visible, while little Weena's head showed as a round black projection. The thudding sound of a machine below grew louder and more oppressive. Everything save that little disk above was profoundly dark, and when I looked up again Weena had disappeared.

"I was in an agony of discomfort. I had some thought of trying to go up the shaft again and leave the Underworld alone. But even while I turned this over in my mind I continued to descend. At last, with intense relief, I saw dimly coming up, a foot to the right of me, a slender loophole in the wall. Swinging myself in, I found it was the aperture of a narrow horizontal tunnel in which I could lie down and rest. It was not too soon. My arms ached, my back was cramped, and I was trembling with the prolonged terror of a fall. Besides this, the unbroken darkness had had a distressing effect upon my eyes. The air was full of the throb-and-hum of machinery pumping air down the shaft.

"I do not know how long I lay. I was roused by a soft hand touching my face. Starting up in the darkness, I snatched at my matches, and, hastily striking one, I saw three stooping white creatures similar to the one I had seen above ground in the ruin, hastily retreating before the light. Living, as they did, in what appeared to me impenetrable darkness, their eyes were abnormally large and sensitive, just as are the pupils of the abysmal fishes, and they reflected the light in the same way. I have no doubt they could see me in that rayless obscurity, and they did not seem to have any fear of me apart from the light. But, so soon as I struck a match in order to see them, they fled incontinently, vanishing into dark gutters and tunnels, from which their eyes glared at me in the strangest fashion.

"I tried to call to them, but the language they had was apparently different from that of the Overworld people; so that I was needs left to my own unaided efforts, and the thought of flight before exploration was even then in my mind. But I said to myself, 'You are in for it now,' and, feeling my way along the tunnel, I found the noise of machinery grow louder. Presently the walls fell away from me, and I came to a large open space, and, striking another match, saw that I had entered a vast arched cavern, which stretched into utter darkness beyond the range of my light. The view I had of it was as much as one could see in the burning of a match.

"Necessarily my memory is vague. Great shapes like big machines rose out of the dimness, and cast grotesque black shadows, in which dim spectral Morlocks sheltered from the glare. The place, by the bye, was very stuffy and oppressive, and the faint halitus of freshly shed blood was in the air. Some way down the central vista was a little table of white metal, laid with what seemed a meal. The Morlocks at any rate were carnivorous! Even at the time, I remember wondering what large animal could have survived to furnish the red joint I saw. It was all very indistinct: the heavy smell, the big unmeaning shapes, the obscene figures lurking in the shadows and only waiting for the darkness to come at me again! Then the match burnt down, and stung my fingers, and fell, a wriggling red spot in the blackness.

"I have thought since how particularly ill-equipped I was for such an experience. When I had started with the Time Machine, I had started with the absurd assumption that the men of the Future would certainly be infinitely ahead of ourselves in all their appliances. I had come without arms, without medicine, without anything to smoke—at times I missed tobacco frightfully!—even without enough matches. If only I had thought of a Kodak! I could have flashed that glimpse of the Underworld in a second, and examined it at leisure. But, as it was, I stood there with only the weapons and the powers that Nature had endowed me with—hands, feet, and teeth; these, and four safety matches that still remained to me.

"I was afraid to push my way in among all this machinery in the dark, and it was only with my last glimpse of light I discovered that my store of matches had run low. It had never occurred to me until that moment that there was any need to economize them, and I had wasted almost half the box in astonishing the Overworlders, to whom fire was a novelty. Now, as I say, I had four left, and while I stood in the dark, a hand touched mine, lank fingers came feeling over my face, and I was sensible of a peculiar unpleasant odour. I fancied I heard the breathing of a crowd of those dreadful little beings about me. I felt the box of matches in my hand being gently disengaged, and other hands behind me plucking at my clothing. The sense of these unseen creatures examining me was indescribably unpleasant. The sudden realization of my ignorance of their ways of thinking and doing came home to me very vividly in the darkness. I shouted at them as loudly as I could. They started away, and then I could feel them approaching me again. They clutched at me more boldly, whispering odd sounds to each other. I shivered violently, and shouted again—rather discordantly. This time they were not so seriously alarmed, and they made a queer laughing noise as they came back to me. I will confess I was horribly frightened. I determined to strike another match and escape under the protection of its glare. I did so, and, eking out the flicker with a scrap of paper from my pocket, I made good my retreat to the narrow tunnel. But I had scarce entered this when my light was blown out, and in the blackness I could hear the Morlocks rustling like wind among leaves, and pattering like the rain, as they hurried after me.

"In a moment I was clutched by several hands, and there was no mistaking that they were trying to haul me back. I struck another light, and waved it in their dazzled faces. You can scarce imagine how nauseatingly inhuman they looked— those pale, chinless faces and great, lidless, pinkish-grey eyes!—as they stared in their blindness and bewilderment. But I did not stay to look, I promise you: I retreated again, and when my second match had ended, I struck my third.

It had almost burnt through when I reached the opening into the shaft. I lay down on the edge, for the throb of the great pump below made me giddy. Then I felt sideways for the projecting hooks, and, as I did so, my feet were grasped from behind, and I was violently tugged backward. I lit my last match . . . and it incontinently went out. But I had my hand on the climbing bars now, and, kicking violently, I disengaged myself from the clutches of the Morlocks, and was speedily clambering up the shaft, while they stayed peering and blinking up at me: all but one little wretch who followed me for some way and well-nigh secured my boot as a trophy.

"That climb seemed interminable to me. With the last twenty or thirty feet of it a deadly nausea came upon me. I had the greatest difficulty in keeping my hold. The last few yards were a frightful struggle against this faintness. Several times my head swam, and I felt all the sensations of falling. At last, however, I got over the well-mouth somehow, and staggered out of the ruin into the blinding sunlight. I fell upon my face. Even the soil smelt sweet and clean. Then I remember Weena kissing my hands and ears, and the voices of others among the Eloi. Then, for a time, I was insensible.

CHAPTER 10

WHEN THE NIGHT CAME

"Now, indeed, I seemed in a worse case than before. Hitherto, except during my night's anguish at the loss of the Time Machine, I had felt a sustaining hope of ultimate escape, but that hope was staggered by these new discoveries. Hitherto I had merely thought myself impeded by the childish simplicity of the little people, and by some unknown forces which I had only to understand to overcome; but there was an altogether new element in the sickening quality of the Morlocks—a something inhuman and malign. Instinctively I loathed them. Before, I had felt as a man might feel who had fallen into a pit: my concern was with the pit and how to get out of it. Now I felt like a beast in a trap, whose enemy would come upon him soon.

"The enemy I dreaded may surprise you. It was the darkness of the new moon. Weena had put this into my head by some at first incomprehensible remarks about the Dark Nights. It was not now such a very difficult problem to guess what the coming Dark Nights might mean. The moon was on the wane: each night there was a longer interval of darkness. And I now understood to some slight degree at least the reason of the fear of the little Upperworld people for the dark. I wondered vaguely what foul villainy it might be that the Morlocks did under the new moon. I felt pretty sure now that my second hypothesis was all wrong. The Upperworld people might once have been the favoured aristocracy, and the Morlocks their mechanical servants; but that had long since passed away. The two species that had resulted from the evolution of man were sliding down towards, or had already arrived at, an altogether new relationship. The Eloi, like the Carlovingian kings, had decayed to a mere beautiful futility. They still possessed the earth on sufferance: since the Morlocks, subterranean for innumerable generations, had come at last to find the daylit surface intolerable. And the Morlocks made their garments, I inferred, and maintained them in their habitual needs, perhaps through the survival of an old habit of service. They did it as a standing horse paws with his foot, or as a man enjoys killing animals in sport: because ancient and departed necessities had impressed it on the organism. But, clearly, the old order was already in part reversed. The nemesis of the delicate ones was creeping on apace. Ages ago, thousands of generations ago, man had thrust his brother man out of the ease and the sunshine. And now that brother was coming back—changed! Already the Eloi had begun to learn one old lesson anew. They were becoming reacquainted with Fear. And suddenly there came into my head the memory of the meat I had seen in the Underworld. It seemed odd how it floated into my mind: not stirred up as it were by the current of my meditations, but coming in almost like a question from outside. I tried to recall the form of it. I had a vague sense of something familiar, but I could not tell what it was at the time.

"Still, however helpless the little people in the presence of their mysterious Fear, I was differently constituted. I came out of this age of ours, this ripe prime of the human race, when Fear does not paralyze and mystery has lost its terrors. I at least would defend myself. Without further delay I determined to make myself arms and a fastness where I might sleep. With that refuge as a base, I could face this strange world with some of that confidence I had lost in realizing to what creatures night by night I lay exposed. I felt I could never sleep again until my bed was secure from them. I shuddered with horror to think how they must already have examined me.

"I wandered during the afternoon along the valley of the Thames, but found nothing that commended itself to my mind as inaccessible. All the buildings and trees seemed easily practicable to such dexterous climbers as the Morlocks, to judge by their wells, must be. Then the tall pinnacles of the Palace of Green Porcelain and the polished gleam of its walls came back to my memory; and in the evening, taking Weena like a child upon my shoulder, I went up the hills towards the southwest. The distance, I had reckoned, was seven or eight miles, but it must have been nearer eighteen. I had first seen the place on a moist afternoon when distances are deceptively diminished. In addition, the heel of one of my shoes was loose, and a nail was working through the sole—they were comfortable old shoes I wore about indoors—so that I was lame. And it was already long past sunset when I came in sight of the palace, silhouetted black against the pale yellow of the sky.

"Weena had been hugely delighted when I began to carry her, but after a time she desired me to let her down, and ran along by the side of me, occasionally darting off on either hand to pick flowers to stick in my pockets. My pockets had always puzzled Weena, but at the last she had concluded that they were an eccentric kind of vase for floral decoration. At least she utilized them for that purpose. And that reminds me! In changing my jacket I found . . ."

The Time Traveller paused, put his hand into his pocket, and silently placed two withered flowers, not unlike very large white mallows, upon the little table. Then he resumed his narrative.

"As the hush of evening crept over the world and we proceeded over the hill crest towards Wimbledon, Weena grew tired and wanted to return to the house of grey stone. But I pointed out the distant pinnacles of the Palace of Green Porcelain to her, and contrived to make her understand that we were seeking a refuge there from her Fear. You know that great pause that comes upon things before the dusk? Even the breeze stops in the trees. To me there is always an air of expectation about that evening stillness. The sky was clear, remote, and empty save for a few horizontal bars far down in the sunset. Well, that night the expectation took the colour of my fears. In that darkling calm my senses seemed preternaturally sharpened. I fancied I could even feel the hollowness of the ground beneath my feet: could, indeed, almost see through it the Morlocks on their ant-hill going hither and thither and waiting for the dark. In my excitement I fancied that they would receive my invasion of their burrows as a declaration of war. And why had they taken my Time Machine?

"So we went on in the quiet, and the twilight deepened into night. The clear blue of the distance faded, and one star after another came out. The ground grew dim and the trees black. Weena's fears and her fatigue grew upon her. I took her in my arms and talked to her and caressed her. Then, as the darkness grew deeper, she put her arms round my neck, and, closing her eyes, tightly pressed her face against my shoulder. So we went down a long slope into a valley, and there in the dimness I almost walked into a little river. This I waded, and went up the opposite side of the valley, past a number of sleeping-houses, and by a statue—a Faun, or some such figure, *minus* the head. Here, too, were acacias. So far I had seen nothing of the Morlocks, but it was yet early in the night, and the darker hours before the old moon rose were still to come.

"From the brow of the next hill I saw a thick wood spreading wide and black before me. I hesitated at this. I could see no end to it, either to the right or the left. Feeling tired—my feet in particular were very sore—I carefully lowered Weena from my shoulder as I halted and sat down upon the turf. I could no longer see the Palace of Green Porcelain, and I was in doubt of my direction. I looked into the thickness of the wood and thought of what it might hide. Under that dense tangle of branches one would be out of sight of the stars. Even were there no other lurking danger—a danger I did not care to let my imagination loose upon—there would still be all the roots to stumble over and the tree boles to strike against. I was very tired, too, after the excitements of the day; so I decided that I would not face it, but would pass the night upon the open hill.

"Weena, I was glad to find, was fast asleep. I carefully wrapped her in my jacket, and sat down beside her to wait for the moonrise. The hillside was quiet and deserted, but from the black of the wood there came now and then a stir of living things. Above me shone the stars, for the night was very clear. I felt a certain sense of friendly comfort in their twinkling. All the old constellations had gone from the sky, however: that slow movement which is imperceptible in a hundred human lifetimes, had long since rearranged them in unfamiliar groupings. But the Milky Way, it seemed to me, was still the same tattered streamer of stardust as of yore. Southward (as I judged it) was a very bright red star that was new to me: it was even more splendid than our own green Sirius. And amid all these scintillating points of light one bright planet shone kindly and steadily like the face of an old friend.

"Looking at these stars suddenly dwarfed my own troubles and all the gravities of terrestrial life. I thought of their unfathomable distance, and the slow inevitable drift of their movements out of the unknown past into the unknown future. I thought of the great precessional cycle that the pole of the earth describes. Only forty times had that silent revolution occurred during all the years that I had traversed. And during these few revolutions all the activity, all the traditions, the complex organizations, the nations, languages, literatures, aspirations, even the mere memory of Man as I knew him, had been swept out of existence. Instead were these frail creatures who had forgotten their high ancestry, and the white Things of which I went in terror. Then I thought of the Great Fear that was between the two species, and for the first time, with a sudden shiver, came the clear knowledge of what the meat I had seen might be. Yet it was too horrible! I looked at little Weena sleeping beside me, her face white and star-like under the stars, and forthwith dismissed the thought.

"Through that long night I held my mind off the Morlocks as well as I could, and whiled away the time by trying to fancy I could find signs of the old constellations in the new confusion. The sky kept very clear, except for a hazy cloud or so. No doubt I dozed at times. Then, as my vigil wore on, came a faintness in the eastward sky, like the reflection of some colourless fire, and the old moon rose, thin and peaked and white. And close behind, and overtaking it, and overflowing it, the dawn came, pale at first, and then growing pink and warm. No Morlocks had approached us. Indeed, I had seen none upon the hill that night. And in the confidence of renewed day it almost seemed to me that my fear had been unreasonable. I stood up and found my foot with the loose heel swollen at the ankle and painful under the heel; so I sat down again, took off my shoes, and flung them away.

"I awakened Weena, and we went down into the wood, now green and pleasant instead of black and forbidding. We found some fruit wherewith to break our fast. We soon met others of the dainty ones, laughing and dancing in the sunlight as though there was no such thing in nature as the night. And then I thought once more of the meat that I had seen. I felt assured now of what it was, and from the bottom of my heart I pitied this last feeble rill from the great flood of humanity. Clearly, at some time in the Long-Ago of human decay the Morlocks' food had run short. Possibly they had lived on rats and suchlike vermin. Even now man is far less discriminating and exclusive in his food than he was—far less than any monkey. His prejudice against human flesh is no deep-seated instinct. And so these inhuman sons of men——! I tried to look at the thing in a scientific spirit. After all, they were less human and more remote than our cannibal ancestors of three or four thousand years ago. And the intelligence that would have made this state of things a torment had gone.

287

Why should I trouble myself? These Eloi were mere fatted cattle, which the ant-like Morlocks preserved and preyed upon—probably saw to the breeding of. And there was Weena dancing at my side!

"Then I tried to preserve myself from the horror that was coming upon me, by regarding it as a rigorous punishment of human selfishness. Man had been content to live in ease and delight upon the labours of his fellow-man, had taken Necessity as his watchword and excuse, and in the fulness of time Necessity had come home to him. I even tried a Carlyle-like scorn of this wretched aristocracy-in-decay. But this attitude of mind was impossible. However great their intellectual degradation, the Eloi had kept too much of the human form not to claim my sympathy, and to make me perforce a sharer in their degradation and their Fear.

"I had at that time very vague ideas as to the course I should pursue. My first was to secure some safe place of refuge, and to make myself such arms of metal or stone as I could contrive. That necessity was immediate. In the next place, I hoped to procure some means of fire, so that I should have the weapon of a torch at hand, for nothing, I knew, would be more efficient against these Morlocks. Then I wanted to arrange some contrivance to break open the doors of bronze under the White Sphinx. I had in mind a battering-ram. I had a persuasion that if I could enter these doors and carry a blaze of light before me I should discover the Time Machine and escape. I could not imagine the Morlocks were strong enough to move it far away. Weena I had resolved to bring with me to our own time. And, turning such schemes over in my mind, I pursued our way towards the building which my fancy had chosen as our dwelling.

CHAPTER 11

THE PALACE OF GREEN PORCELAIN

"I found the Palace of Green Porcelain, when we approached it about noon, deserted and falling into ruin. Only ragged vestiges of glass remained in its windows, and great sheets of the green facing had fallen away from the corroded metallic framework. It lay very high upon a turfy down, and looking northeastward before I entered it, I was surprised to see a large estuary, or even creek, where I judged Wandsworth and Battersea must once have been. I thought then—though I never followed up the thought—of what might have happened, or might be happening, to the living things in the sea.

"The material of the Palace proved on examination to be indeed porcelain, and along the face of it I saw an inscription in some unknown character. I thought, rather foolishly, that Weena might help me to interpret this, but I only learnt that the bare idea of writing had never entered her head. She always seemed to me, I fancy, more human than she was, perhaps because her affection was so human.

"Within the big valves of the door—which were open and broken—we found, instead of the customary hall, a long gallery lit by many side windows. At the first glance I was reminded of a museum. The tiled floor was thick with dust, and a remarkable array of miscellaneous objects was shrouded in the same grey covering. Then I perceived, standing strange and gaunt in the centre of the hall, what was clearly the lower part of a huge skeleton. I recognized by the oblique feet that it was some extinct creature after the fashion of the Megatherium. The skull and the upper bones lay beside it in the thick dust, and in one place, where rainwater had dropped through a leak in the roof, the thing itself had been worn away. Further in the gallery was the huge skeleton barrel of a

Brontosaurus. My museum hypothesis was confirmed. Going towards the side, I found what appeared to be sloping shelves, and, clearing away the thick dust, I found the old familiar glass cases of our own time. But they must have been air-tight, to judge from the fair preservation of some of their contents.

"Clearly we stood among the ruins of some latter-day South Kensington! Here, apparently, was the Palaeontological Section, and a very splendid array of fossils it must have been, though the inevitable process of decay that had been staved off for a time, and had, through the extinction of bacteria and fungi, lost ninety-nine hundredths of its force, was, nevertheless, with extreme sureness if with extreme slowness, at work again upon all its treasures. Here and there I found traces of the little people in the shape of rare fossils broken to pieces or threaded in strings upon reeds. And the cases had in some instances been bodily removed—by the Morlocks as I judged. The place was very silent. The thick dust deadened our footsteps. Weena, who had been rolling a sea-urchin down the sloping glass of a case, presently came, as I stared about me, and very quietly took my hand and stood beside me.

"And at first I was so much surprised by this ancient monument of an intellectual age, that I gave no thought to the possibilities it presented. Even my preoccupation about the Time Machine receded a little from my mind.

"To judge from the size of the place, this Palace of Green Porcelain had a great deal more in it than a Gallery of Palaeontology; possibly historical galleries; it might be, even, a library! To me, at least in my present circumstances, these would be vastly more interesting than this spectacle of old-time geology in decay. Exploring, I found another short gallery running transversely to the first. This appeared to be devoted to minerals, and the sight of a block of sulphur set my mind running on gunpowder. But I could find no saltpetre; indeed, no nitrates of any kind. Doubtless they had deliquesced ages ago. Yet the sulphur hung in my mind, and set up a train of thinking. As for the rest of the contents of that gallery, though, on the whole, they were the best preserved of all I saw, I had little interest. I am no specialist in mineralogy, and I went on down a very ruinous aisle running parallel to the first hall I had entered. Apparently this section had been devoted to natural history, but everything had long since passed out of recognition. A few shrivelled and blackened vestiges of what had once been stuffed animals, desiccated mummies in jars that had once held spirit, a brown dust of departed plants: that was all! I was sorry for that, because I should have been glad to trace the patient readjustments by which the conquest of animated nature had been attained. Then we came to a gallery of simply colossal proportions, but singularly ill-lit, the floor of it running downward at a slight angle from the end at which I entered. At intervals white globes hung from the ceiling—many of them cracked and smashed—which suggested that originally the place had been artificially lit. Here I was more in my element, for rising on either side of me were the huge bulks of big machines, all greatly corroded and many broken down, but some still fairly complete. You know I have a certain weakness for mechanism, and I was inclined to linger among these: the more so as for the most part they had the interest of puzzles, and I could make only the vaguest guesses at what they were for. I fancied that if I could solve their puzzles I should find myself in possession of powers that might be of use against the Morlocks.

"Suddenly Weena came very close to my side. So suddenly that she startled me. Had it not been for her I do not think I should have noticed that the floor of the gallery sloped at all. The end I had come in at was quite above ground, and was lit by rare slit-like windows. As you went down the length, the ground came up against these windows, until at last there was a pit like the 'area' of a London house before each, and only a narrow line of daylight at the top. I went slowly along, puzzling about the machines, and had been too intent upon them to notice the gradual diminution of the light, until Weena's increasing apprehensions drew my attention. Then I saw that the gallery ran down at last into a thick darkness. I hesitated, and then, as I looked round me, I saw that the dust was less abundant and its surface less even. Further away towards the dimness, it appeared to be broken by a number of small narrow footprints. My sense of the immediate presence of the Morlocks revived at that. I felt that I was wasting my time in this academic examination of machinery. I called to mind that it was already far advanced in the afternoon, and that I had still no weapon, no refuge, and no means of making a fire. And then down in the remote blackness of the gallery I heard a peculiar pattering and the same odd noises I had heard down the well.

"I took Weena's hand. Then, struck with a sudden idea, I left her and turned to a machine from which projected a lever not unlike those in a signal-box. Clambering upon the stand, and grasping this lever in my hands, I put all my weight upon it sideways. Suddenly Weena, deserted in the central aisle, began to whimper. I had judged the strength of the lever pretty correctly, for it snapped after a minute's strain, and I rejoined her with a mace in my hand more than sufficient, I judged, for any Morlock skull I might encounter. And I longed very much to kill a Morlock or so. Very inhuman, you may think, to want to go killing one's own descendants! But it was impossible, somehow, to feel any humanity in the things. Only my disinclination to leave Weena, and a persuasion that if I began to slake my thirst for murder my Time Machine might suffer, restrained me from going straight down the gallery and killing the brutes I heard.

"Well, mace in one hand and Weena in the other, I went out of that gallery and into another and still larger one, which at the first glance reminded me of a military chapel hung with tattered flags. The brown and charred rags that hung from the sides of it I presently recognized as the decaying vestiges of books. They had long since dropped to pieces, and every semblance of print had left them. But here and there were warped boards and cracked metallic clasps that told the tale well enough. Had I been a literary man I might, perhaps, have moralized upon the futility of all ambition. But as it was, the thing that struck me with keenest force was the enormous waste of labour to which this sombre wilderness of rotting paper testified. At the time I will confess that I thought chiefly of the *Philosophical Transactions* and my own seventeen papers upon physical optics.

"Then, going up a broad staircase, we came to what may once have been a gallery of technical chemistry. And here I had not a little hope of useful discoveries. Except at one end where the roof had collapsed, this gallery was well preserved. I went eagerly to every unbroken case. And at last, in one of the really air-tight cases, I found a box of matches. Very eagerly I tried them. They were perfectly good. They were not even damp. I turned to Weena. 'Dance,' I cried to her in her own tongue. For now I had a weapon indeed against the horrible creatures we feared. And so, in that derelict museum, upon the thick soft carpeting of dust, to Weena's huge delight, I solemnly performed a kind of composite dance, whistling 'The Land of the Leal' as cheerfully as I could. In part it was a modest cancan, in part a step dance, in part a skirt dance (so far as my tail-coat permitted), and in part original. For I am naturally inventive, as you know.

"Now, I still think that for this box of matches to have escaped the wear of time for immemorial years was a most strange, as for me it was a most fortunate, thing. Yet, oddly enough, I found a far unlikelier substance, and that was camphor. I found it in a sealed jar, that by chance, I suppose, had been really hermetically sealed. I fancied at first that it was paraffin wax, and smashed the glass accordingly. But the odour of camphor was unmistakable. In the universal decay this volatile substance had chanced to survive, perhaps through many thousands of centuries. It reminded me of a sepia painting I had once seen done from the ink of a fossil Belemnite that must have perished and become fossilized millions of years ago. I was about to throw it away, but I remembered that it was inflammable and burnt with a good bright flame—was, in fact, an excellent candle—and I put it in my pocket. I found no explosives, however, nor any means of breaking down the bronze doors. As yet my iron crowbar was the most helpful thing I had chanced upon. Nevertheless I left that gallery greatly elated.

"I cannot tell you all the story of that long afternoon. It would require a great effort of memory to recall my explorations in at all the proper order. I remember a long gallery of rusting stands of arms, and how I hesitated between my crowbar and a hatchet or a sword. I could not carry both, however, and my bar of iron promised best against the bronze gates. There were numbers of guns, pistols, and rifles. The most were masses of rust, but many were of some new metal and still fairly sound. But any cartridges or powder there may once have been had rotted into dust. One corner I saw was charred and shattered: perhaps, I thought, by an explosion among the specimens. In another place was a vast array of idols—Polynesian, Mexican, Grecian, Phoenician, every country on earth, I should think. And here, yielding to an irresistible impulse, I wrote my name upon the nose of a steatite monster from South America that particularly took my fancy.

"As the evening drew on, my interest waned. I went through gallery after gallery, dusty, silent, often ruinous, the exhibits sometimes mere heaps of rust and lignite, sometimes fresher. In one place I suddenly found myself near the model of a tin mine, and then by the merest accident I discovered, in an air-tight case, two dynamite cartridges! I shouted 'Eureka,' and smashed the case with joy. Then came a doubt. I hesitated. Then, selecting a little side gallery, I made my essay. I never felt such a disappointment as I did in waiting five, ten, fifteen minutes for an explosion that never came. Of course the things were dummies, as I might have guessed from their presence. I really believe that, had they not been so, I should have rushed off incontinently and blown sphinx, bronze doors, and (as it proved) my chances of finding the Time Machine, all together into nonexistence.

"It was after that, I think, that we came to a little open court within the palace. It was turfed, and had three fruit-trees. So we rested and refreshed ourselves. Towards sunset I began to consider our position. Night was creeping upon us, and my inaccessible hiding-place had still to be found. But that troubled me very little now. I had in my possession a thing that was, perhaps, the best of all defences against the Morlocks—I had matches! I had the camphor in my pocket, too, if a blaze were needed. It seemed to me that the best thing we could do would be to pass the night in the open, protected by a fire. In the morning there was the getting of the Time Machine. Towards that, as yet, I had only my iron mace. But now, with my growing knowledge, I felt very differently towards those bronze doors. Up to this, I had refrained from forcing them, largely because of the mystery on the other side. They had never impressed me as being very strong, and I hoped to find my bar of iron not altogether inadequate for the work.

CHAPTER 12

IN THE DARKNESS

"We emerged from the Palace while the sun was still in part above the horizon. I was determined to reach the White Sphinx early the next morning, and ere the dusk I purposed pushing through the woods that had stopped me on the previous journey. My plan was to go as far as possible that night, and then, building a fire, to sleep in the protection of its glare. Accordingly, as we went along I gathered any sticks or dried grass I saw, and presently had my arms full of such litter. Thus loaded, our progress was slower than I had anticipated, and besides, Weena was tired. And I, also, began to suffer from sleepiness too; so that it was full night before we reached the wood. Upon the shrubby hill of its edge Weena would have stopped, fearing the darkness before us; but a singular sense of impending calamity, that should indeed have served me as a warning, drove me onward. I had been without sleep for a night and two days, and I was feverish and irritable. I felt sleep coming upon me, and the Morlocks with it.

"While we hesitated, among the black bushes behind us, and dim against their blackness, I saw three crouching figures. There was scrub and long grass all about us, and I did not feel safe from their insidious approach. The forest, I calculated, was rather less than a mile across. If we could get through it to the bare hillside, there, as it seemed to me, was an altogether safer resting-place: I thought that with my matches and my camphor I could contrive to keep my path illuminated through the woods. Yet it was evident that if I was to flourish matches with my hands I should have to abandon my firewood: so, rather reluctantly, I put it down. And then it came into my head that I would amaze our friends behind by lighting it. I was to discover the atrocious folly of this proceeding, but it came to my mind as an ingenious move for covering our retreat.

"I don't know if you have ever thought what a rare thing flame must be in the absence of man and in a temperate climate. The sun's heat is rarely strong enough to burn, even when it is focussed by dewdrops, as is sometimes the case in more tropical districts. Lightning may blast and blacken, but it rarely gives rise to wide-spread fire. Decaying vegetation may occasionally smoulder with the heat of its fermentation, but this rarely results in flame. In this decadence, too, the art of fire-making had been forgotten on the earth. The red tongues that went licking up my heap of wood were an altogether new and strange thing to Weena.

"She wanted to run to it and play with it. I believe she would have cast herself into it had I not restrained her. But I caught her up, and, in spite of her struggles, plunged boldly before me into the wood. For a little way the glare of my fire lit the path. Looking back presently, I could see, through the crowded stems, that from my heap of sticks the blaze had spread to some bushes adjacent, and a curved line of fire was creeping up the grass of the hill. I laughed at that, and turned again to the dark trees before me. It was very black, and Weena clung to me convulsively, but there was still, as my eyes grew accustomed to the darkness, sufficient light for me to avoid the stems. Overhead it was simply black, except where a gap of remote blue sky shone down upon us here and there. I lit none of my matches because I had no hands free. Upon my left arm I carried my little one, in my right hand I had my iron bar.

"For some way I heard nothing but the crackling twigs under my feet, the faint rustle of the breeze above, and my own breathing and the throb of the blood-vessels in my ears. Then I seemed to know of a pattering about me. I pushed on grimly. The pattering grew more distinct, and then I caught the same queer sounds and voices I had heard in the Underworld. There were evidently several of the Morlocks, and they were closing in upon me. Indeed, in another minute I felt a tug at my coat, then something at my arm. And Weena shivered violently, and became quite still.

"It was time for a match. But to get one I must put her down. I did so, and, as I fumbled with my pocket, a struggle began in the darkness about my knees, perfectly silent on her part and with the same peculiar cooing sounds from the Morlocks. Soft little hands, too, were creeping over my coat and back, touching even my neck. Then the match scratched and fizzed. I held it flaring, and saw the white backs of the Morlocks in flight amid the trees. I hastily took a lump of camphor from my pocket, and prepared to light it as soon as the match should wane. Then I looked at Weena. She was lying clutching my feet and quite motionless, with her face to the ground. With a sudden fright I stooped to her. She seemed scarcely to breathe. I lit the block of camphor and flung it to the ground, and as it split and flared up and drove back the Morlocks and the shadows, I knelt down and lifted her. The wood behind seemed full of the stir and murmur of a great company!

"She seemed to have fainted. I put her carefully upon my shoulder and rose to push on, and then there came a horrible realization. In maneuvering with my matches and Weena,

I had turned myself about several times, and now I had not the faintest idea in what direction lay my path. For all I knew, I might be facing back towards the Palace of Green Porcelain. I found myself in a cold sweat. I had to think rapidly what to do. I determined to build a fire and encamp where we were. I put Weena, still motionless, down upon a turfy bole, and very hastily, as my first lump of camphor waned, I began collecting sticks and leaves. Here and there out of the darkness round me the Morlocks' eyes shone like carbuncles.

"The camphor flickered and went out. I lit a match, and as I did so, two white forms that had been approaching Weena dashed hastily away. One was so blinded by the light that he came straight for me and I felt his bones grind under the blow of my fist. He gave a whoop of dismay, staggered a little way, and fell down. I lit another piece of camphor, and went on gathering my bonfire. Presently I noticed how dry was some of the foliage above me, for since my arrival on the Time Machine, a matter of a week, no rain had fallen. So, instead of casting about among the trees for fallen twigs, I began leaping up and dragging down branches. Very soon I had a choking smoky fire of green wood and dry sticks, and could economize my camphor. Then I turned to where Weena lay beside my iron mace. I tried what I could to revive her, but she lay like one dead. I could not even satisfy myself whether or not she breathed.

"Now, the smoke of the fire beat over towards me, and it must have made me heavy of a sudden. Moreover, the vapour of camphor was in the air. My fire would not need replenishing for an hour or so. I felt very weary after my exertion, and sat down. The wood, too, was full of a slumbrous murmur that I did not understand. I seemed just to nod and open my eyes. But all was dark, and the Morlocks had their hands upon me. Flinging off their clinging fingers I hastily felt in my pocket for the match-box, and—it had gone! Then they gripped and closed with me again. In a moment I knew what had happened. I had slept, and my fire had gone out, and the bitterness of death came over my soul. The forest seemed full of the smell of burning wood. I was caught by the neck, by the hair, by the arms, and pulled down. It was indescribably horrible in the darkness to feel all those soft creatures heaped upon me. I felt as if I was in a monstrous spider's web. I was overpowered, and went down. I felt little teeth nipping at my neck. I rolled over, and as I did so my hand came against my iron lever. It gave me strength. I struggled up, shaking the human rats from me, and, holding the bar short, I thrust where I judged their faces might be. I could feel the succulent giving of flesh and bone under my blows, and for a moment I was free.

"The strange exultation that so often seems to accompany hard fighting came upon me. I knew that both I and Weena were lost, but I determined to make the Morlocks pay for their meat. I stood with my back to a tree, swinging the iron bar before me. The whole wood was full of the stir and cries of them. A minute passed. Their voices seemed to rise to a higher pitch of excitement, and their movements grew faster. Yet none came within reach. I stood glaring at the blackness. Then suddenly came hope. What if the Morlocks were afraid? And close on the heels of that came a strange thing. The darkness seemed to grow luminous. Very dimly I began to see the Morlocks about me—three battered at my feet—and then I recognized, with incredulous surprise, that the others were running, in an incessant stream, as it seemed, from behind me, and away through the wood in front. And their backs seemed no longer white, but reddish. As I stood agape, I saw a little red spark go drifting across a gap of starlight between the branches, and vanish. And at that I understood the smell of burning wood, the slumbrous murmur that was growing now into a gusty roar, the red glow, and the Morlocks' flight.

"Stepping out from behind my tree and looking back, I saw, through the black pillars of the nearer trees, the flames of the burning forest. It was my first fire coming after me. With that I looked for Weena, but she was gone. The hissing and crackling behind me, the explosive thud as each fresh tree burst into flame, left little time for reflection. My iron bar still gripped, I followed in the Morlocks' path. It was a close race. Once the flames crept forward so swiftly on my right as I ran, that I was outflanked, and had to strike off to the left. But at last I emerged upon a small open space, and as I did so, a Morlock came blundering towards me, and past me, and went on straight into the fire!

"And now I was to see the most weird and horrible thing, I think, of all that I beheld in that future age. This whole space was as bright as day with the reflection of the fire. In the centre was a hillock or tumulus, surmounted by a scorched hawthorn. Beyond this was another arm of the burning forest, with yellow tongues already writhing from it, completely encircling the space with a fence of fire. Upon the hillside were some thirty or forty Morlocks, dazzled by the light and heat, and blundering hither and thither against each other in their bewilderment. At first I did not realize their blindness, and struck furiously at them with my bar, in a frenzy of fear, as they approached me, killing one and crippling several more. But when I had watched the gestures of one of them groping under the hawthorn against the red sky, and heard their moans, I was assured of their absolute helplessness and misery in the glare, and I struck no more of them.

"Yet every now and then one would come straight towards me, setting loose a quivering horror that made me quick to elude him. At one time the flames died down somewhat, and

I feared the foul creatures would presently be able to see me. I was even thinking of beginning the fight by killing some of them before this should happen; but the fire burst out again brightly, and I stayed my hand. I walked about the hill among them and avoided them, looking for some trace of Weena. But Weena was gone.

"At last I sat down on the summit of the hillock, and watched this strange incredible company of blind things groping to and fro, and making uncanny noises to each one, as the glare of the fire beat on them. The coiling uprush of smoke streamed across the sky, and through the rare tatters of that red canopy, remote as though they belonged to another universe, shone the little stars. Two or three Morlocks came blundering into me, and I drove them off with blows of my fists, trembling as I did so.

"For the most part of that night I was persuaded it was a nightmare. I bit myself and screamed in a passionate desire to awake. I beat the ground with my hands, and got up and sat down again, and wandered here and there, and again sat down. Then I would fall to rubbing my eyes and calling upon God to let me awake. Thrice I saw Morlocks put their heads down in a kind of agony and rush into the flames. But, at last, above the subsiding red of the fire, above the streaming masses of black smoke and the whitening and blackening tree stumps, and the diminishing numbers of these dim creatures, came the white light of the day.

"I searched again for traces of Weena, but there were none. It was plain that they had left her poor little body in the forest. I cannot describe how it relieved me to think that it had escaped the awful fate to which it seemed destined. As I thought of that, I was almost moved to begin a massacre of the helpless abominations about me, but I contained myself. The hillock, as I have said, was a kind of island in the forest.

From its summit I could now make out through a haze of smoke the Palace of Green Porcelain, and from that I could get my bearings for the White Sphinx. And so, leaving the remnant of these damned souls still going hither and thither and moaning, as the day grew clearer, I tied some grass about my feet and limped on across smoking ashes and among black stems that still pulsated internally with fire, towards the hiding-place of the Time Machine. I walked slowly, for I was almost exhausted, as well as lame, and I felt the intensest wretchedness for the horrible death of little Weena. It seemed an overwhelming calamity. Now, in this old familiar room, it is more like the sorrow of a dream than an actual loss. But that morning it left me absolutely lonely again—terribly alone. I began to think of this house of mine, of this fireside, of some of you, and with such thoughts came a longing that was pain.

"But, as I walked over the smoking ashes under the bright morning sky, I made a discovery. In my trouser pocket were still some loose matches. The box must have leaked before it was lost.

CHAPTER 13

THE TRAP OF THE WHITE SPHINX

"About eight or nine in the morning I came to the same seat of yellow metal from which I had viewed the world upon the evening of my arrival. I thought of my hasty conclusions upon that evening, and could not refrain from laughing bitterly at my confidence. Here was the same beautiful scene, the same abundant foliage, the same splendid palaces and magnificent ruins, the same silver river running between its fertile banks. The gay robes of the beautiful people moved hither and thither among the trees. Some were bathing in exactly the place where I had saved Weena, and that suddenly gave me a keen stab of pain. And like blots upon the landscape rose the cupolas above the ways to the Underworld. I understood now what all the beauty of the Overworld people covered. Very pleasant was their day, as pleasant as the day of the cattle in the field. Like the cattle, they knew of no enemies, and provided against no needs. And their end was the same.

"I grieved to think how brief the dream of the human intellect had been. It had committed suicide. It had set itself steadfastly towards comfort and ease, a balanced society with security and permanency as its watchword, it had attained its hopes—to come to this at last. Once, life and property must have reached almost absolute safety. The rich had been assured of his wealth and comfort, the toiler assured of his life and work. No doubt in that perfect world there had been no unemployed problem, no social question left unsolved. And a great quiet had followed.

"It is a law of nature we overlook, that intellectual versatility is the compensation for change, danger, and trouble. An animal perfectly in harmony with its environment is a perfect mechanism. Nature never appeals to intelligence until habit and instinct are useless. There is no intelligence where there is no change and no need of change. Only those animals partake of intelligence that have to meet a huge variety of needs and dangers.

"So, as I see it, the Upperworld man had drifted towards his feeble prettiness, and the Underworld to mere mechanical industry. But that perfect state had lacked one thing even for mechanical perfection—absolute permanency. Apparently as time went on, the feeding of the Underworld, however it was effected, had become disjointed. Mother Necessity, who had been staved off for a few thousand years, came back again, and she began below. The Underworld being in contact with machinery, which, however perfect, still needs some little thought outside habit, had probably retained perforce rather more initiative, if less of every other human character, than the Upper. And when other meat failed them, they turned to what old habit had hitherto forbidden. So I say I saw it in my last view of the world of Eight Hundred and Two Thousand Seven Hundred and One. It may be as wrong an explanation as mortal wit could invent. It is how the thing shaped itself to me, and as that I give it to you.

"After the fatigues, excitements, and terrors of the past days, and in spite of my grief, this seat and the tranquil view and the warm sunlight were very pleasant. I was very tired and sleepy, and soon my theorizing passed into dozing. Catching myself at that, I took my own hint, and, spreading myself out upon the turf, I had a long and refreshing sleep.

"I awoke a little before sunsetting. I now felt safe against being caught napping by the Morlocks, and, stretching myself, I came on down the hill towards the White Sphinx. I had my crowbar in one hand, and the other hand played with the matches in my pocket.

"And now came a most unexpected thing. As I approached the pedestal of the sphinx I found the bronze valves were open. They had slid down into grooves.

"At that I stopped short before them, hesitating to enter.

"Within was a small apartment, and on a raised place in the corner of this was the Time Machine. I had the small levers in my pocket. So here, after all my elaborate preparations for the siege of the White Sphinx, was a meek surrender. I threw my iron bar away, almost sorry not to use it.

"A sudden thought came into my head as I stooped towards the portal. For once, at least, I grasped the mental operations of the Morlocks. Suppressing a strong inclination to laugh, I

305

stepped through the bronze frame and up to the Time Machine. I was surprised to find it had been carefully oiled and cleaned. I have suspected since that the Morlocks had even partially taken it to pieces while trying in their dim way to grasp its purpose.

"Now as I stood and examined it, finding a pleasure in the mere touch of the contrivance, the thing I had expected happened. The bronze panels suddenly slid up and struck the frame with a clang. I was in the dark—trapped. So the Morlocks thought. At that I chuckled gleefully.

"I could already hear their murmuring laughter as they came towards me. Very calmly I tried to strike the match. I had only to fix on the levers and depart then like a ghost. But I had overlooked one little thing. The matches were of that abominable kind that light only on the box.

"You may imagine how all my calm vanished. The little brutes were close upon me. One touched me. I made a sweeping blow in the dark at them with the levers, and began to scramble into the saddle of the machine. Then came one hand upon me and then another. Then I had simply to fight against their persistent fingers for my levers, and at the same time feel for the studs over which these fitted. One, indeed, they almost got away from me. As it slipped from my hand, I had to butt in the dark with my head—I could hear the Morlock's skull ring—to recover it. It was a nearer thing than the fight in the forest, I think, this last scramble.

"But at last the lever was fixed and pulled over. The clinging hands slipped from me. The darkness presently fell from my eyes. I found myself in the same grey light and tumult I have already described.

CHAPTER 14

THE FURTHER VISION

"I have already told you of the sickness and confusion that comes with time travelling. And this time I was not seated properly in the saddle, but sideways and in an unstable fashion. For an indefinite time I clung to the machine as it swayed and vibrated, quite unheeding how I went, and when I brought myself to look at the dials again I was amazed to find where I had arrived. One dial records days, another thousands of days, another millions of days, and another thousands of millions. Now, instead of reversing the levers I had pulled them over so as to go forward with them, and when I came to look at these indicators I found that the thousands hand was sweeping round as fast as the seconds hands of a watch—into futurity. Very cautiously, for I remembered my former head-long fall, I began to reverse my motion. Slower and slower went the circling hands until the thousands one seemed motionless and the daily one was no longer a mere mist upon its scale. Still slower, until the grey haze around me became distincter and dim outlines of an undulating waste grew visible.

"I stopped. I was on a bleak moorland, covered with a sparse vegetation, and grey with a thin hoarfrost. The time was midday, the orange sun, shorn of its effulgence, brooded near the meridian in a sky of drabby grey. Only a few black bushes broke the monotony of the scene. The great buildings of the decadent men among whom, it seemed to me, I had been so recently, had vanished and left no trace: not a mound even marked their position. Hill and valley, sea and river—all, under the wear and work of the rain and frost, had melted into new forms. No doubt, too, the rain and snow had long since washed out the Morlock tunnels. A nipping breeze stung

307

my hands and face. So far as I could see there were neither
hills, nor trees, nor rivers: only an uneven stretch of cheerless
plateau.

"Then suddenly a dark bulk rose out of the moor, something that gleamed like a serrated row of iron plates, and vanished almost immediately in a depression. And then I became
aware of a number of faint-grey things, coloured to almost the
exact tint of the frost-bitten soil, which were browsing here
and there upon its scanty grass, and running to and fro. I saw
one jump with a sudden start, and then my eye detected perhaps a score of them. At first I thought they were rabbits, or
some small breed of kangaroo. Then, as one came hopping
near me, I perceived that it belonged to neither of these
groups. It was plantigrade, its hind legs rather the longer; it
was tailless, and covered with a straight greyish hair that
thickened about the head into a Skye terrier's mane. As I had
understood that in the Golden Age man had killed out almost
all the other animals, sparing only a few of the more ornamental, I was naturally curious about the creatures. They did
not seem afraid of me, but browsed on, much as rabbits
would do in a place unfrequented by men; and it occurred
to me that I might perhaps secure a specimen.

"I got off the machine, and picked up a big stone. I had
scarcely done so when one of the little creatures came within
easy range. I was so lucky as to hit it on the head, and it
rolled over at once and lay motionless. I ran to it at once. It
remained still, almost as if it were killed. I was surprised to see
that the thing had five feeble digits to both its fore and hind
feet—the fore feet, indeed, were almost as human as the fore
feet of a frog. It had, moreover, a roundish head, with a
projecting forehead and forward-looking eyes, obscured by its
lank hair. A disagreeable apprehension flashed across my
mind. As I knelt down and seized my capture, intending to

308

examine its teeth and other anatomical points which might show human characteristics, the metallic-looking object, to which I have already alluded, reappeared above a ridge in the moor, coming towards me and making a strange clattering sound as it came. Forthwith the grey animals about me began to answer with a short, weak yelping—as if of terror—and bolted off in a direction opposite to that from which this new creature approached. They must have hidden in burrows or behind bushes and tussocks, for in a moment not one of them was visible.

"I rose to my feet, and stared at this grotesque monster. I can only describe it by comparing it to a centipede. It stood about three feet high, and had a long segmented body, perhaps thirty feet long, with curiously overlapping greenish-black plates. It seemed to crawl upon a multitude of feet, looping its body as it advanced. Its blunt round head, with a polygonal arrangement of black eye spots, carried two flexible, writhing, horn-like antennae. It was coming along, I should judge, at a pace of about eight or ten miles an hour, and it left me little time for thinking. Leaving my grey animal, or grey man, whichever it was, on the ground, I set off for the machine. Halfway I paused, regretting that abandonment, but a glance over my shoulder destroyed any such regret. When I gained the machine the monster was scarce fifty yards away. It was certainly not a vertebrated animal. It had no snout, and its mouth was fringed with jointed dark-coloured plates. But I did not care for a nearer view.

"I traversed one day and stopped again, hoping to find the colossus gone and some vestige of my victim; but, I should judge, the giant centipede did not trouble itself about bones. At any rate both had vanished. The faintly human touch of these little creatures perplexed me greatly. If you come to think, there is no reason why a degenerate humanity should not come at last to differentiate into as many species as the descendants of the mud fish who fathered all the land vertebrates. I saw no more of any insect colossus, as to my thinking the segmented creature must have been. Evidently the physiological difficulty that at present keeps all the insects small had been surmounted at last, and this division of the animal kingdom had arrived at the long-awaited supremacy which its enormous energy and vitality deserve. I made several attempts to kill or capture another of the greyish vermin, but none of my missiles were so successful as my first; and, after perhaps a dozen disappointing throws, that left my arm aching, I felt a gust of irritation at my folly in coming so far into futurity without weapons or equipment. I resolved to run on for one glimpse of the still remoter future—one peep into the deeper abyss of time—and then to return to you and my own epoch. Once more I remounted the machine, and once more the world grew hazy and grey.

"As I drove on, a peculiar change crept over the appearance of things. The palpitating greyness grew darker; then—though I was still travelling with prodigious velocity—the blinking succession of day and night, which was usually indicative of a slower pace, returned, and grew more and more marked. This puzzled me very much at first. The alternations of night and day grew slower and slower, and so did the passage of the sun across the sky, until they seemed to stretch through centuries. At last a steady twilight brooded over the earth, a twilight only broken now and then when a comet glared across the darkling sky. The band of light that had indicated the sun had long since disappeared; for the sun had ceased to set—it simply rose and fell in the west, and grew ever broader and more red. All trace of the moon had vanished. The circling of the stars, growing slower and slower, had given place to creeping points of light. At last, some time

310

before I stopped, the sun, red and very large, halted motion-less upon the horizon, a vast dome glowing with a dull heat, and now and then suffering a momentary extinction. At one time it had for a little while glowed more brilliantly again, but it speedily reverted to its sullen red-heat. I perceived by this slowing down of its rising and setting that the work of the tidal drag was done. The earth had come to rest with one face to the sun, even as in our own time the moon faces the earth. Very cautiously, for I remembered my former headlong fall, I began to reverse my motion. Slower and slower went the cir-cling hands until the thousands one seemed motionless, and the daily one was no longer a mere mist upon its scale. Still slower, until the dim outlines of a desolate beach grew visible.

"I stopped very gently and sat upon the Time Machine, looking round. The sky was no longer blue. Northeastward it was inky black, and out of the blackness shone brightly and steadily the pale white stars. Overhead it was a deep Indian red and starless, and southeastward it grew brighter to a glowing scarlet where, cut by the horizon, lay the huge hull of the sun, red and motionless. The rocks about me were of a harsh reddish colour, and all the trace of life that I could see at first was the intensely green vegetation that covered every projecting point on their southeastern face. It was the same rich green that one sees on forest moss or on the lichen in caves: plants which like these grow in a perpetual twilight.

"The machine was standing on a sloping beach. The sea stretched away to the southwest, to rise into a sharp bright horizon against the wan sky. There were no breakers and no waves, for not a breath of wind was stirring. Only a slight oily swell rose and fell like a gentle breathing, and showed that the eternal sea was still moving and living. And along the margin where the water sometimes broke was a thick incrus-tation of salt—pink under the lurid sky. There was a sense of

311

oppression in my head, and I noticed that I was breathing very fast. The sensation reminded me of my only experience of mountaineering, and from that I judged the air to be more rarefied than it is now.

"Far away up the desolate slope I heard a harsh scream, and saw a thing like a huge white butterfly go slanting and fluttering up into the sky and, circling, disappear over some low hillocks beyond. The sound of its voice was so dismal that I shivered and seated myself more firmly upon the machine. Looking round me again, I saw that, quite near, what I had taken to be a reddish mass of rock was moving slowly towards me. Then I saw the thing was really a monstrous crab-like creature. Can you imagine a crab as large as yonder table, with its many legs moving slowly and uncertainly, its big claws swaying, its long antennae, like carters' whips, waving and feeling, and its stalked eyes gleaming at you on either side of its metallic front? Its back was corrugated and ornamented with ungainly bosses, and a greenish incrustation blotched it here and there. I could see the many palps of its complicated mouth flickering and feeling as it moved.

"As I stared at this sinister apparition crawling towards me, I felt a tickling on my cheek as though a fly had lighted there. I tried to brush it away with my hand, but in a moment it returned, and almost immediately came another by my ear. I struck at this, and caught something thread-like. It was drawn swiftly out of my hand. With a frightful qualm, I turned, and saw that I had grasped the antenna of another monster crab that stood just behind me. Its evil eyes were wriggling on their stalks, its mouth was all alive with appetite, and its vast ungainly claws, smeared with an algal slime, were descending upon me. In a moment my hand was on the lever, and I had placed a month between myself and these monsters. But I was still on the same beach, and I saw them distinctly now as soon

312

as I stopped. Dozens of them seemed to be crawling here and there, in the sombre light, among the foliated sheets of intense green.

"I cannot convey the sense of abominable desolation that hung over the world. The red eastern sky, the northward blackness, the salt Dead Sea, the stony beach crawling with these foul, slow-stirring monsters, the uniform poisonous-looking green of the lichenous plants, the thin air that hurts one's lungs: all contributed to an appalling effect. I moved on a hundred years, and there was the same red sun—a little larger, a little duller—the same dying sea, the same chill air, and the same crowd of earthy crustacea creeping in and out among the green weed and the red rocks. And in the westward sky I saw a curved pale line like a vast new moon.

"So I travelled, stopping ever and again, in great strides of a thousand years or more, drawn on by the mystery of the earth's fate, watching with a strange fascination the sun grow larger and duller in the westward sky, and the life of the old earth ebb away. At last, more than thirty million years hence, the huge red-hot dome of the sun had come to obscure nearly a tenth part of the darkling heavens. Then I stopped once more, for the crawling multitude of crabs had disappeared, and the red beach, save for its livid green liverworts and lichens, seemed lifeless. And now it was flecked with white. A bitter cold assailed me. Rare white flakes ever and again came eddying down. To the northeastward, the glare of snow lay under the starlight of the sable sky, and I could see an undulating crest of hillocks pinkish-white. There were fringes of ice along the sea margin, with drifting masses further out; but the main expanse of that salt ocean, all bloody under the eternal sunset, was still unfrozen.

"I looked about me to see if any traces of animal-life remained. A certain indefinable apprehension still kept me in the saddle of the machine. But I saw nothing moving, in earth or sky or sea. The green slime on the rocks alone testified that life was not extinct. A shallow sandbank had appeared in the sea and the water had receded from the beach. I fancied I saw some black object flopping about upon this bank, but it became motionless as I looked at it, and I judged that my eye had been deceived, and that the black object was merely a rock. The stars in the sky were intensely bright and seemed to me to twinkle very little.

"Suddenly I noticed that the circular westward outline of the sun had changed; that a concavity, a bay, had appeared in the curve. I saw this grow larger. For a minute perhaps I stared aghast at this blackness that was creeping over the day, and then I realized that an eclipse was beginning. Either the moon or the planet Mercury was passing across the sun's disk. Naturally, at first I took it to be the moon, but there is much to incline me to believe that what I really saw was the transit of an inner planet passing very near to the earth.

"The darkness grew apace; a cold wind began to blow in freshening gusts from the east, and the showering white flakes in the air increased in number. From the edge of the sea came a ripple and whisper. Beyond these lifeless sounds the world was silent. Silent? It would be hard to convey the stillness of it. All the sounds of man, the bleating of sheep, the cries of birds, the hum of insects, the stir that makes the background of our lives—all that was over. As the darkness thickened, the eddying flakes grew more abundant, dancing before my eyes; and the cold of the air more intense. At last, one by one, swiftly, one after the other, the white peaks of the distant hills vanished into blackness. The breeze rose to a moaning wind. I saw the black central shadow of the eclipse sweeping towards me. In another moment the pale stars alone were visible. All else was rayless obscurity. The sky was absolutely black.

"A horror of this great darkness came on me. The cold, that smote to my marrow, and the pain I felt in breathing overcame me. I shivered, and a deadly nausea seized me. Then like a red-hot bow in the sky appeared the edge of the sun. I got off the machine to recover myself. I felt giddy and incapable of facing the return journey. As I stood sick and confused I saw again the moving thing upon the shoal—there was no mistake now that it was a moving thing—against the red water of the sea. It was a round thing, the size of a football perhaps, or, it may be, bigger, and tentacles trailed down from it; it seemed black against the weltering blood-red water, and it was hopping fitfully about. Then I felt I was fainting. But a terrible dread of lying helpless in that remote and awful twilight sustained me while I clambered upon the saddle.

CHAPTER 15

THE TIME TRAVELLER'S RETURN

"So I came back. For a long time I must have been insensible upon the machine. The blinking succession of the days and nights was resumed, the sun got golden again, the sky blue. I breathed with greater freedom. The fluctuating contours of the land ebbed and flowed. The hands spun backward upon the dials. At last I saw again the dim shadows of houses, the evidences of decadent humanity. These, too, changed and passed, and others came. Presently, when the million dial was at zero, I slackened speed. I began to recognize our own petty and familiar architecture, the thousands hand ran back to the starting-point, the night and day flapped slower and slower. Then the old walls of the laboratory came round me. Very gently, now, I slowed the mechanism down.

"I saw one little thing that seemed odd to me. I think I have told you that when I set out, before my velocity became very high, Mrs. Watchett had walked across the room, travelling, as it seemed to me, like a rocket. As I returned, I passed again across that minute when she traversed the laboratory. But now her every motion appeared to be the exact inversion of her previous ones. The door at the lower end opened, and she glided quietly up the laboratory, back foremost, and disappeared behind the door by which she had previously entered. Just before that I seemed to see Hillyer for a moment; but he passed like a flash.

"Then I stopped the machine, and saw about me again the old familiar laboratory, my tools, my appliances just as I had left them. I got off the thing very shakily, and sat down upon my bench. For several minutes I trembled violently. Then I became calmer. Around me was my old workshop again, exactly as it had been. I might have slept there, and the whole thing have been a dream.

"And yet, not exactly! The thing had started from the southeast corner of the laboratory. It had come to rest again in the northwest, against the wall where you saw it. That gives you the exact distance from my little lawn to the pedestal of the White Sphinx, into which the Morlocks had carried my machine.

"For a time my brain went stagnant. Presently I got up and came through the passage here, limping, because my heel was still painful, and feeling sorely begrimed. I saw the *Pall Mall Gazette* on the table by the door. I found the date was indeed today, and looking at the timepiece, saw the hour was almost eight o'clock. I heard your voices and the clatter of plates. I hesitated—I felt so sick and weak. Then I sniffed good wholesome meat, and opened the door on you. You know the rest. I washed, and dined, and now I am telling you the story.

CHAPTER 16

AFTER THE STORY

"I know," he said, after a pause, "that all this will be absolutely incredible to you, but to me the one incredible thing is that I am here tonight in this old familiar room, looking into your friendly faces, and telling you all these strange adventures." He looked at the Medical Man. "No. I cannot expect you to believe it. Take it as a lie—or a prophecy. Say I dreamed it in the workshop. Consider I have been speculating upon the destinies of our race, until I have hatched this fiction. Treat my assertion of its truth as a mere stroke of art to enhance its interest. And, taking it as a story, what do you think of it?"

He took up his pipe, and began, in his old accustomed manner, to tap with it nervously upon the bars of the grate. There was a momentary stillness. Then chairs began to creak and shoes to scrape upon the carpet. I took my eyes off the Time Traveller's face, and looked round at his audience. They were in the dark, and little spots of colour swam before them. The Medical Man seemed absorbed in the contemplation of our host. The Editor was looking hard at the end of his cigar—the sixth. The Journalist fumbled for his watch. The others, as far as I remember, were motionless.

The Editor stood up with a sigh. "What a pity it is you're not a writer of stories!" he said, putting his hand on the Time Traveller's shoulder.

"You don't believe it?"

"Well——"

"I thought not."

The Time Traveller turned to us. "Where are the matches?" he said. He lit one and spoke over his pipe, puffing. "To tell you the truth . . . I hardly believe it myself. . . . And yet . . ."

317

His eye fell with a mute inquiry upon the withered white flowers upon the little table. Then he turned over the hand holding his pipe, and I saw he was looking at some half-healed scars on his knuckles.

The Medical Man rose, came to the lamp, and examined the flowers. "The gynoeceum's odd," he said. The Psychologist leant forward to see, holding out his hand for a specimen.

"I'm hanged if it isn't a quarter to one," said the Journalist. "How shall we get home?"

"Plenty of cabs at the station," said the Psychologist.

"It's a curious thing," said the Medical Man; "but I certainly don't know the natural order of these flowers. May I have them?"

The Time Traveller hesitated. Then suddenly, "Certainly not."

"Where did you really get them?" said the Medical Man.

The Time Traveller put his hand to his head. He spoke like one who was trying to keep hold of an idea that eluded him. "They were put into my pocket by Weena, when I travelled into Time." He stared round the room. "I'm damned if it isn't all going. This room and you and the atmosphere of every day is too much for my memory. Did I ever make a Time Machine, or a model of a Time Machine? Or is it all only a dream? They say life is a dream, a precious poor dream at times—but I can't stand another that won't fit. It's madness. And where did the dream come from? . . . I must look at that machine. If there *is* one!"

He caught up the lamp swiftly, and carried it, flaring red, through the door into the corridor. We followed him. There in the flickering light of the lamp was the machine sure enough, squat, ugly, and askew, a thing of brass, ebony, ivory, and translucent glimmering quartz. Solid to the touch—for I put out my hand and felt the rail of it—and with brown spots and smears upon the ivory, and bits of grass and moss upon the lower parts, and one rail bent awry.

The Time Traveller put the lamp down on the bench, and ran his hand along the damaged rail. "It's all right now," he said. "The story I told you was true. I'm sorry to have brought you out here in the cold." He took up the lamp, and, in an absolute silence, we returned to the smoking-room.

He came into the hall with us, and helped the Editor on with his coat. The Medical Man looked into his face and, with a certain hesitation, told him he was suffering from over-work, at which he laughed hugely. I remember him standing in the open doorway, bawling good night.

I shared a cab with the Editor. He thought the tale a "gaudy lie." For my own part I was unable to come to a conclusion. The story was so fantastic and incredible, the telling so credible and sober. I lay awake most of the night thinking about it. I determined to go next day and see the Time Traveller again. I was told he was in the laboratory and, being on easy terms in the house, I went up to him. The laboratory, however, was empty. I stared for a minute at the Time Machine and put out my hand and touched the lever. At that the squat substantial-looking mass swayed like a bough shaken by the wind. Its instability startled me extremely, and I had a queer reminiscence of the childish days when I used to be forbidden to meddle. I came back through the corridor. The Time Traveller met me in the smoking-room. He was coming from the house. He had a small camera under one arm and a knapsack under the other. He laughed when he saw me, and gave me an elbow to shake. "I'm frightfully busy," said he, "with that thing in there."

"But is it not some hoax?" I said. "Do you really travel through time?"

319

"Really and truly I do." And he looked frankly into my eyes. He hesitated. His eye wandered about the room. "I only want half an hour," he said. "I know why you came, and it's awfully good of you. There's some magazines here. If you'll stop to lunch I'll prove you this time travelling up to the hilt, specimens and all. If you'll forgive my leaving you now?"

I consented, hardly comprehending then the full import of his words, and he nodded and went on down the corridor. I heard the door of the laboratory slam, seated myself in a chair, and took up a daily paper. What was he going to do before lunch-time? Then suddenly I was reminded by an advertisement that I had promised to meet Richardson, the publisher, at two. I looked at my watch, and saw that I could barely save that engagement. I got up and went down the passage to tell the Time Traveller.

As I took hold of the handle of the door I heard an exclamation, oddly truncated at the end, and a click and a thud. A gust of air whirled round me as I opened the door, and from within came the sound of broken glass falling on the floor. The Time Traveller was not there. I seemed to see a ghostly, indistinct figure sitting in a whirling mass of black and brass for a moment—a figure so transparent that the bench behind with its sheets of drawings was absolutely distinct; but this phantasm vanished as I rubbed my eyes. The Time Machine had gone. Save for a subsiding stir of dust, the further end of the laboratory was empty. A pane of the skylight had, apparently, just been blown in.

I felt an unreasonable amazement. I knew that something strange had happened, and for the moment could not distinguish what the strange thing might be. As I stood staring, the door into the garden opened, and the man-servant appeared.

We looked at each other. Then ideas began to come. "Has Mr.—— gone out that way?" said I.

"No, sir. No one has come out this way. I was expecting to find him here."

At that I understood. At the risk of disappointing Richardson I stayed on, waiting for the Time Traveller: waiting for the second, perhaps still stranger story, and the specimens and photographs he would bring with him. But I am beginning now to fear that I must wait a lifetime. The Time Traveller vanished three years ago. And, as everybody knows now, he has never returned.

EPILOGUE

One cannot choose but wonder. Will he ever return? It may be that he swept back into the past, and fell among the blood-drinking, hairy savages of the Age of Unpolished Stone; into the abysses of the Cretaceous Sea; or among the grotesque saurians, the huge reptilian brutes of the Jurassic times. He may even now—if I may use the phrase—be wandering on some plesiosaurus-haunted Oolitic coral reef, or beside the lonely saline seas of the Triassic Age. Or did he go forward, into one of the nearer ages, in which men are still men, but with the riddles of our own time answered and its wearisome problems solved? Into the manhood of the race: for I, for my own part, cannot think that these latter days of weak experiment, fragmentary theory, and mutual discord are indeed man's culminating time! I say, for my own part. He, I know—for the question had been discussed among us long before the Time Machine was made—thought but cheerlessly of the Advancement of Mankind, and saw in the growing pile of civilization only a foolish heaping that must inevitably fall back upon and destroy its makers in the end. If that is so, it remains for us to live as though it were not so. But to me the future is still black and blank—is a vast ignorance, lit at a few casual places by the memory of his story. And I have by me, for my comfort, two strange white flowers—shrivelled now, and brown and flat and brittle—to witness that even when mind and strength had gone, gratitude and a mutual tenderness still lived on in the heart of man.

ACKNOWLEDGMENTS

All possible care has been taken to trace ownership and secure permission for each selection in this series. The Great Books Foundation wishes to thank the following authors, publishers, and representatives for permission to reprint copyrighted material:

Miriam, from SELECTED WRITINGS OF TRUMAN CAPOTE. Copyright 1945 by Conde Naste Publications; renewed 1973 by Conde Naste Publications. Reprinted by permission of Random House, Inc.

Zoo Island, from THE HARVEST, by Tomás Rivera. Copyright 1989 by Tomás Rivera Archives/Concepción Rivera. Reprinted by permission of Arte Publico Press.

At the Pitt-Rivers, from PACK OF CARDS AND OTHER STORIES, by Penelope Lively. Copyright 1978 by Penelope Lively. Reprinted by permission of Grove Press, Inc.

New African, from SARAH PHILLIPS, by Andrea Lee. Copyright 1984 by Andrea Lee. Reprinted by permission of Random House, Inc.

Sponono, from TALES FROM A TROUBLED LAND, by Alan Paton. Copyright 1961 by Alan Paton. First published in *Esquire.* Reprinted by permission of Charles Scribner's Sons, an imprint of Macmillan Publishing Company.

Bobby's Room, from SECRET VILLAGES, by Douglas Dunn. Copyright 1985 by Douglas Dunn. Reprinted by permission of Peters, Fraser & Dunlop Limited.

A Bird in the House, by Margaret Laurence. Copyright 1964 by Margaret Laurence. Reprinted by permission of the Estate of Margaret Laurence.

The Little Cousins, from THE OLD FOREST AND OTHER STORIES, by Peter Taylor. Copyright 1959 by Peter Taylor. First published in *The New Yorker.* Reprinted by permission of Doubleday, a division of Bantam, Doubleday, Dell Publishing Group, Inc.

The Idealist, from TRAVELLER'S SAMPLER, by Frank O'Connor. Copyright 1950, 1956 by Frank O'Connor. Reprinted by permission of Joan Daves Agency.

Special thanks to Ruth Wescoat.

Cover design by Allen Landsberger.

Interior design by William Seabright, William Seabright & Associates.